LEGENDS OF MARVEL

THE AVENGERS

Peter David, Roger Stern, Walter Simonson, Tom DeFalco, Ron Frenz, Kathryn Immonen & Roy Thomas
WRITERS

Dale Keown, Ron Lim, Mike Hawthorne, Ron Frenz, Tom Reilly & Jerry Ordway
PENCILERS

Mark Farmer, Marc Deering, Walden Wong, Scott Hanna, Ron Lim, Sal Buscema, Keith Williams, Tom Reilly & Jerry Ordway
INKERS

Peter Steigerwald, Espen Grundetjern, Tamra Bonvillain, Rachelle Rosenberg, Chris O'Halloran & Jay David Ramos with John Starr
COLOR ARTISTS

John Workman; and VC's Cory Petit, Joe Caramagna & Clayton Cowles
LETTERERS

Dale Keown & Peter Steigerwald; Patch Zircher & Matt Yackey; Kim Jacinto & Java Tartaglia; and Jerry Ordway & Frank D'Armata
COVER ARTISTS

Shannon Andews Ballesteros
ASSISTANT EDITOR

Sarah Brunstad & Alanna Smith
ASSOCIATE EDITORS

Wil Moss & Tom Brevoort
EDITORS

AVENGERS CREATD BY Stan Lee & Jack Kirby

COLLECTION EDITOR **MARK D. BEAZLEY**
ASSISTANT MANAGING EDITOR **MAIA LOWY**
ASSISTANT MANAGING EDITOR **LISA MONTALBANO**
SENIOR EDITOR, SPECIAL PROJECTS **JENNIFER GRÜNWALD**

VP PRODUCTION & SPECIAL PROJECTS **JEFF YOUNGQUIST**
BOOK DESIGNERS **ADAM DEL RE** WITH **SALENA MAHINA**
SVP PRINT, SALES & MARKETING **DAVID GABRIEL**
EDITOR IN CHIEF **C.B. CEBULSKI**

LEGENDS OF MARVEL: AVENGERS. Contains material originally published in magazine form as INCREDIBLE HULK: LAST CALL (2019) #1, AVENGERS: LOKI UNLEASHED (2019) #1, THOR: THE WORTHY (2019) #1 and CAPTAIN AMERICA & THE INVADERS: BAHAMAS TRIANGLE (2019) #1. First printing 2020. ISBN 978-1-302-92195-8. Published by MARVEL WORLDWIDE, INC., a subsidiary of MARVEL ENTERTAINMENT, LLC. OFFICE OF PUBLICATION: 1290 Avenue of the Americas, New York, NY 10104. © 2020 MARVEL No similarity between any of the names, characters, persons, and/or institutions in this magazine with those of any living or dead person or institution is intended, and any such similarity which may exist is purely coincidental. **Printed in Canada.** KEVIN FEIGE, Chief Creative Officer; DAN BUCKLEY, President, Marvel Entertainment; JOHN NEE, Publisher; JOE QUESADA, EVP & Creative Director; TOM BREVOORT, SVP of Publishing; DAVID BOGART, Associate Publisher & SVP of Talent Affairs; Publishing & Partnership; DAVID GABRIEL, VP of Print & Digital Publishing; JEFF YOUNGQUIST, VP of Production & Special Projects; DAN CARR, Executive Director of Publishing Technology; ALEX MORALES, Director of Publishing Operations; DAN EDINGTON, Managing Editor; SUSAN CRESPI, Production Manager; STAN LEE, Chairman Emeritus. For information regarding advertising in Marvel Comics or on Marvel.com, please contact Vit DeBellis, Custom Solutions & Integrated Advertising Manager, at vdebellis@marvel.com. For Marvel subscription inquiries, please call 888-511-5480. **Manufactured between 1/17/2020 and 2/18/2020 by SOLISCO PRINTERS, SCOTT, QC, CANADA.**

10 9 8 7 6 5 4 3 2 1

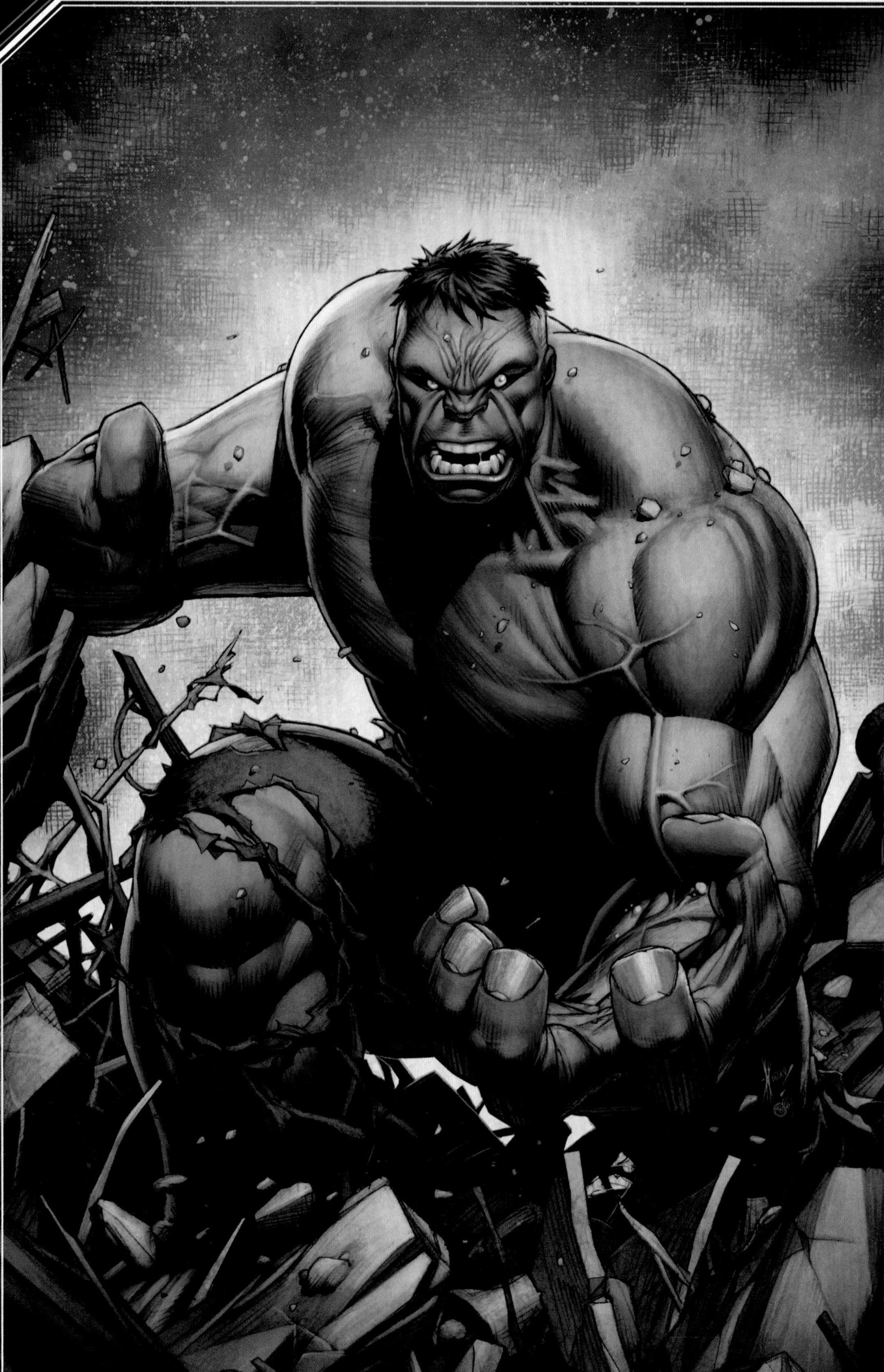

INCREDIBLE HULK: LAST CALL

BRUCE BANNER WAS A BRILLIANT SCIENTIST WITH A BRIGHT FUTURE — UNTIL A GAMMA BOMB TRANSFORMED HIM INTO THE MONSTER KNOWN AS **THE INCREDIBLE HULK**. NOW, ANY TIME BRUCE EXPERIENCES A STRONG SURGE OF EMOTION...THE HULK COMES OUT.

FOR A TIME, BRUCE MANAGED TO CONTROL THE HULK AND WAS EVEN ABLE TO MARRY HIS LONGTIME SWEETHEART, BETTY ROSS. BUT THEIR UNION WAS PLAGUED WITH MISFORTUNE. THROUGHOUT THEIR RELATIONSHIP, VILLAINS TARGETED BETTY OVER AND OVER, INCLUDING ONE OCCASION THAT SAW M.O.D.O.K. TRANSFORM HER INTO THE MONSTROUS HARPY. AND FINALLY, ONE VILLAIN ACHIEVED THE ULTIMATE REVENGE: ABOMINATION INFECTED BETTY WITH A TRANSFUSION OF HIS AND BRUCE'S GAMMA-IRRADIATED BLOOD, FATALLY POISONING HER.

THIS IS A STORY ABOUT WHEN BRUCE WAS ON HIS OWN. ALL ALONE...WITH THE INCREDIBLE HULK.

Peter David	Dale Keown	Mark Farmer, Marc Deering, Walden Wong & Scott Hanna
WRITER	**PENCILERR**	**INKERS**

Peter Steigerwald with John Starr	VC's Cory Petit
COLOR ARTISTS	**LETTERER**

e Keown & Peter Steigerwald	Sarah Brunstad	Wil Moss	Tom Brevoort	
COVER ART	**ASSOCIATE EDITOR**	**EDITOR**	**EXECUTIVE EDITOR**	HULK CREATD BY Stan Lee & Jack Kirby

INCREDIBLE HULK: LAST CALL
variant by Junggeun Yoon

INCREDIBLE HULK: LAST CALL
variant by Adam Kubert & David Curiel

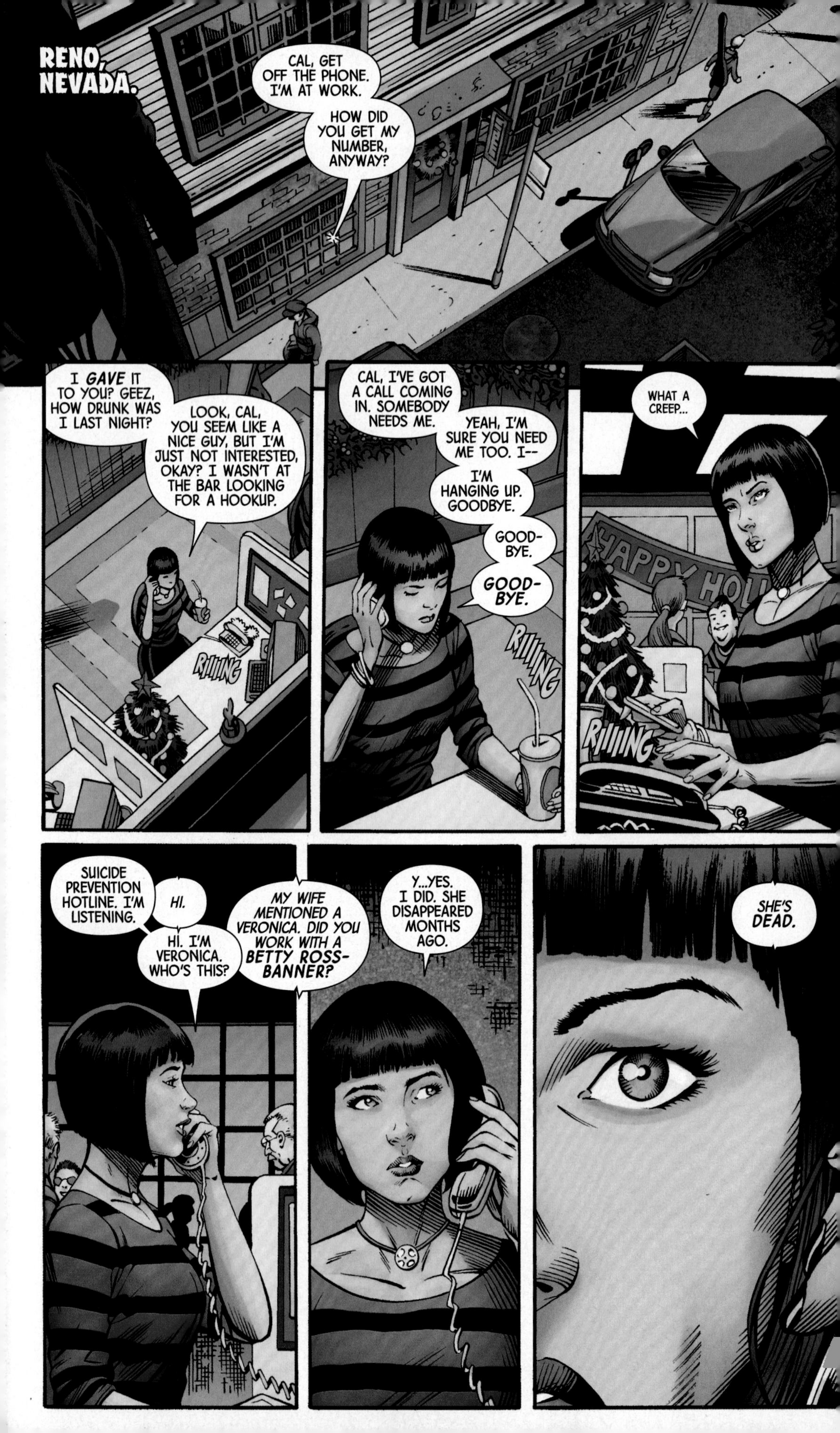
RENO, NEVADA.
CAL, GET OFF THE PHONE. I'M AT WORK.
HOW DID YOU GET MY NUMBER, ANYWAY?
I *GAVE* IT TO YOU? GEEZ, HOW DRUNK WAS I LAST NIGHT?
LOOK, CAL, YOU SEEM LIKE A NICE GUY, BUT I'M JUST NOT INTERESTED, OKAY? I WASN'T AT THE BAR LOOKING FOR A HOOKUP.
RIIING
CAL, I'VE GOT A CALL COMING IN. SOMEBODY NEEDS ME.
YEAH, I'M SURE YOU NEED ME TOO. I--
I'M HANGING UP. GOODBYE.
GOOD-BYE.
GOOD-BYE.
RIIING
WHAT A CREEP...
HAPPY HOL
RIIING
SUICIDE PREVENTION HOTLINE. I'M LISTENING.
HI.
HI. I'M VERONICA. WHO'S THIS?
MY WIFE MENTIONED A VERONICA. DID YOU WORK WITH A **BETTY ROSS-BANNER?**
Y...YES. I DID. SHE DISAPPEARED MONTHS AGO.
SHE'S **DEAD.**

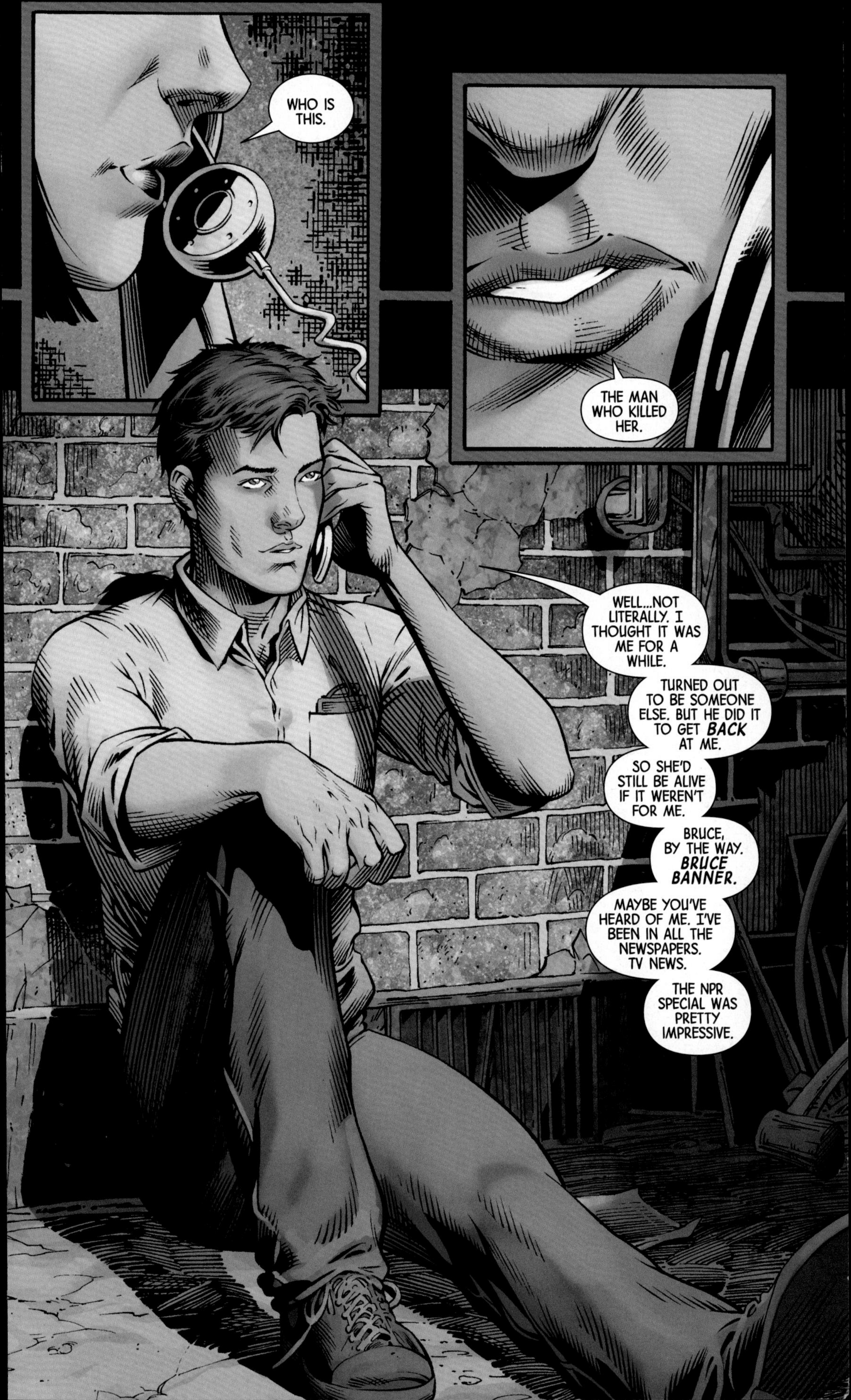
WHO IS THIS.
THE MAN WHO KILLED HER.
WELL...NOT LITERALLY. I THOUGHT IT WAS ME FOR A WHILE.
TURNED OUT TO BE SOMEONE ELSE. BUT HE DID IT TO GET BACK AT ME.
SO SHE'D STILL BE ALIVE IF IT WEREN'T FOR ME.
BRUCE, BY THE WAY. BRUCE BANNER.
MAYBE YOU'VE HEARD OF ME. I'VE BEEN IN ALL THE NEWSPAPERS. TV NEWS.
THE NPR SPECIAL WAS PRETTY IMPRESSIVE.

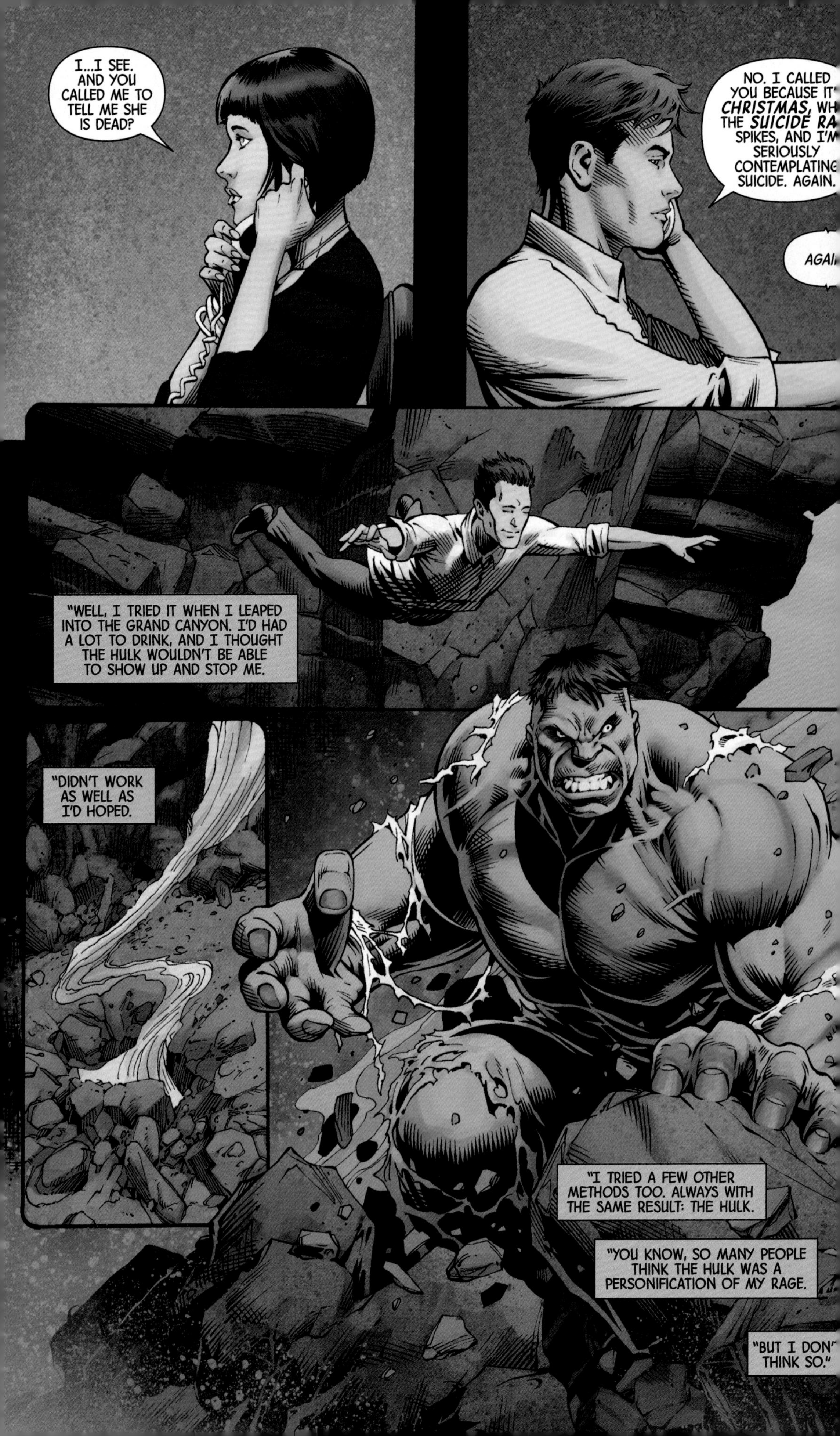
I...I SEE. AND YOU CALLED ME TO TELL ME SHE IS DEAD?
NO. I CALLED YOU BECAUSE IT' *CHRISTMAS,* WH THE *SUICIDE RA* SPIKES, AND I'M SERIOUSLY CONTEMPLATING SUICIDE. AGAIN.
AGAI
"WELL, I TRIED IT WHEN I LEAPED INTO THE GRAND CANYON. I'D HAD A LOT TO DRINK, AND I THOUGHT THE HULK WOULDN'T BE ABLE TO SHOW UP AND STOP ME.
"DIDN'T WORK AS WELL AS I'D HOPED.
"I TRIED A FEW OTHER METHODS TOO. ALWAYS WITH THE SAME RESULT: THE HULK.
"YOU KNOW, SO MANY PEOPLE THINK THE HULK WAS A PERSONIFICATION OF MY RAGE.
"BUT I DON' THINK SO."

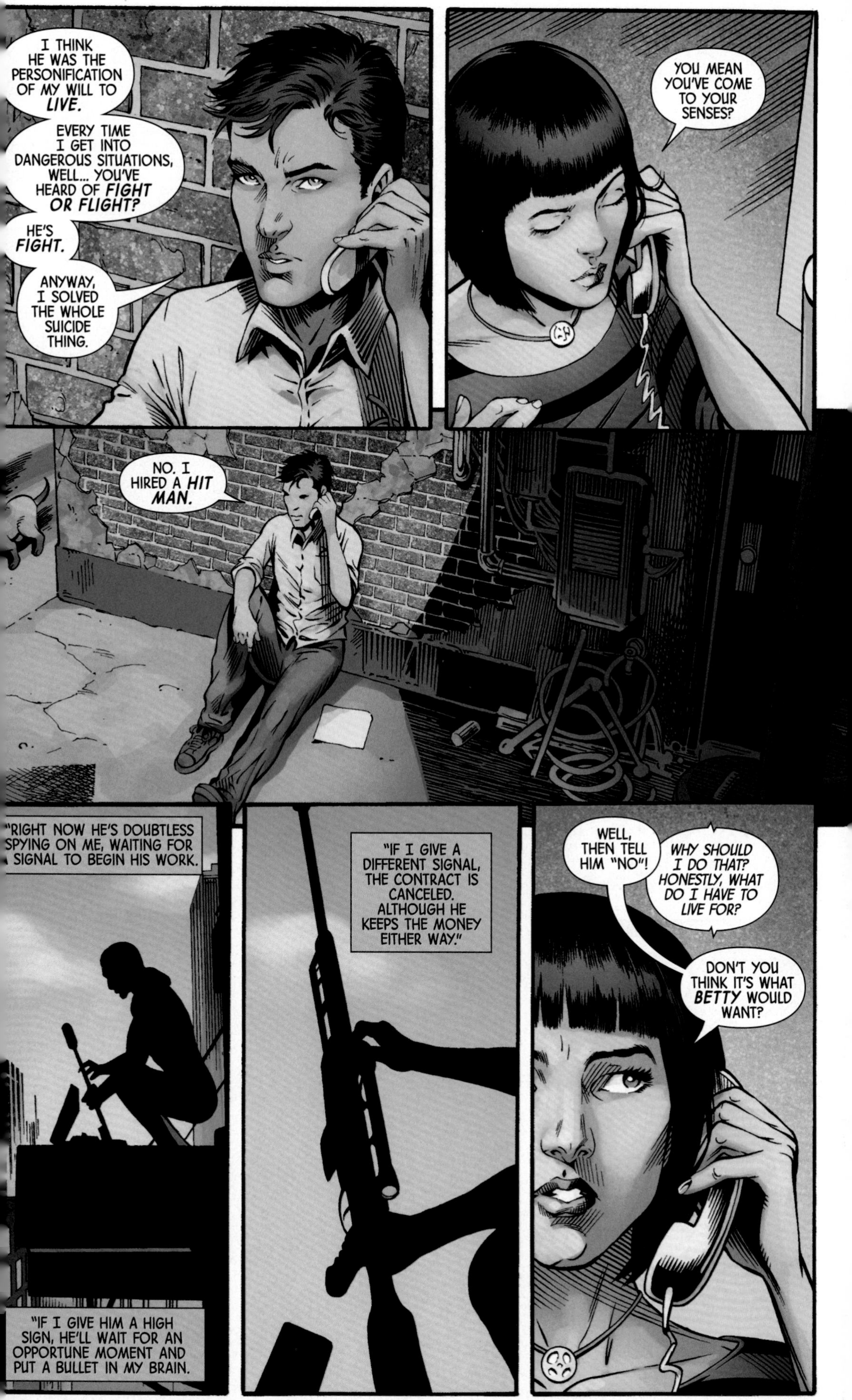
I THINK HE WAS THE PERSONIFICATION OF MY WILL TO *LIVE.*
EVERY TIME I GET INTO DANGEROUS SITUATIONS, WELL... YOU'VE HEARD OF *FIGHT OR FLIGHT?*
HE'S *FIGHT.*
ANYWAY, I SOLVED THE WHOLE SUICIDE THING.
YOU MEAN YOU'VE COME TO YOUR SENSES?
NO. I HIRED A *HIT MAN.*
"RIGHT NOW HE'S DOUBTLESS SPYING ON ME, WAITING FOR A SIGNAL TO BEGIN HIS WORK.
"IF I GIVE HIM A HIGH SIGN, HE'LL WAIT FOR AN OPPORTUNE MOMENT AND PUT A BULLET IN MY BRAIN.
"IF I GIVE A DIFFERENT SIGNAL, THE CONTRACT IS CANCELED. ALTHOUGH HE KEEPS THE MONEY EITHER WAY."
WELL, THEN TELL HIM "NO"!
WHY SHOULD I DO THAT? HONESTLY, WHAT DO I HAVE TO LIVE FOR?
DON'T YOU THINK IT'S WHAT *BETTY* WOULD WANT?

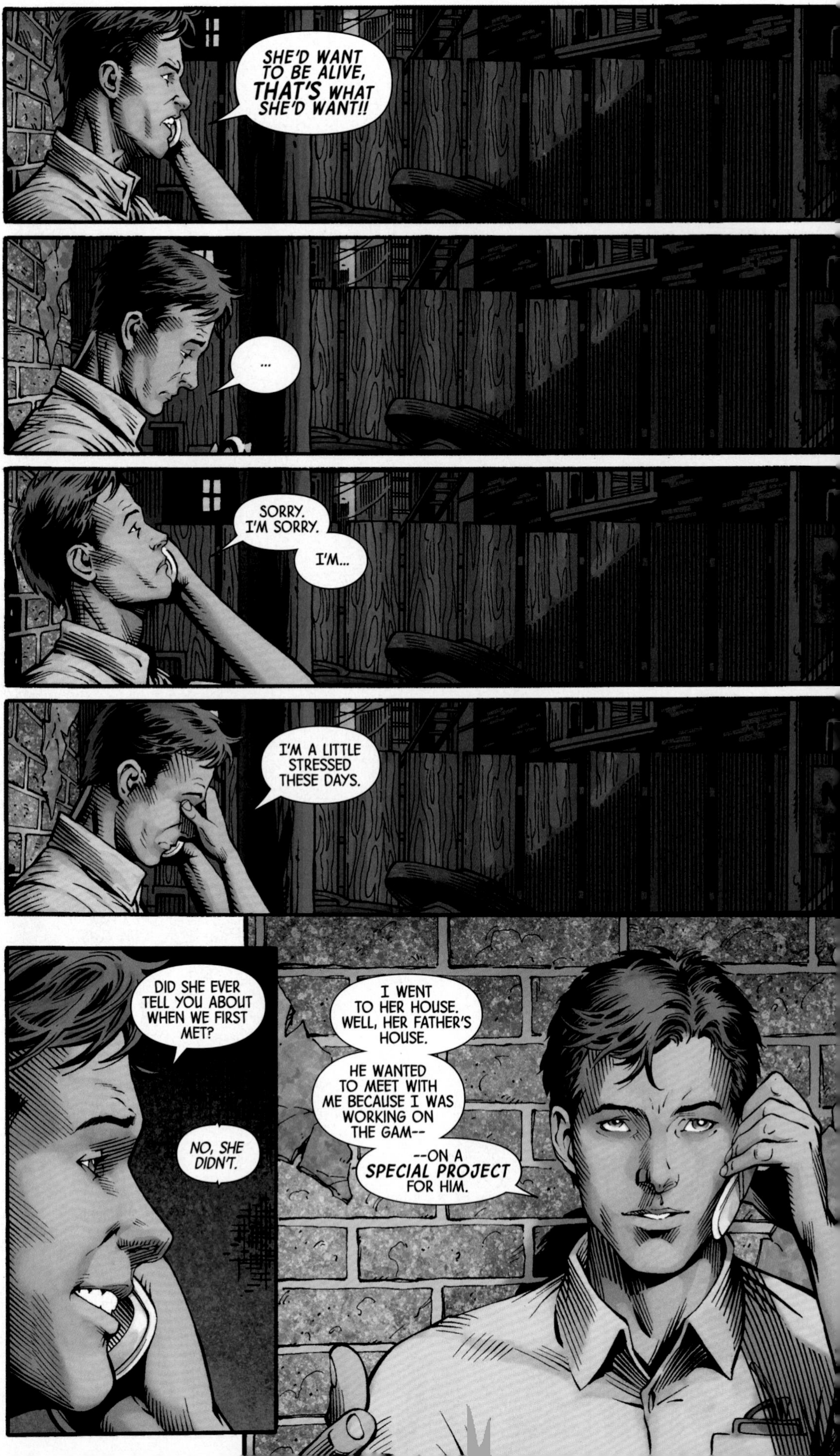

SHE'D WANT TO BE ALIVE, THAT'S WHAT SHE'D WANT!!
...
SORRY. I'M SORRY.
I'M...
I'M A LITTLE STRESSED THESE DAYS.
DID SHE EVER TELL YOU ABOUT WHEN WE FIRST MET?
NO, SHE DIDN'T.
I WENT TO HER HOUSE. WELL, HER FATHER'S HOUSE.
HE WANTED TO MEET WITH ME BECAUSE I WAS WORKING ON THE GAM--
--ON A SPECIAL PROJECT FOR HIM.

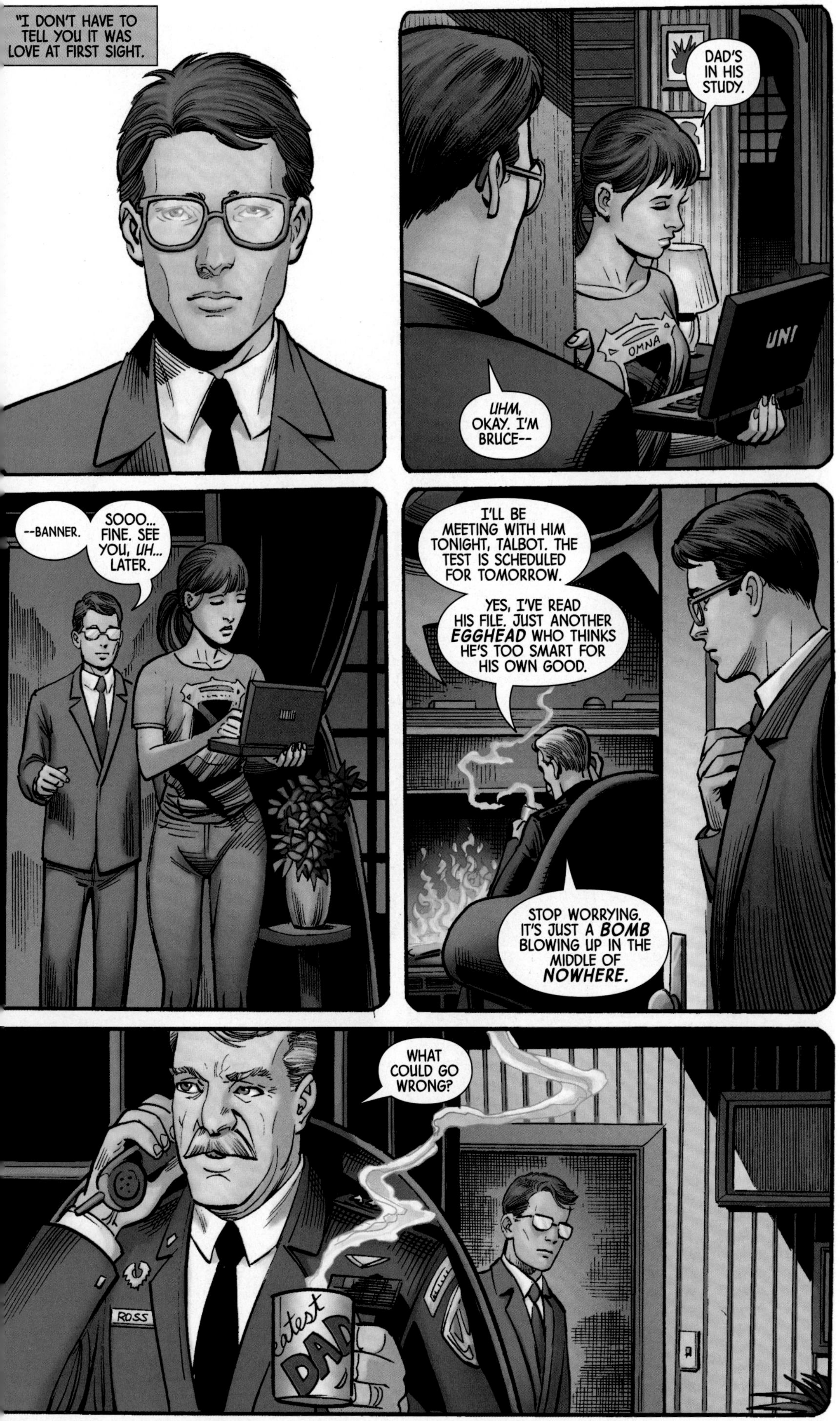
"I DON'T HAVE TO TELL YOU IT WAS LOVE AT FIRST SIGHT.
DAD'S IN HIS STUDY.
UHM, OKAY. I'M BRUCE--
--BANNER.
SOOO... FINE. SEE YOU, UH... LATER.
I'LL BE MEETING WITH HIM TONIGHT, TALBOT. THE TEST IS SCHEDULED FOR TOMORROW.
YES, I'VE READ HIS FILE. JUST ANOTHER EGGHEAD WHO THINKS HE'S TOO SMART FOR HIS OWN GOOD.
STOP WORRYING. IT'S JUST A BOMB BLOWING UP IN THE MIDDLE OF NOWHERE.
WHAT COULD GO WRONG?
ROSS

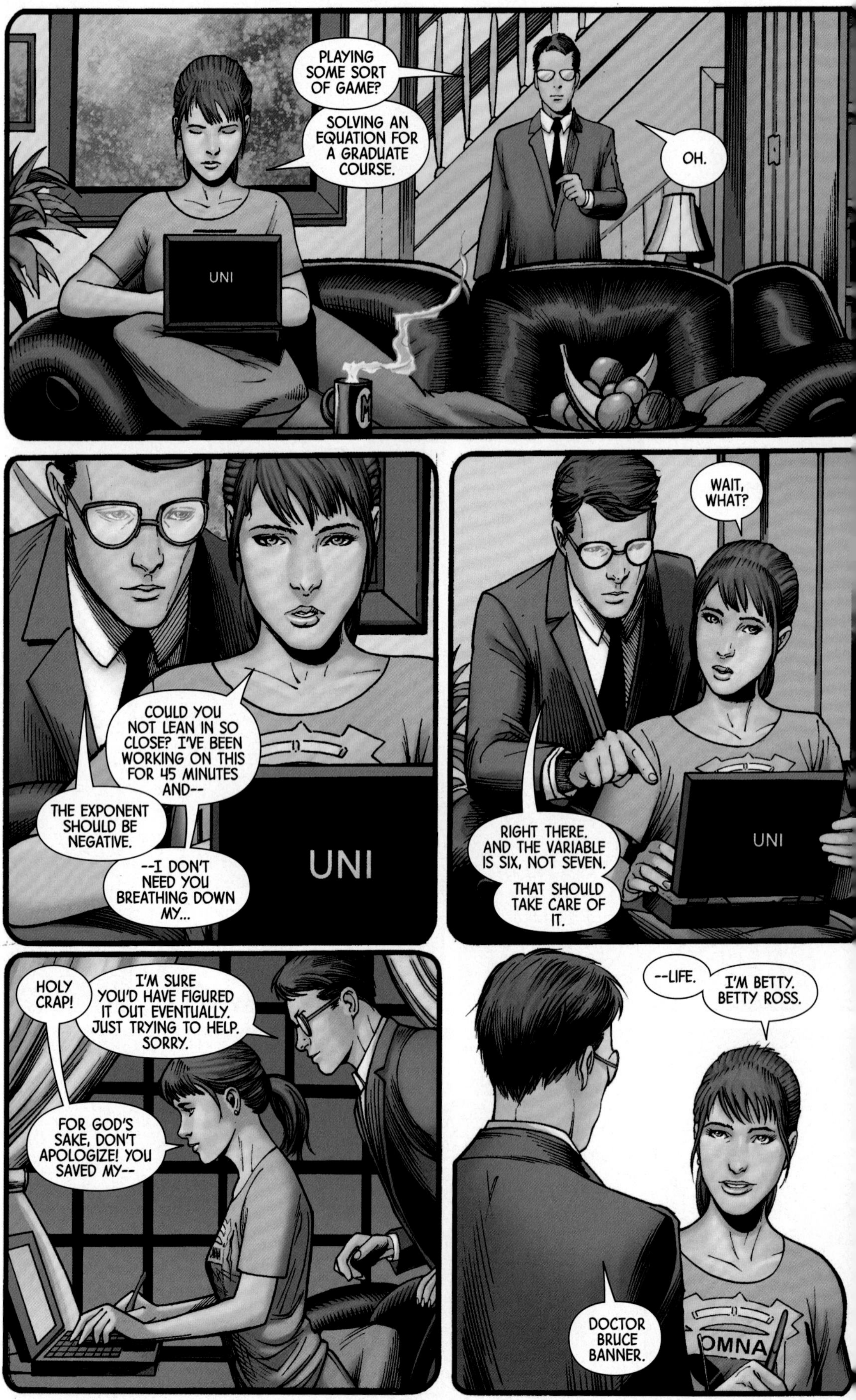

PLAYING SOME SORT OF GAME?
SOLVING AN EQUATION FOR A GRADUATE COURSE.
OH.
UNI
COULD YOU NOT LEAN IN SO CLOSE? I'VE BEEN WORKING ON THIS FOR 45 MINUTES AND--
THE EXPONENT SHOULD BE NEGATIVE.
--I DON'T NEED YOU BREATHING DOWN MY...
UNI
WAIT, WHAT?
RIGHT THERE. AND THE VARIABLE IS SIX, NOT SEVEN.
THAT SHOULD TAKE CARE OF IT.
UNI
HOLY CRAP!
I'M SURE YOU'D HAVE FIGURED IT OUT EVENTUALLY. JUST TRYING TO HELP. SORRY.
FOR GOD'S SAKE, DON'T APOLOGIZE! YOU SAVED MY--
--LIFE.
I'M BETTY. BETTY ROSS.
DOCTOR BRUCE BANNER.
OMNA

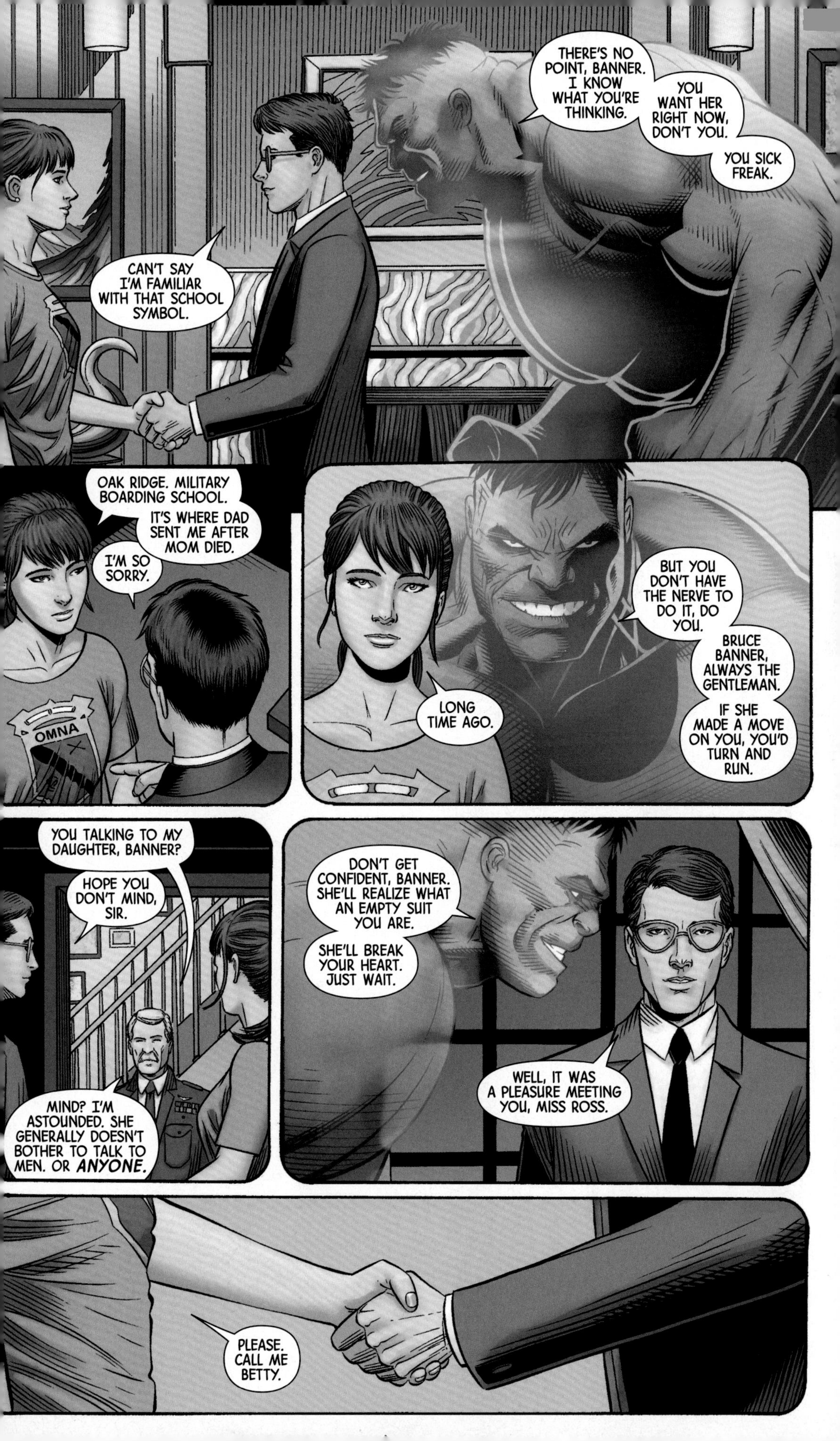
THERE'S NO POINT, BANNER. I KNOW WHAT YOU'RE THINKING.
YOU WANT HER RIGHT NOW, DON'T YOU.
YOU SICK FREAK.
CAN'T SAY I'M FAMILIAR WITH THAT SCHOOL SYMBOL.
OAK RIDGE. MILITARY BOARDING SCHOOL.
IT'S WHERE DAD SENT ME AFTER MOM DIED.
I'M SO SORRY.
OMNA
LONG TIME AGO.
BUT YOU DON'T HAVE THE NERVE TO DO IT, DO YOU.
BRUCE BANNER, ALWAYS THE GENTLEMAN.
IF SHE MADE A MOVE ON YOU, YOU'D TURN AND RUN.
YOU TALKING TO MY DAUGHTER, BANNER?
HOPE YOU DON'T MIND, SIR.
MIND? I'M ASTOUNDED. SHE GENERALLY DOESN'T BOTHER TO TALK TO MEN. OR *ANYONE.*
DON'T GET CONFIDENT, BANNER. SHE'LL REALIZE WHAT AN EMPTY SUIT YOU ARE.
SHE'LL BREAK YOUR HEART. JUST WAIT.
WELL, IT WAS A PLEASURE MEETING YOU, MISS ROSS.
PLEASE. CALL ME BETTY.

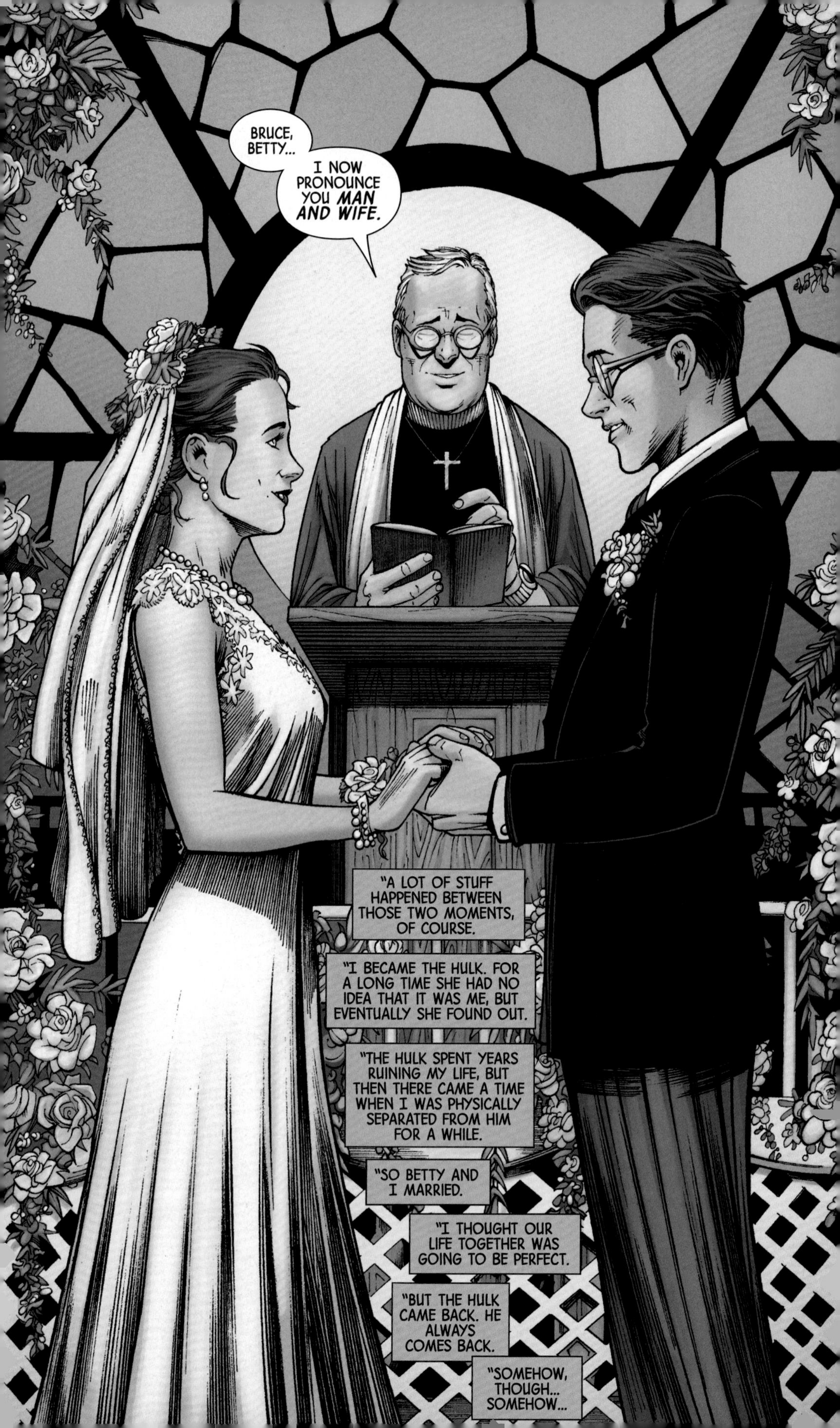
BRUCE, BETTY...
I NOW PRONOUNCE YOU *MAN AND WIFE.*
"A LOT OF STUFF HAPPENED BETWEEN THOSE TWO MOMENTS, OF COURSE.
"I BECAME THE HULK. FOR A LONG TIME SHE HAD NO IDEA THAT IT WAS ME, BUT EVENTUALLY SHE FOUND OUT.
"THE HULK SPENT YEARS RUINING MY LIFE, BUT THEN THERE CAME A TIME WHEN I WAS PHYSICALLY SEPARATED FROM HIM FOR A WHILE.
"SO BETTY AND I MARRIED.
"I THOUGHT OUR LIFE TOGETHER WAS GOING TO BE PERFECT.
"BUT THE HULK CAME BACK. HE ALWAYS COMES BACK.
"SOMEHOW, THOUGH... SOMEHOW...

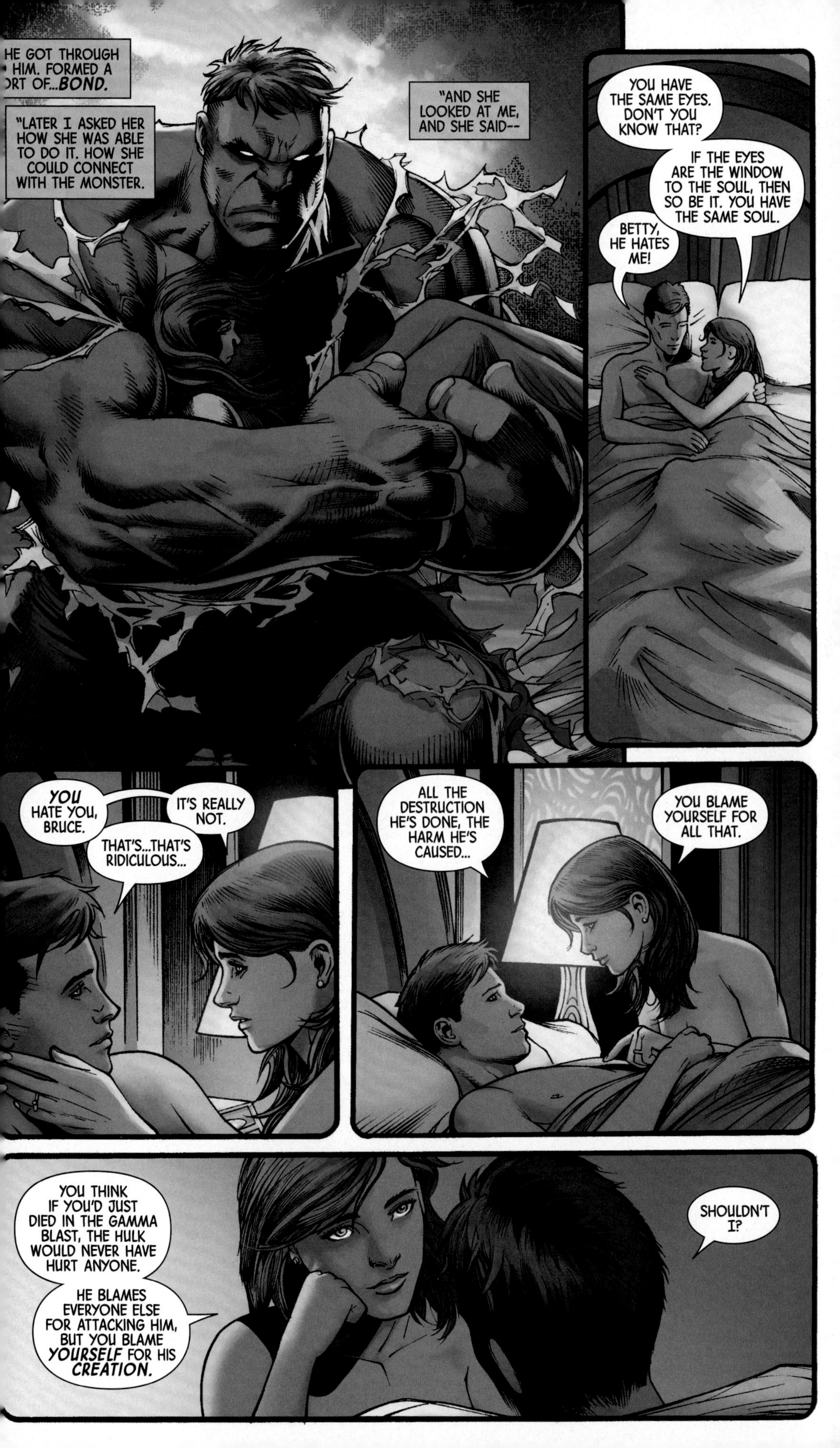
HE GOT THROUGH HIM. FORMED A ORT OF...BOND.
"LATER I ASKED HER HOW SHE WAS ABLE TO DO IT. HOW SHE COULD CONNECT WITH THE MONSTER.
"AND SHE LOOKED AT ME, AND SHE SAID--
YOU HAVE THE SAME EYES. DON'T YOU KNOW THAT?
IF THE EYES ARE THE WINDOW TO THE SOUL, THEN SO BE IT. YOU HAVE THE SAME SOUL.
BETTY, HE HATES ME!
YOU HATE YOU, BRUCE.
THAT'S...THAT'S RIDICULOUS...
IT'S REALLY NOT.
ALL THE DESTRUCTION HE'S DONE, THE HARM HE'S CAUSED...
YOU BLAME YOURSELF FOR ALL THAT.
YOU THINK IF YOU'D JUST DIED IN THE GAMMA BLAST, THE HULK WOULD NEVER HAVE HURT ANYONE.
HE BLAMES EVERYONE ELSE FOR ATTACKING HIM, BUT YOU BLAME YOURSELF FOR HIS CREATION.
SHOULDN'T I?

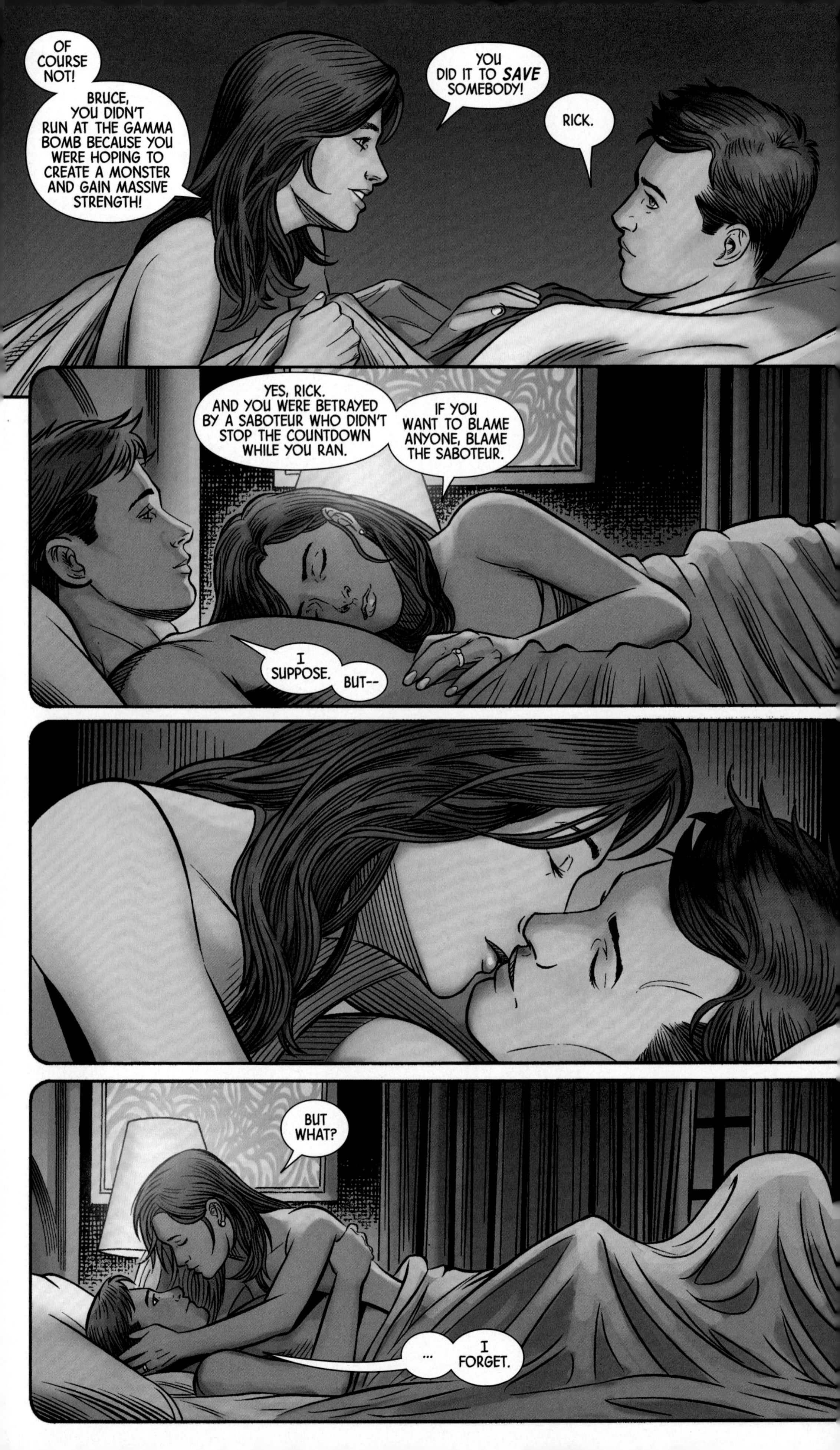
OF COURSE NOT!
BRUCE, YOU DIDN'T RUN AT THE GAMMA BOMB BECAUSE YOU WERE HOPING TO CREATE A MONSTER AND GAIN MASSIVE STRENGTH!
YOU DID IT TO SAVE SOMEBODY!
RICK.
YES, RICK. AND YOU WERE BETRAYED BY A SABOTEUR WHO DIDN'T STOP THE COUNTDOWN WHILE YOU RAN.
IF YOU WANT TO BLAME ANYONE, BLAME THE SABOTEUR.
I SUPPOSE.
BUT--
BUT WHAT?
...
I FORGET.

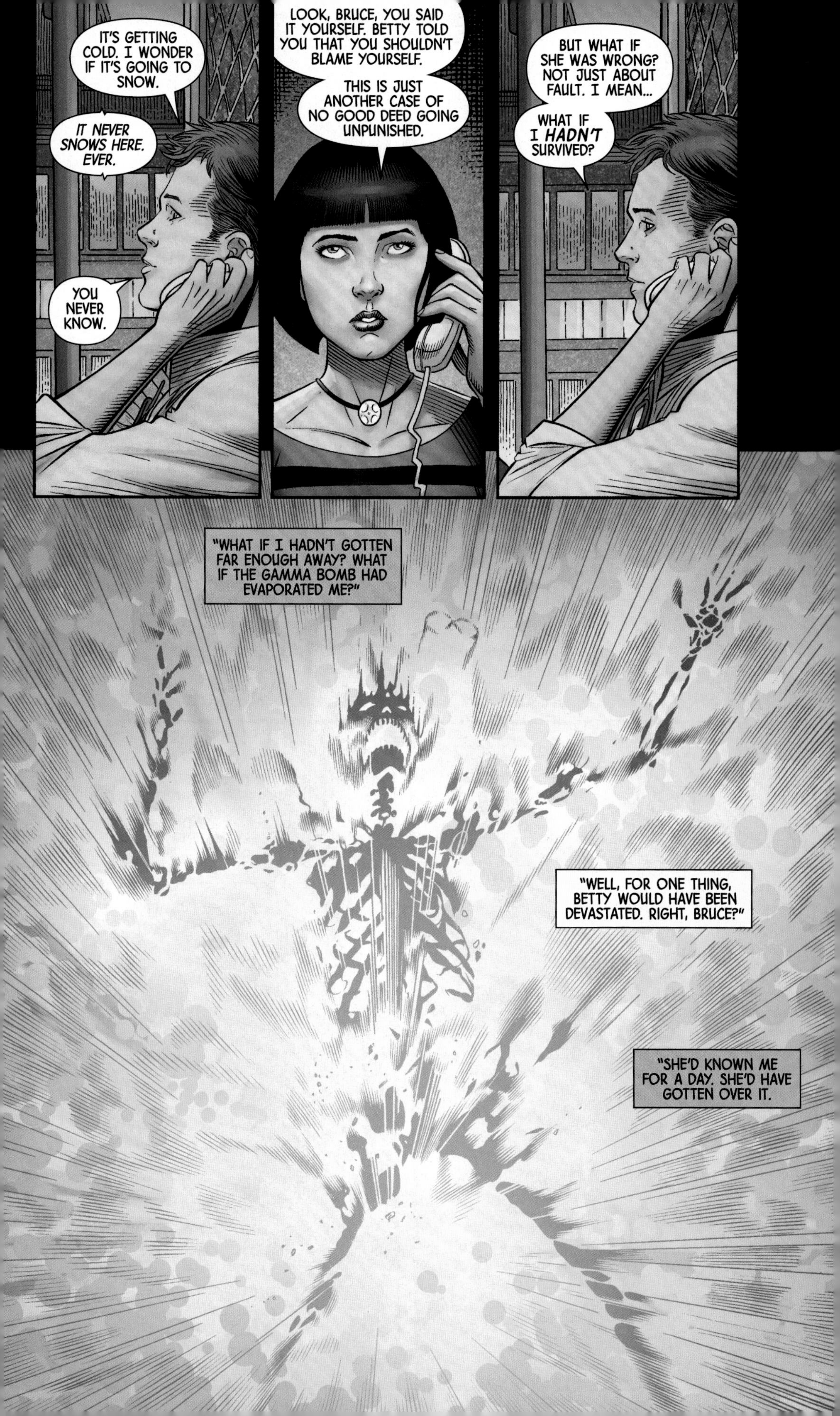
IT'S GETTING COLD. I WONDER IF IT'S GOING TO SNOW.
IT NEVER SNOWS HERE. EVER.
YOU NEVER KNOW.
LOOK, BRUCE, YOU SAID IT YOURSELF. BETTY TOLD YOU THAT YOU SHOULDN'T BLAME YOURSELF.
THIS IS JUST ANOTHER CASE OF NO GOOD DEED GOING UNPUNISHED.
BUT WHAT IF SHE WAS WRONG? NOT JUST ABOUT FAULT. I MEAN...
WHAT IF I HADN'T SURVIVED?
"WHAT IF I HADN'T GOTTEN FAR ENOUGH AWAY? WHAT IF THE GAMMA BOMB HAD EVAPORATED ME?"
"WELL, FOR ONE THING, BETTY WOULD HAVE BEEN DEVASTATED. RIGHT, BRUCE?"
"SHE'D KNOWN ME FOR A DAY. SHE'D HAVE GOTTEN OVER IT.

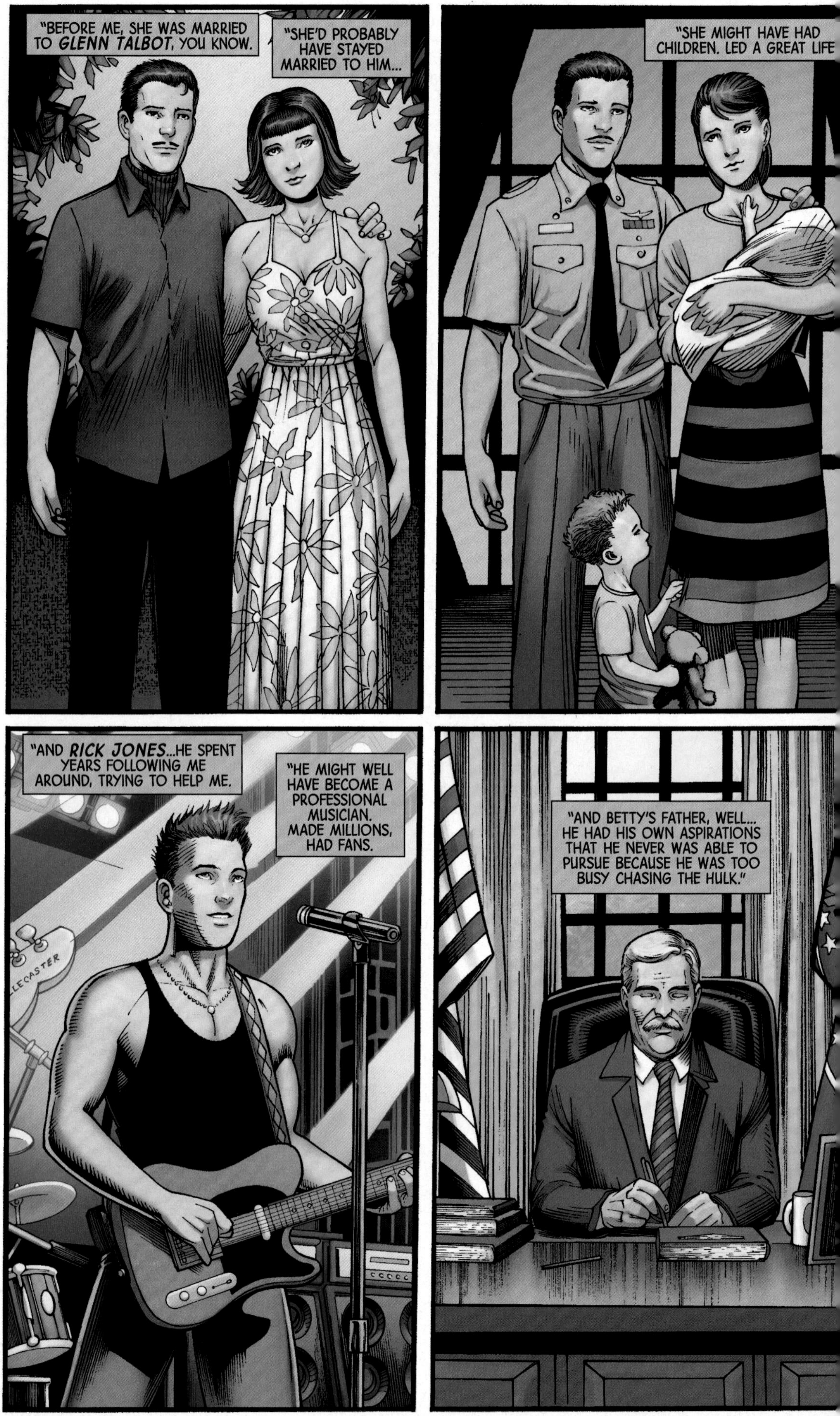
"BEFORE ME, SHE WAS MARRIED TO GLENN TALBOT, YOU KNOW.
"SHE'D PROBABLY HAVE STAYED MARRIED TO HIM...
"SHE MIGHT HAVE HAD CHILDREN. LED A GREAT LIFE
"AND RICK JONES...HE SPENT YEARS FOLLOWING ME AROUND, TRYING TO HELP ME.
"HE MIGHT WELL HAVE BECOME A PROFESSIONAL MUSICIAN. MADE MILLIONS, HAD FANS.
LECASTER
"AND BETTY'S FATHER, WELL... HE HAD HIS OWN ASPIRATIONS THAT HE NEVER WAS ABLE TO PURSUE BECAUSE HE WAS TOO BUSY CHASING THE HULK."

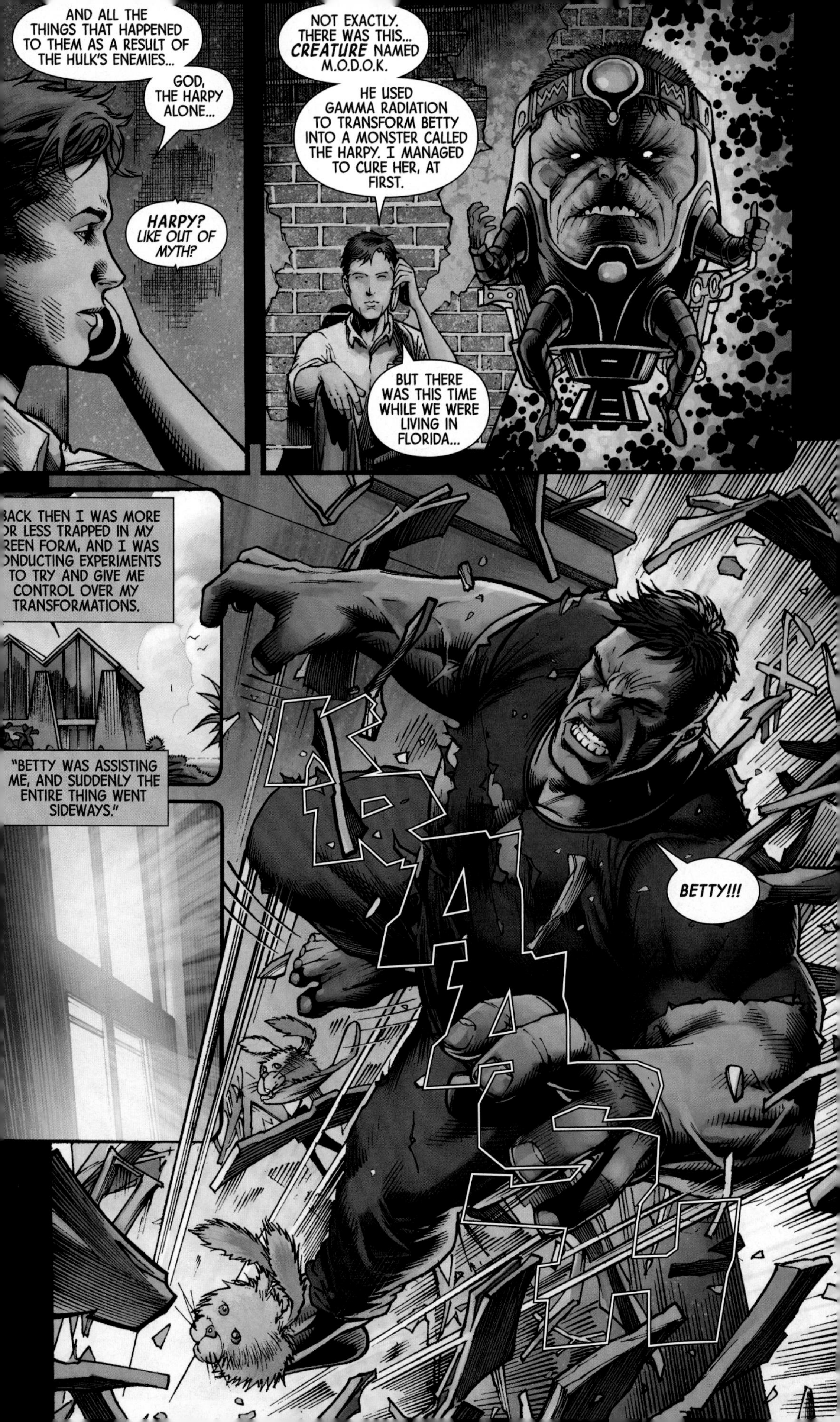
AND ALL THE THINGS THAT HAPPENED TO THEM AS A RESULT OF THE HULK'S ENEMIES...
GOD, THE HARPY ALONE...
HARPY? LIKE OUT OF MYTH?
NOT EXACTLY. THERE WAS THIS... CREATURE NAMED M.O.D.O.K.
HE USED GAMMA RADIATION TO TRANSFORM BETTY INTO A MONSTER CALLED THE HARPY. I MANAGED TO CURE HER, AT FIRST.
BUT THERE WAS THIS TIME WHILE WE WERE LIVING IN FLORIDA...
BACK THEN I WAS MORE OR LESS TRAPPED IN MY GREEN FORM, AND I WAS CONDUCTING EXPERIMENTS TO TRY AND GIVE ME CONTROL OVER MY TRANSFORMATIONS.
"BETTY WAS ASSISTING ME, AND SUDDENLY THE ENTIRE THING WENT SIDEWAYS."
KRAASH
BETTY!!!

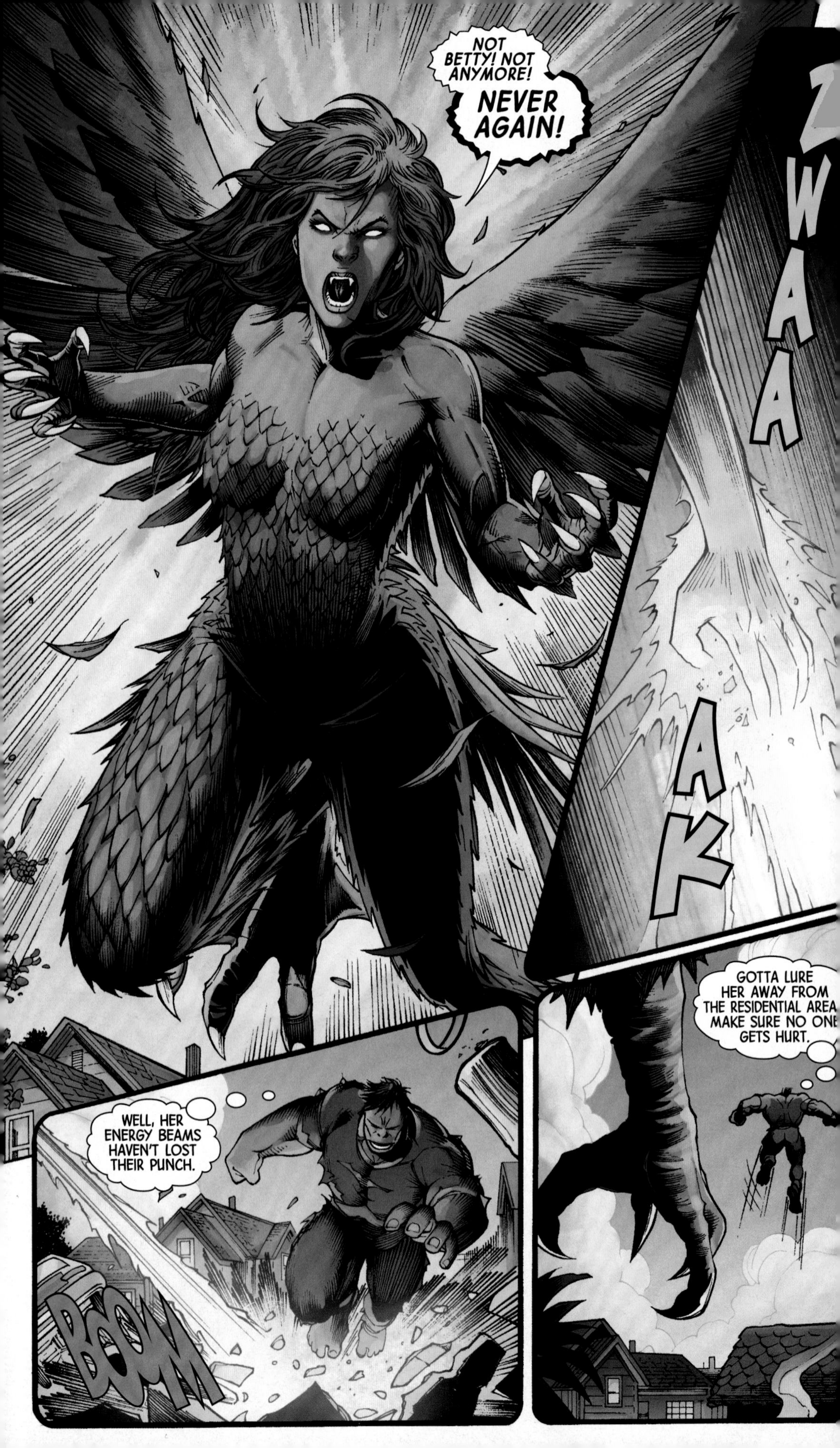
NOT BETTY! NOT ANYMORE!
NEVER AGAIN!
ZWAAAAK
WELL, HER ENERGY BEAMS HAVEN'T LOST THEIR PUNCH.
BOOM
GOTTA LURE HER AWAY FROM THE RESIDENTIAL AREA. MAKE SURE NO ONE GETS HURT.

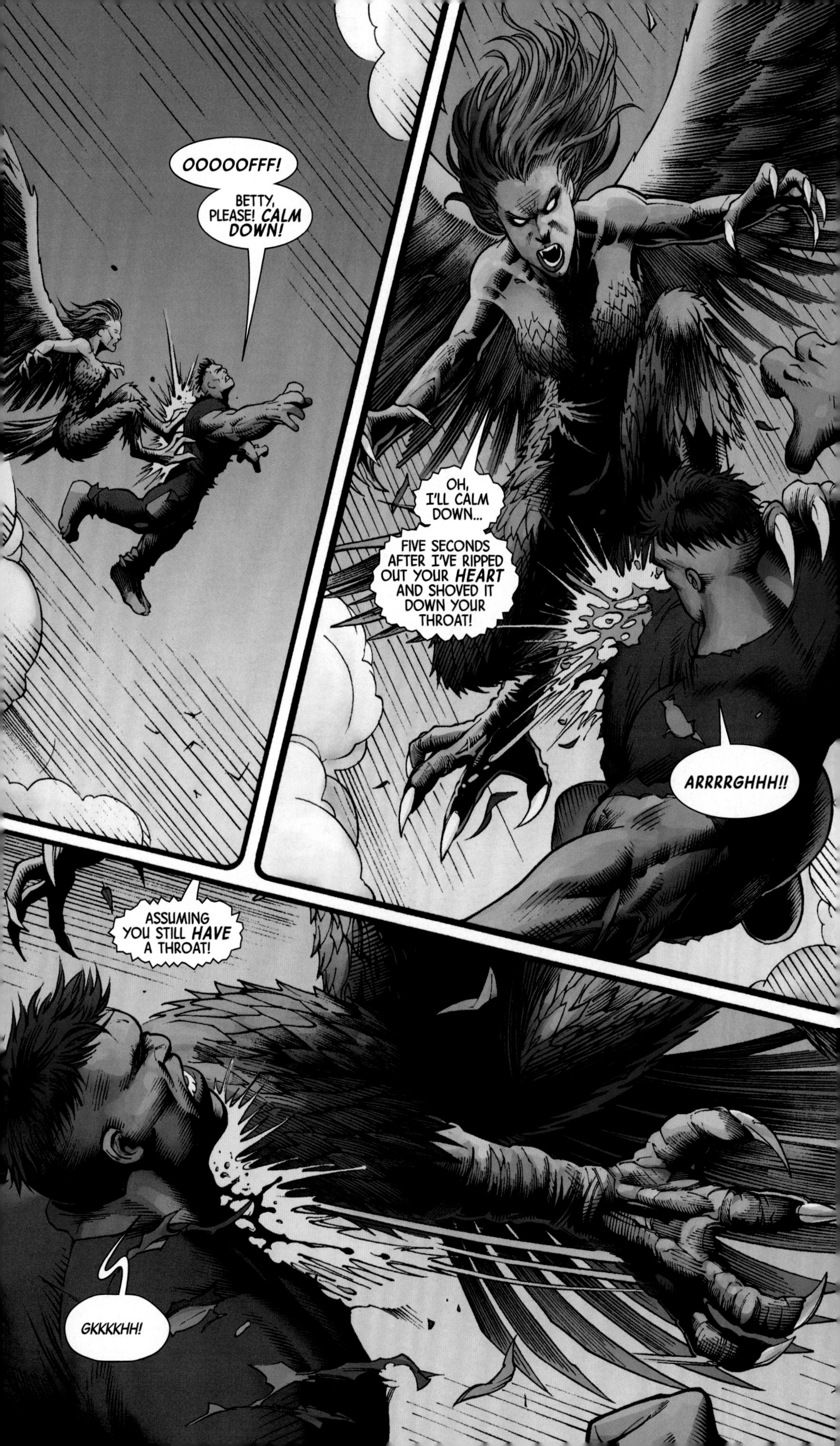
OOOOOFFF!
BETTY, PLEASE! CALM DOWN!
OH, I'LL CALM DOWN...
FIVE SECONDS AFTER I'VE RIPPED OUT YOUR HEART AND SHOVED IT DOWN YOUR THROAT!
ARRRRGHHH!!
ASSUMING YOU STILL HAVE A THROAT!
GKKKKHH!

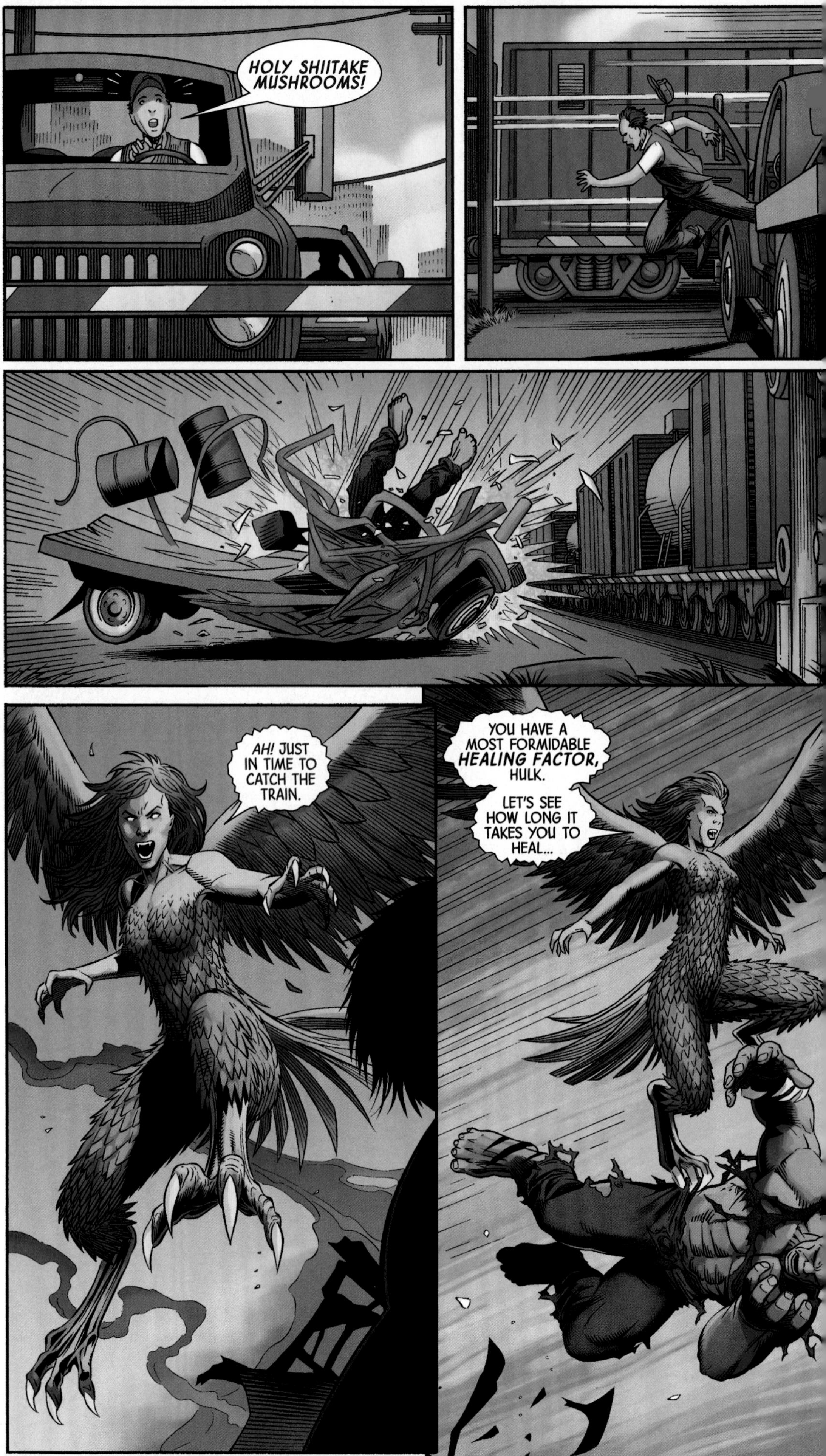
HOLY SHIITAKE MUSHROOMS!
AH! JUST IN TIME TO CATCH THE TRAIN.
YOU HAVE A MOST FORMIDABLE *HEALING FACTOR,* HULK.
LET'S SEE HOW LONG IT TAKES YOU TO HEAL...

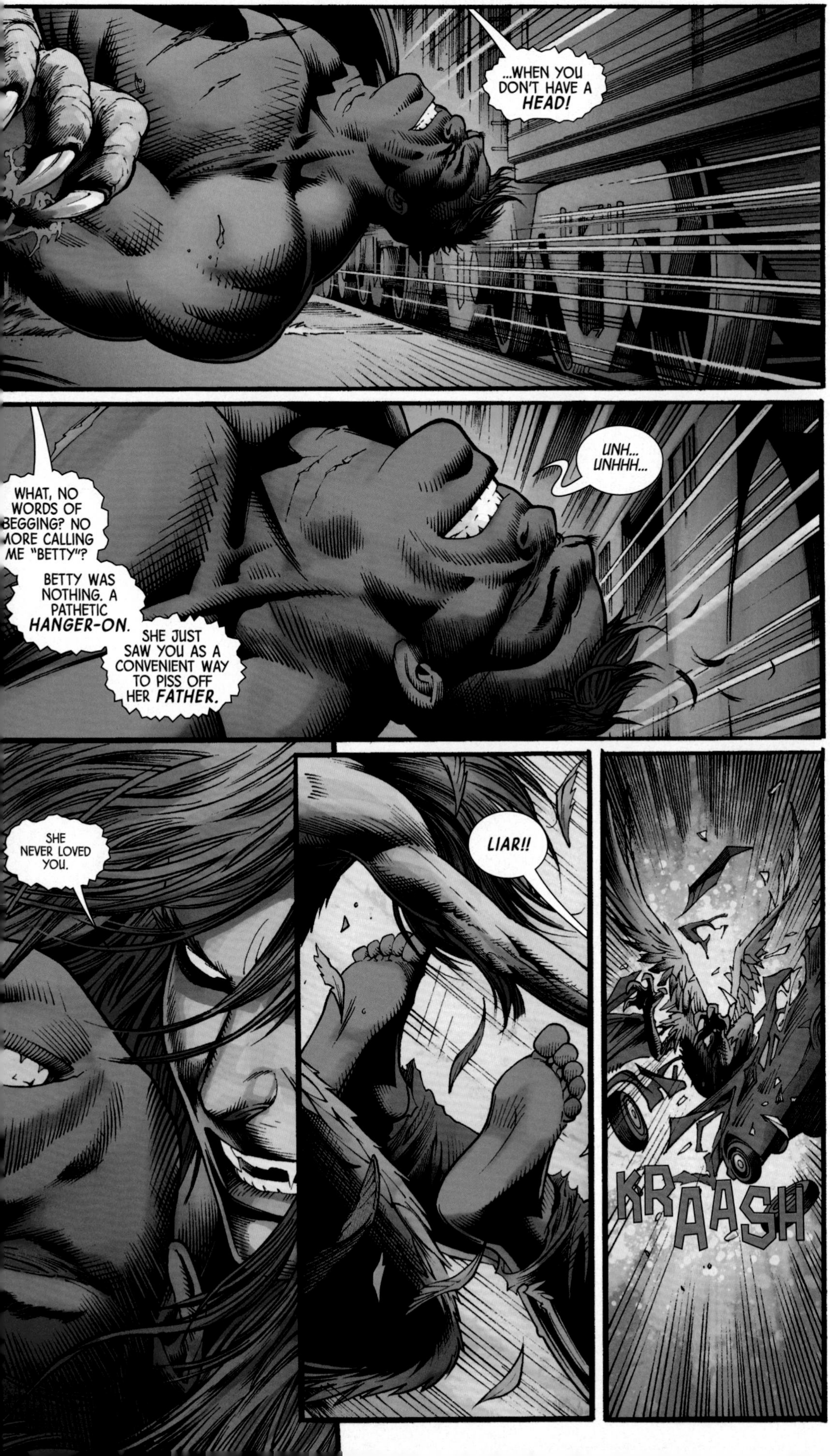
...WHEN YOU DON'T HAVE A HEAD!
WHAT, NO WORDS OF BEGGING? NO MORE CALLING ME "BETTY"?
BETTY WAS NOTHING. A PATHETIC HANGER-ON.
SHE JUST SAW YOU AS A CONVENIENT WAY TO PISS OFF HER FATHER.
UNH... UNHHH...
SHE NEVER LOVED YOU.
LIAR!!
KRAASH

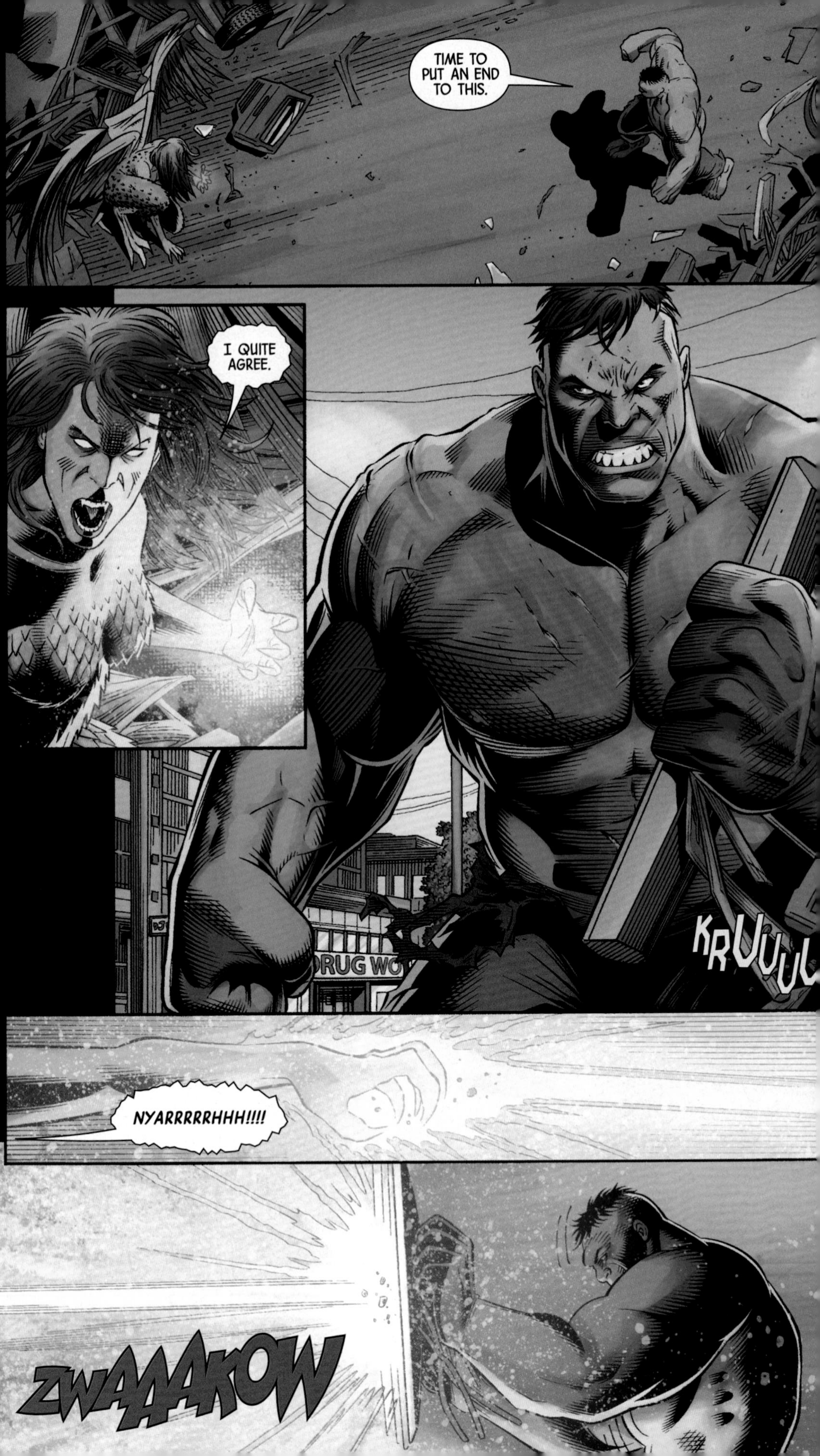
TIME TO PUT AN END TO THIS.
I QUITE AGREE.
KRUUUU
NYARRRRRHHH!!!!
ZWAAAKOW

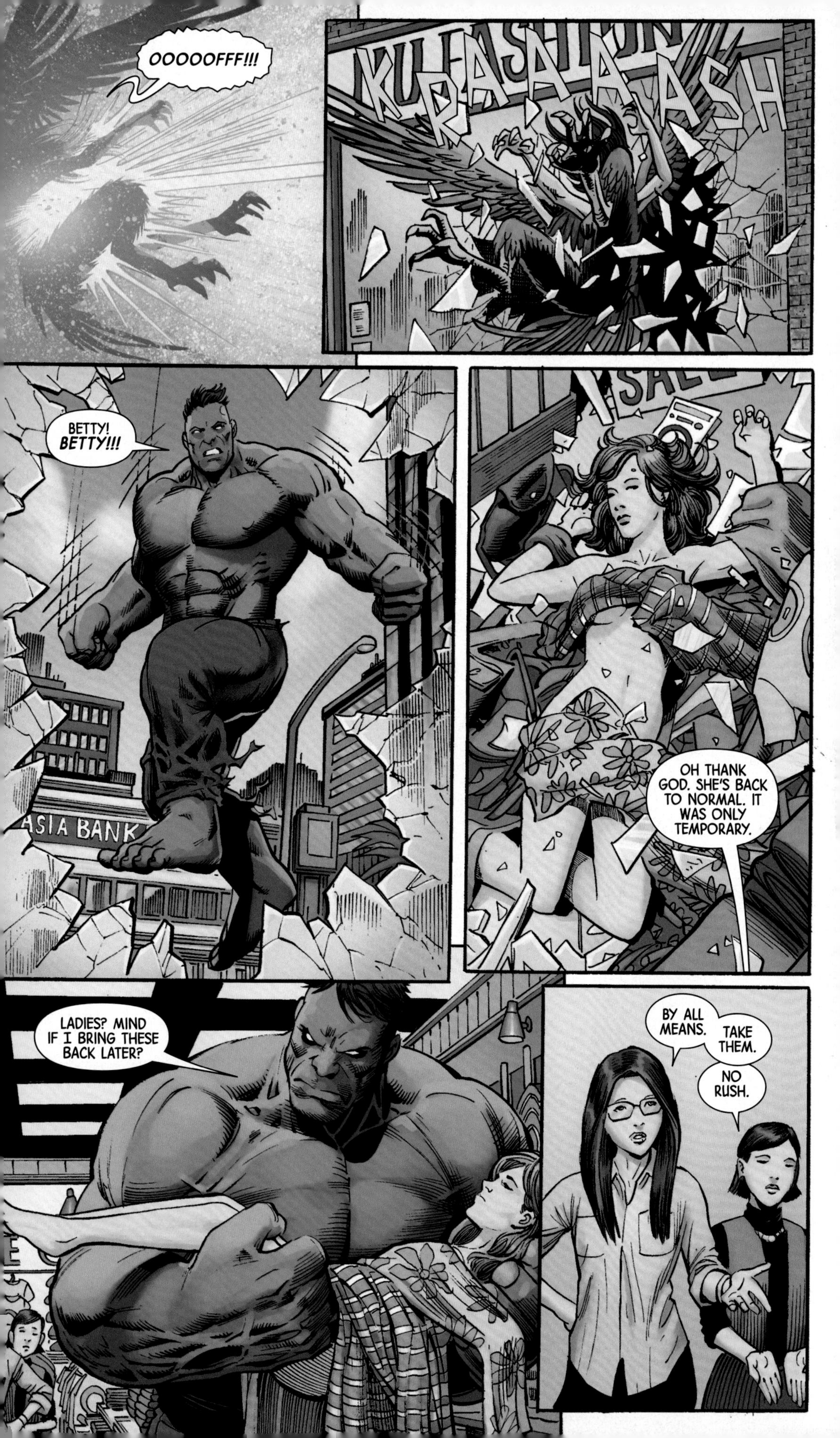
OOOOOFFF!!!
KRASHHH
KRAAASSH
BETTY! BETTY!!!
ASIA BANK
SALE
OH THANK GOD. SHE'S BACK TO NORMAL. IT WAS ONLY TEMPORARY.
LADIES? MIND IF I BRING THESE BACK LATER?
BY ALL MEANS.
TAKE THEM.
NO RUSH.

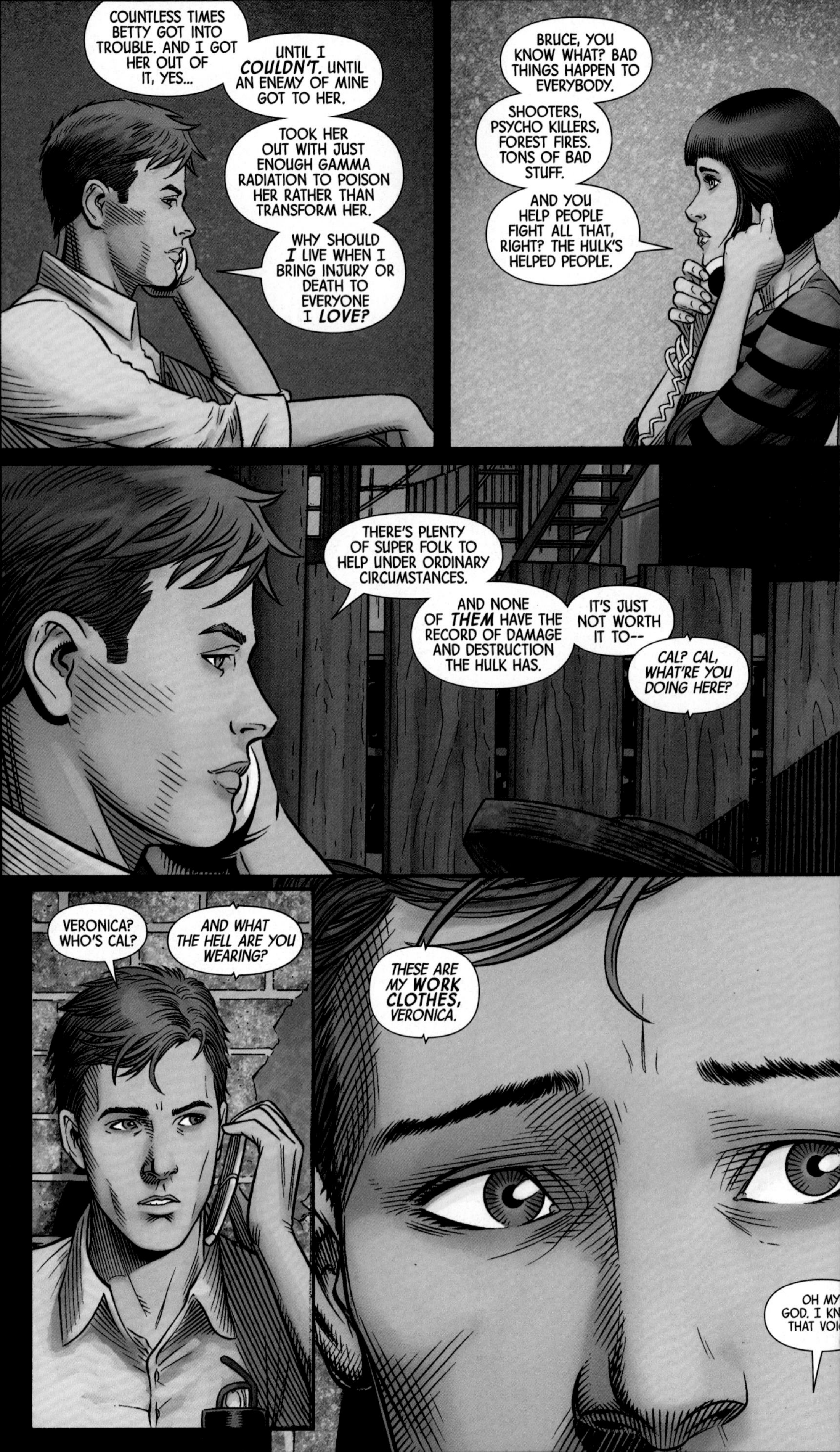
COUNTLESS TIMES BETTY GOT INTO TROUBLE. AND I GOT HER OUT OF IT, YES...
UNTIL I COULDN'T. UNTIL AN ENEMY OF MINE GOT TO HER.
TOOK HER OUT WITH JUST ENOUGH GAMMA RADIATION TO POISON HER RATHER THAN TRANSFORM HER.
WHY SHOULD I LIVE WHEN I BRING INJURY OR DEATH TO EVERYONE I LOVE?
BRUCE, YOU KNOW WHAT? BAD THINGS HAPPEN TO EVERYBODY.
SHOOTERS, PSYCHO KILLERS, FOREST FIRES. TONS OF BAD STUFF.
AND YOU HELP PEOPLE FIGHT ALL THAT, RIGHT? THE HULK'S HELPED PEOPLE.
THERE'S PLENTY OF SUPER FOLK TO HELP UNDER ORDINARY CIRCUMSTANCES.
AND NONE OF THEM HAVE THE RECORD OF DAMAGE AND DESTRUCTION THE HULK HAS.
IT'S JUST NOT WORTH IT TO--
CAL? CAL, WHAT'RE YOU DOING HERE?
VERONICA? WHO'S CAL?
AND WHAT THE HELL ARE YOU WEARING?
THESE ARE MY WORK CLOTHES, VERONICA.
OH MY GOD. I KN THAT VOI

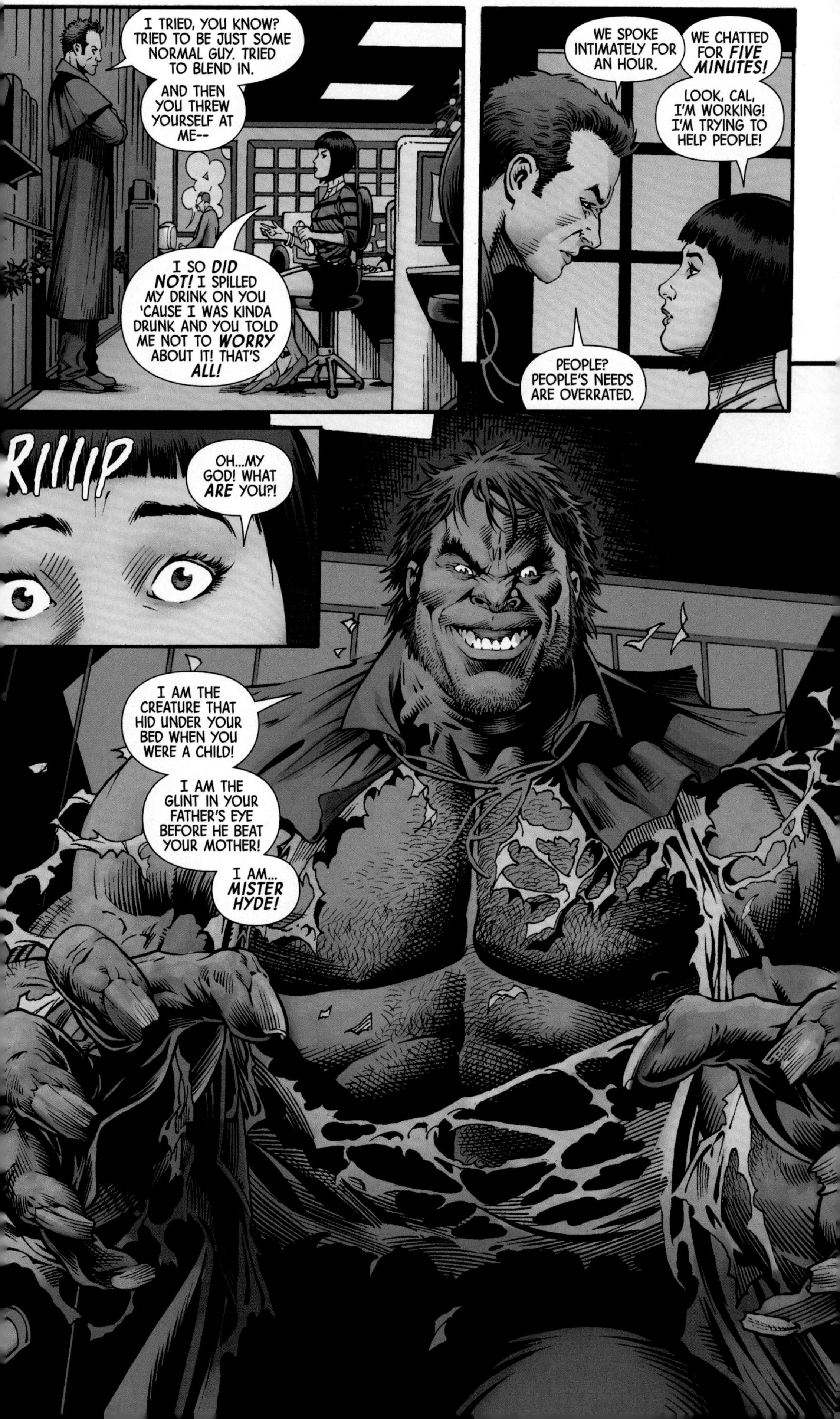
I TRIED, YOU KNOW? TRIED TO BE JUST SOME NORMAL GUY. TRIED TO BLEND IN.
AND THEN YOU THREW YOURSELF AT ME--
I SO DID NOT! I SPILLED MY DRINK ON YOU 'CAUSE I WAS KINDA DRUNK AND YOU TOLD ME NOT TO WORRY ABOUT IT! THAT'S ALL!
WE SPOKE INTIMATELY FOR AN HOUR.
WE CHATTED FOR FIVE MINUTES!
LOOK, CAL, I'M WORKING! I'M TRYING TO HELP PEOPLE!
PEOPLE? PEOPLE'S NEEDS ARE OVERRATED.
RIIIP
OH...MY GOD! WHAT ARE YOU?!
I AM THE CREATURE THAT HID UNDER YOUR BED WHEN YOU WERE A CHILD!
I AM THE GLINT IN YOUR FATHER'S EYE BEFORE HE BEAT YOUR MOTHER!
I AM... MISTER HYDE!

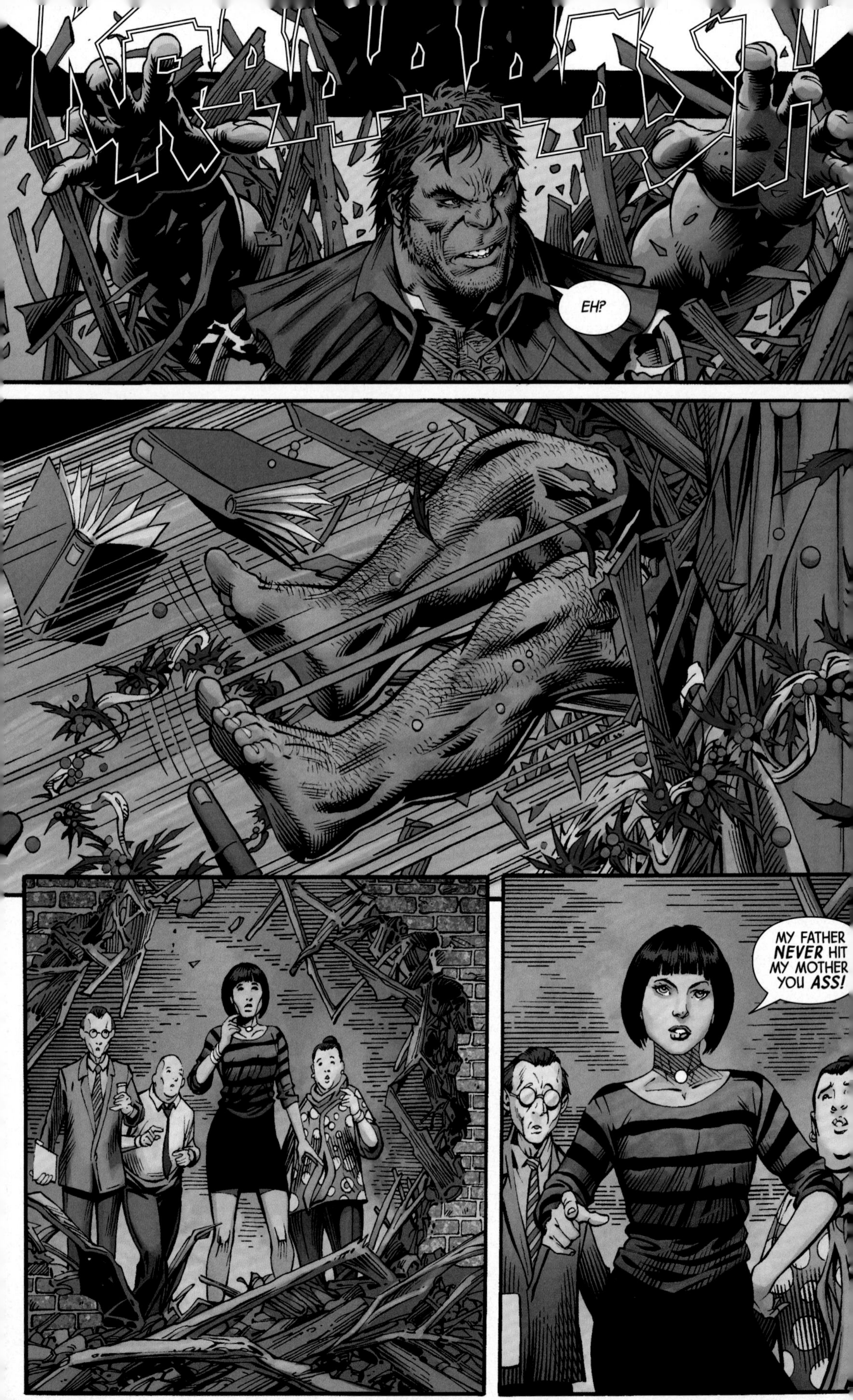
EH?
MY FATHER **NEVER** HIT MY MOTHER YOU **ASS!**

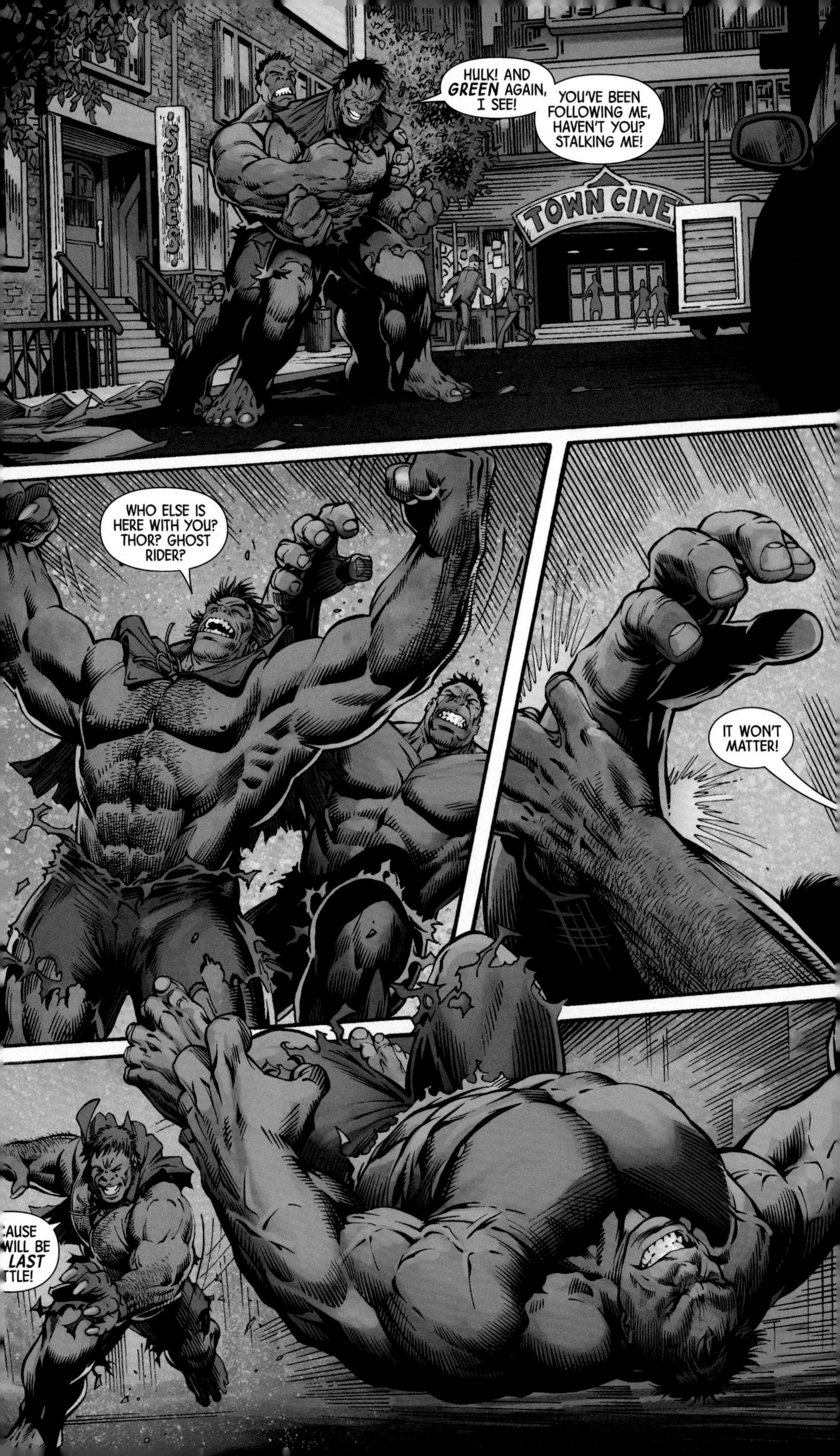

HULK! AND GREEN AGAIN, I SEE!
YOU'VE BEEN FOLLOWING ME, HAVEN'T YOU? STALKING ME!
TOWN CINE
SHOES
WHO ELSE IS HERE WITH YOU? THOR? GHOST RIDER?
IT WON'T MATTER!
CAUSE WILL BE LAST TTLE!

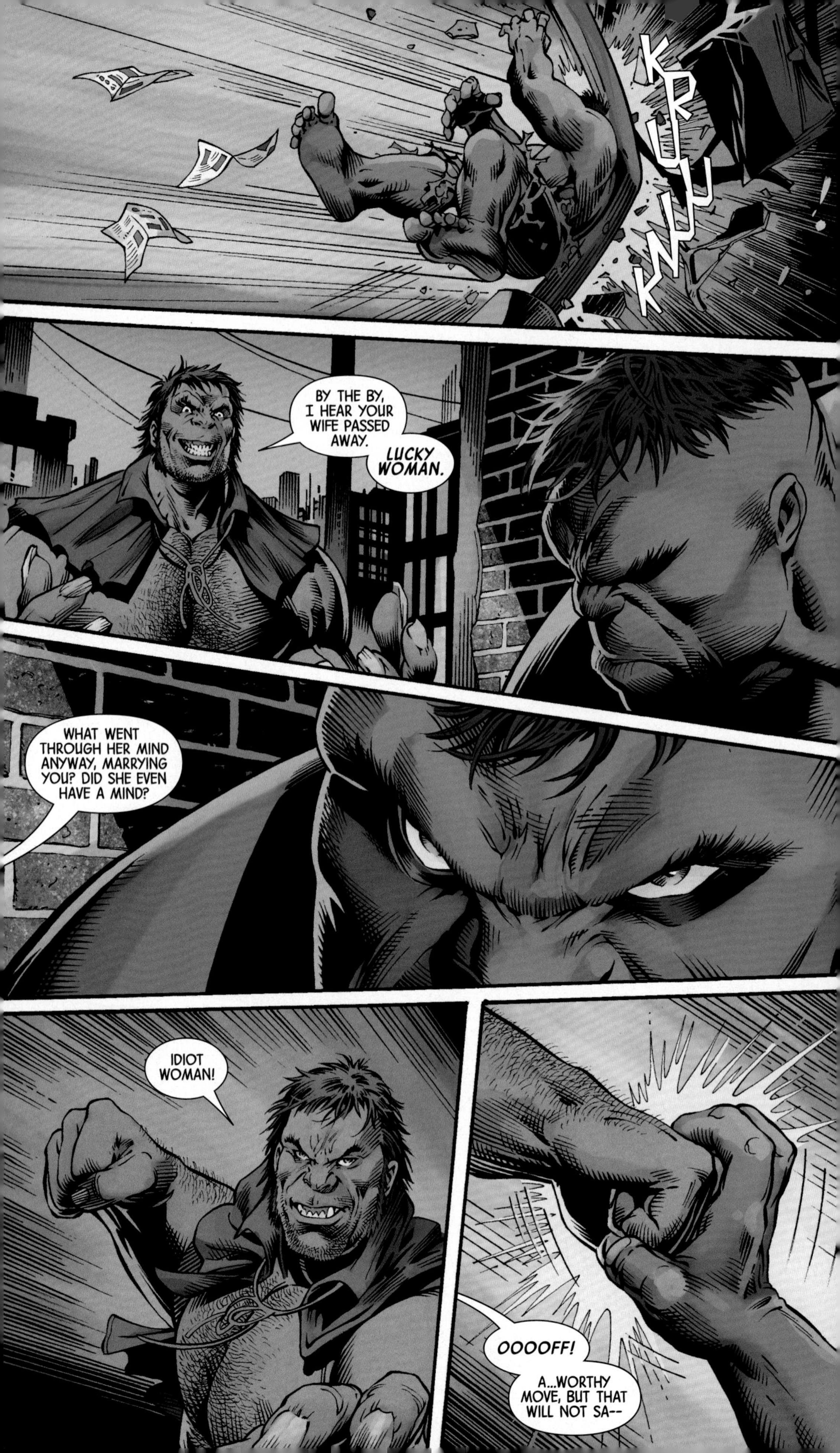
KRUUUNK!
BY THE BY, I HEAR YOUR WIFE PASSED AWAY.
LUCKY WOMAN.
WHAT WENT THROUGH HER MIND ANYWAY, MARRYING YOU? DID SHE EVEN HAVE A MIND?
IDIOT WOMAN!
OOOOFF!
A...WORTHY MOVE, BUT THAT WILL NOT SA--

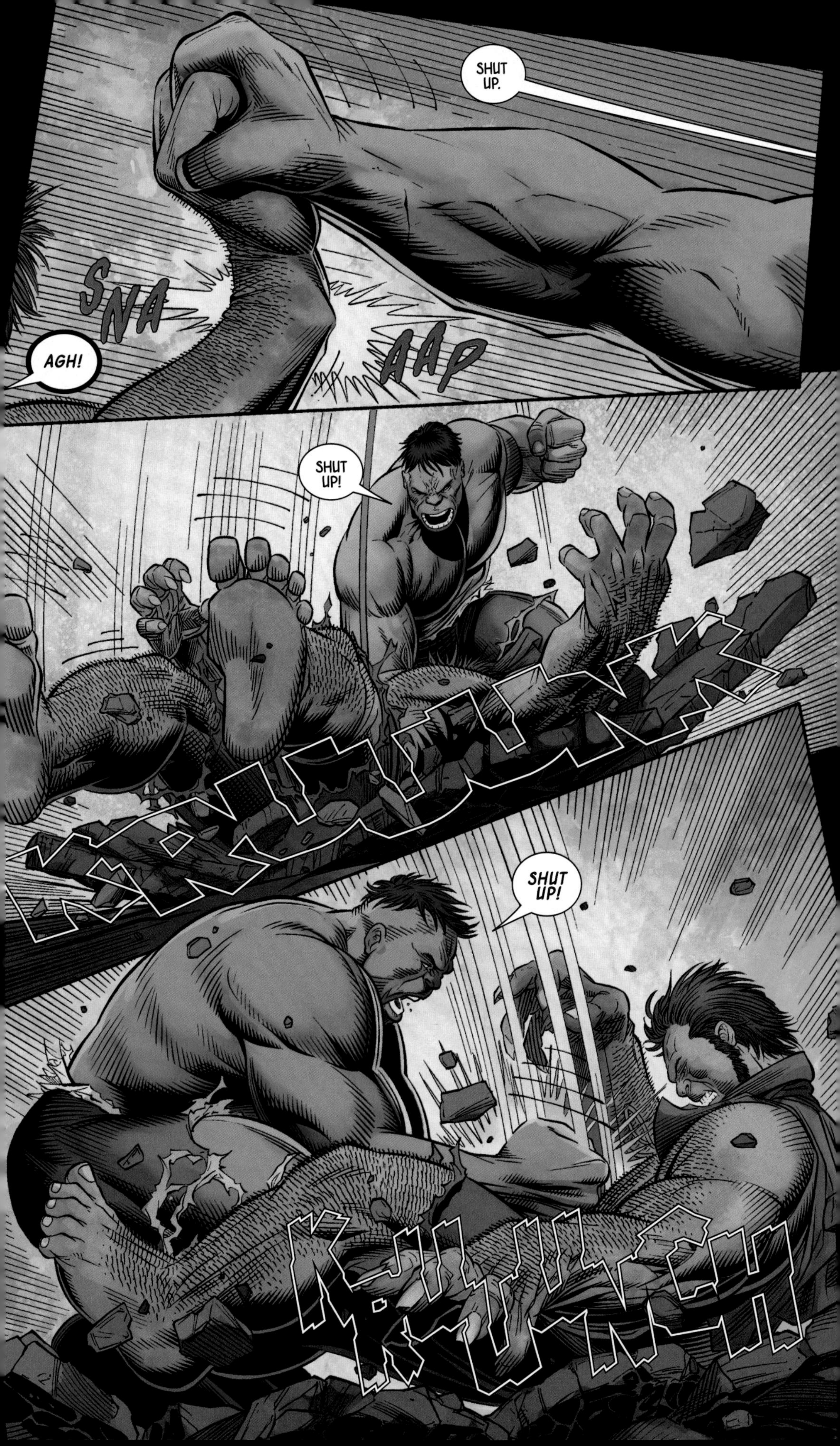
SHUT UP.
SNA
AAP
AGH!
SHUT UP!
SHUT UP!
KRUNCH

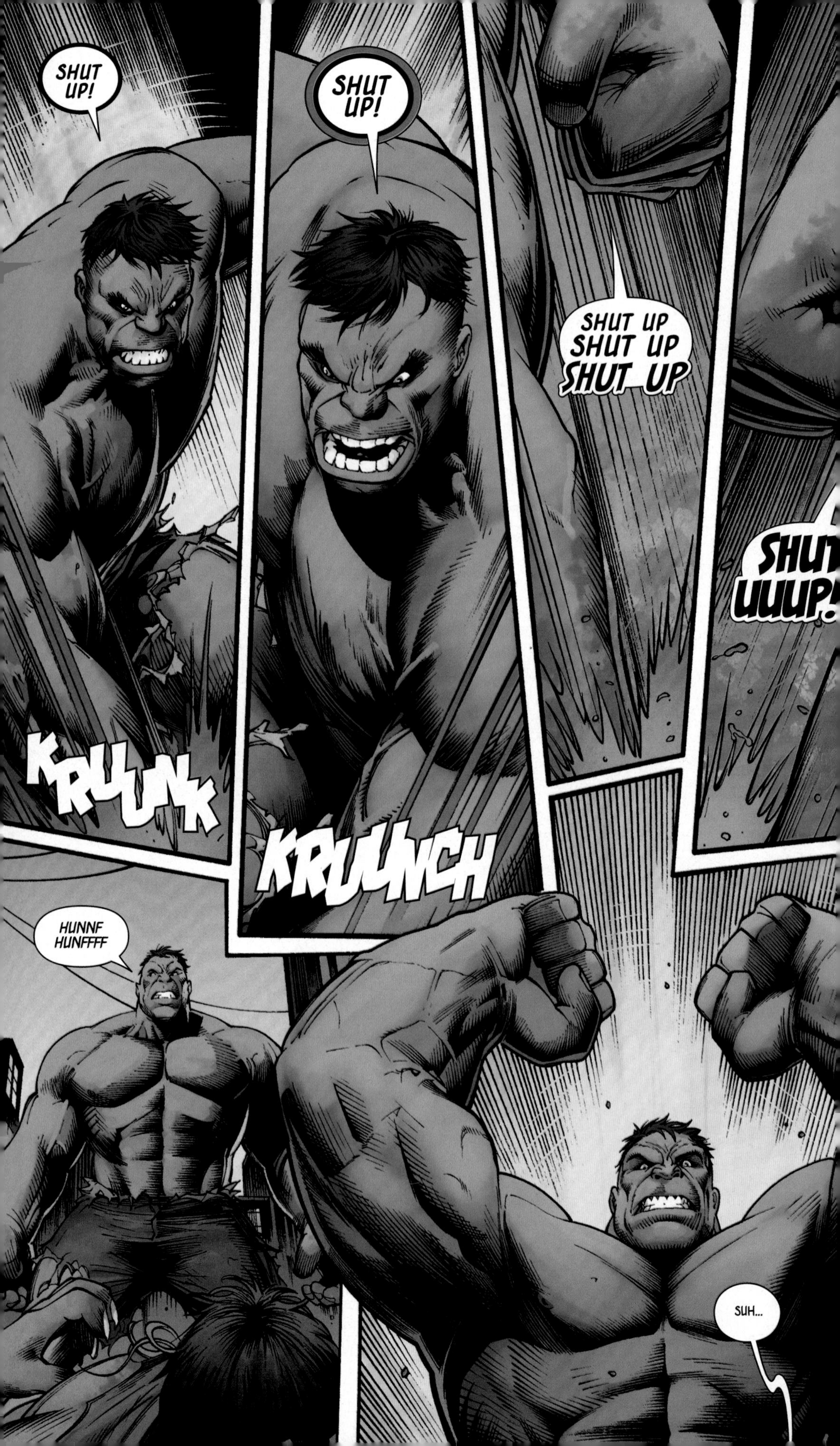
SHUT UP!
SHUT UP!
SHUT UP
SHUT UP
SHUT UP
SHUT UUUP!
KRUUNK
KRUUNCH
HUNNF HUNFFFF
SUH...

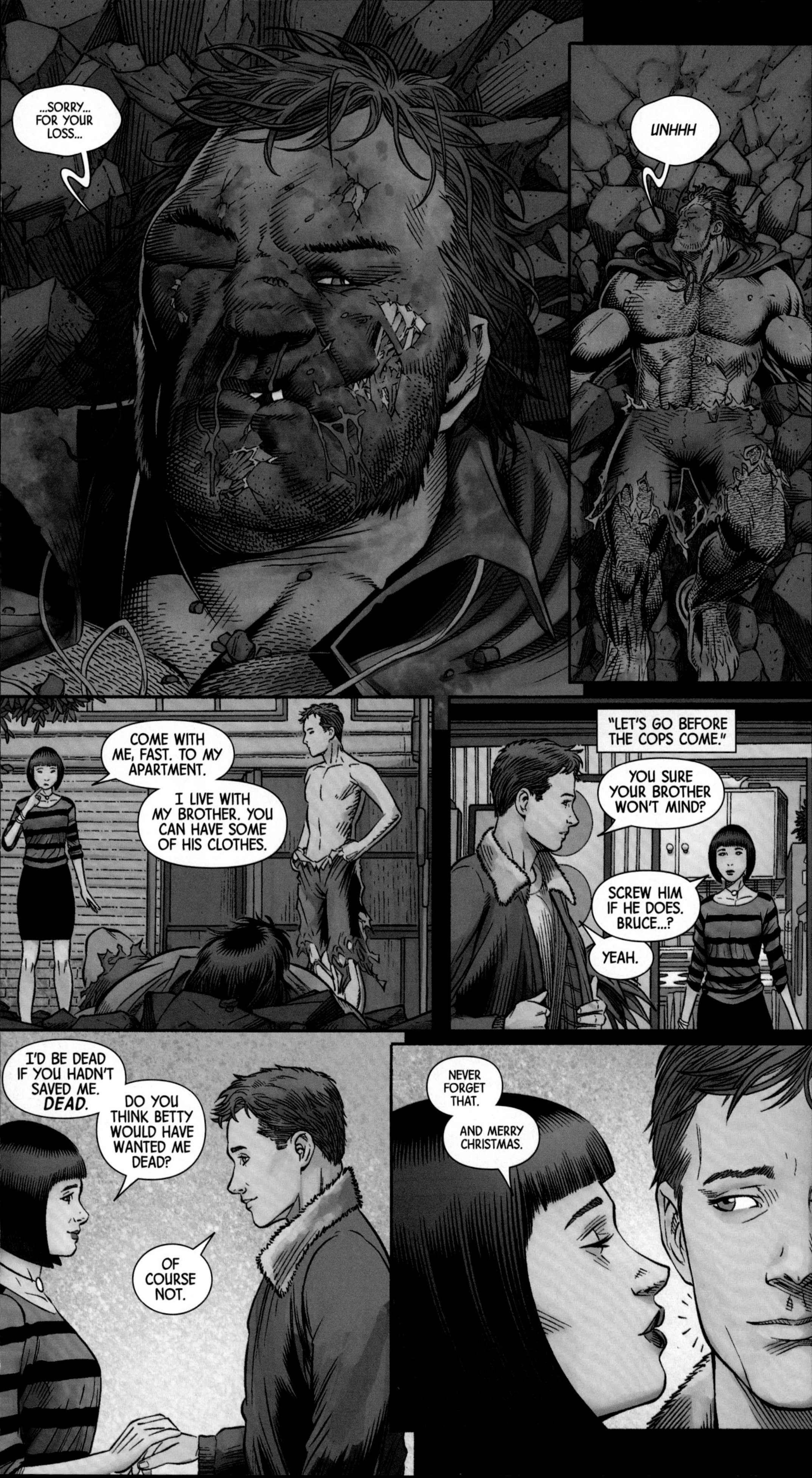
...SORRY... FOR YOUR LOSS...
UNHHH
COME WITH ME, FAST. TO MY APARTMENT.
I LIVE WITH MY BROTHER. YOU CAN HAVE SOME OF HIS CLOTHES.
"LET'S GO BEFORE THE COPS COME."
YOU SURE YOUR BROTHER WON'T MIND?
SCREW HIM IF HE DOES. BRUCE...?
YEAH.
I'D BE DEAD IF YOU HADN'T SAVED ME. DEAD.
DO YOU THINK BETTY WOULD HAVE WANTED ME DEAD?
OF COURSE NOT.
NEVER FORGET THAT.
AND MERRY CHRISTMAS.

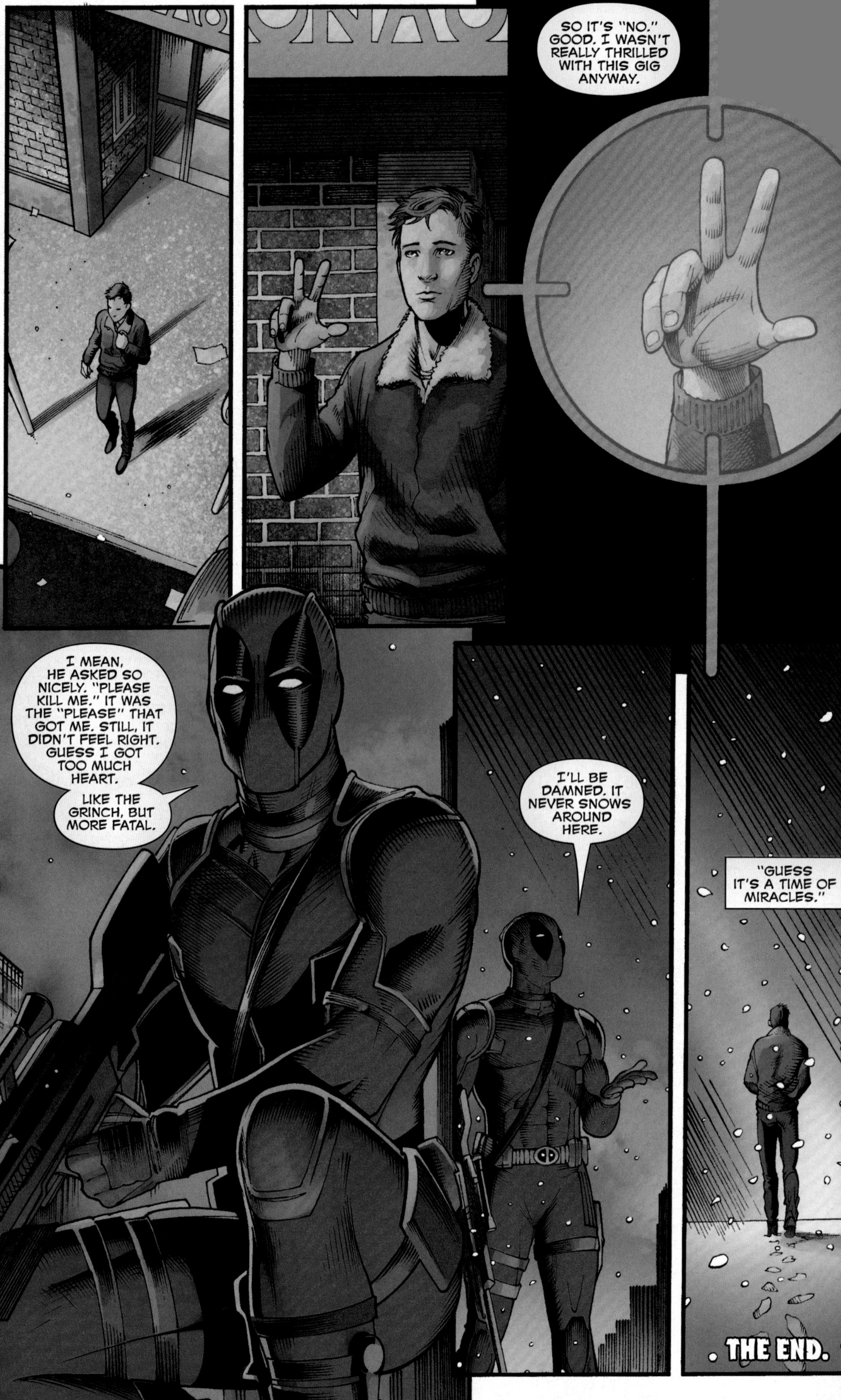
SO IT'S "NO." GOOD. I WASN'T REALLY THRILLED WITH THIS GIG ANYWAY.
I MEAN, HE ASKED SO NICELY. "PLEASE KILL ME." IT WAS THE "PLEASE" THAT GOT ME. STILL, IT DIDN'T FEEL RIGHT. GUESS I GOT TOO MUCH HEART.
LIKE THE GRINCH, BUT MORE FATAL.
I'LL BE DAMNED. IT NEVER SNOWS AROUND HERE.
"GUESS IT'S A TIME OF MIRACLES."
THE END.

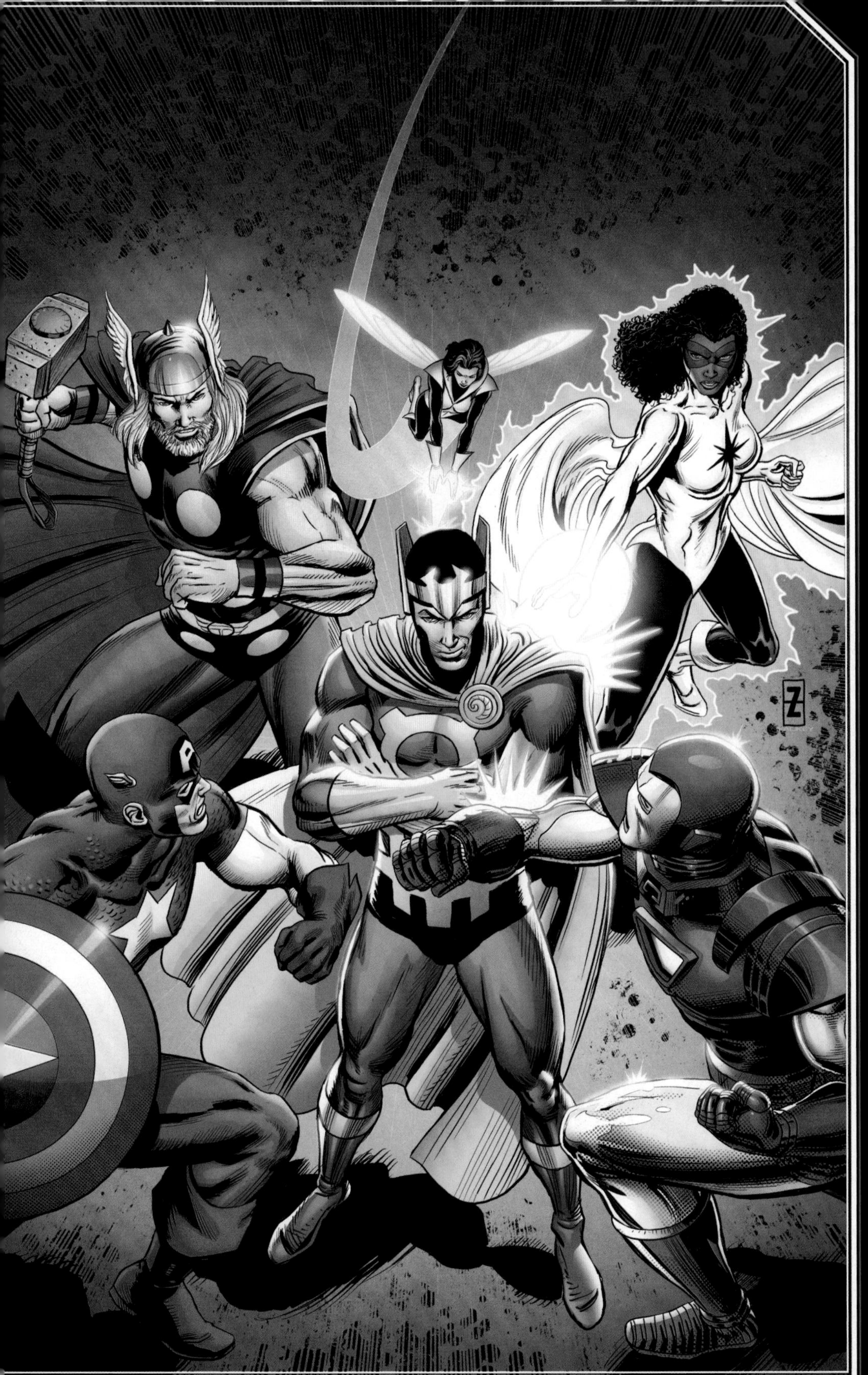

EARTH'S MIGHTIEST HEROES DEFENDED AVENGERS MANSION AFTER IT WAS BESIEGED BY THE MASTERS OF EVIL, BUT THEIR VICTORY WAS NOT WITHOUT HARDSHIP. NOW, AS THEY TRY TO REBUILD THEIR HOME AND REGAIN THEIR STRENGTH, THERE MAY BE A...FAMILIAR THREAT ON ITS WAY.

TAKES PLACE AFTER THE EVENTS OF *AVENGERS* #277!

Roger Stern **WRITER**
Dale Keown **PENCILER**
Scott Hanna **INKER**
Espen Grundetjern **COLOR ARTIST**
VC's Cory Peti **LETTERER**

Patch Zircher & Matt Yackey **COVER ART**
Shannon Andrews Ballesteros **ASSISTANT EDITOR**
Alanna Smith **ASSOCIATE EDITOR**
Tom Brevoort **EDITOR**
AVENGERS CREATD BY Stan Lee & Jack Ki

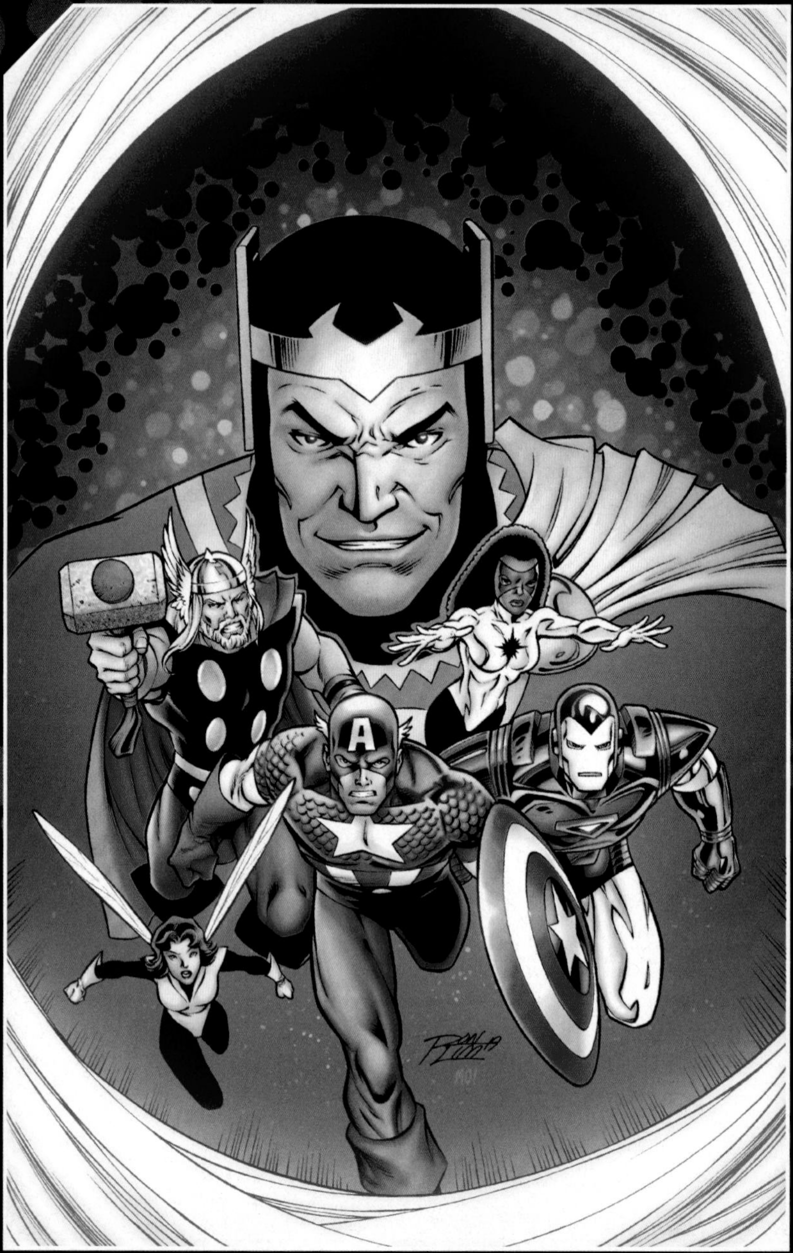

AVENGERS: LOKI UNLEASHED
variant by Ron Lim, Rafael Fonteriz & Morry Hollowell

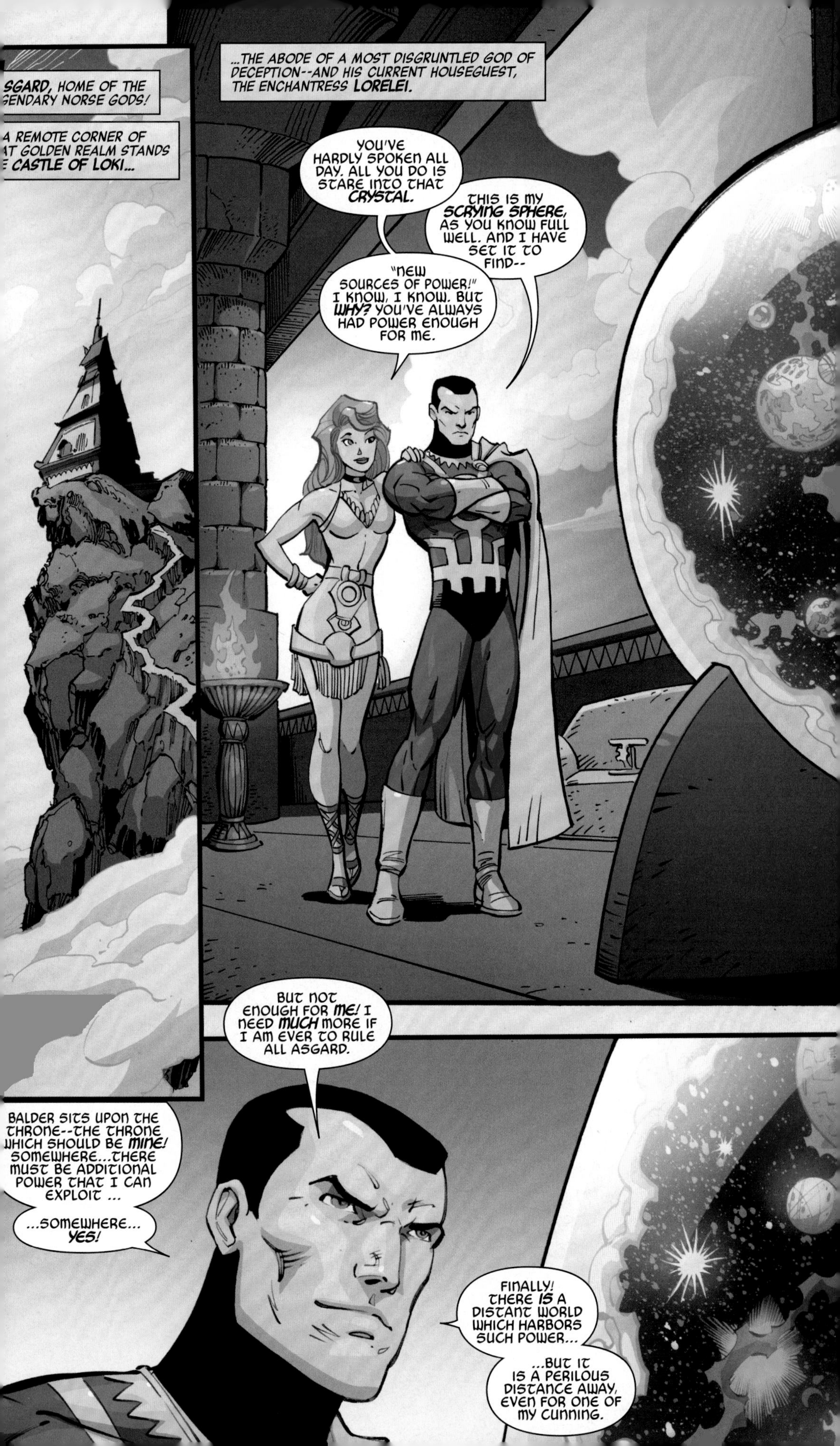
SGARD, HOME OF THE
GENDARY NORSE GODS!
A REMOTE CORNER OF
AT GOLDEN REALM STANDS
E CASTLE OF LOKI...
...THE ABODE OF A MOST DISGRUNTLED GOD OF DECEPTION--AND HIS CURRENT HOUSEGUEST, THE ENCHANTRESS LORELEI.
YOU'VE HARDLY SPOKEN ALL DAY. ALL YOU DO IS STARE INTO THAT CRYSTAL.
THIS IS MY SCRYING SPHERE, AS YOU KNOW FULL WELL. AND I HAVE SET IT TO FIND--
"NEW SOURCES OF POWER!" I KNOW, I KNOW. BUT WHY? YOU'VE ALWAYS HAD POWER ENOUGH FOR ME.
BUT NOT ENOUGH FOR ME! I NEED MUCH MORE IF I AM EVER TO RULE ALL ASGARD.
BALDER SITS UPON THE THRONE--THE THRONE WHICH SHOULD BE MINE! SOMEWHERE...THERE MUST BE ADDITIONAL POWER THAT I CAN EXPLOIT ...
...SOMEWHERE... YES!
FINALLY! THERE IS A DISTANT WORLD WHICH HARBORS SUCH POWER...
...BUT IT IS A PERILOUS DISTANCE AWAY, EVEN FOR ONE OF MY CUNNING.

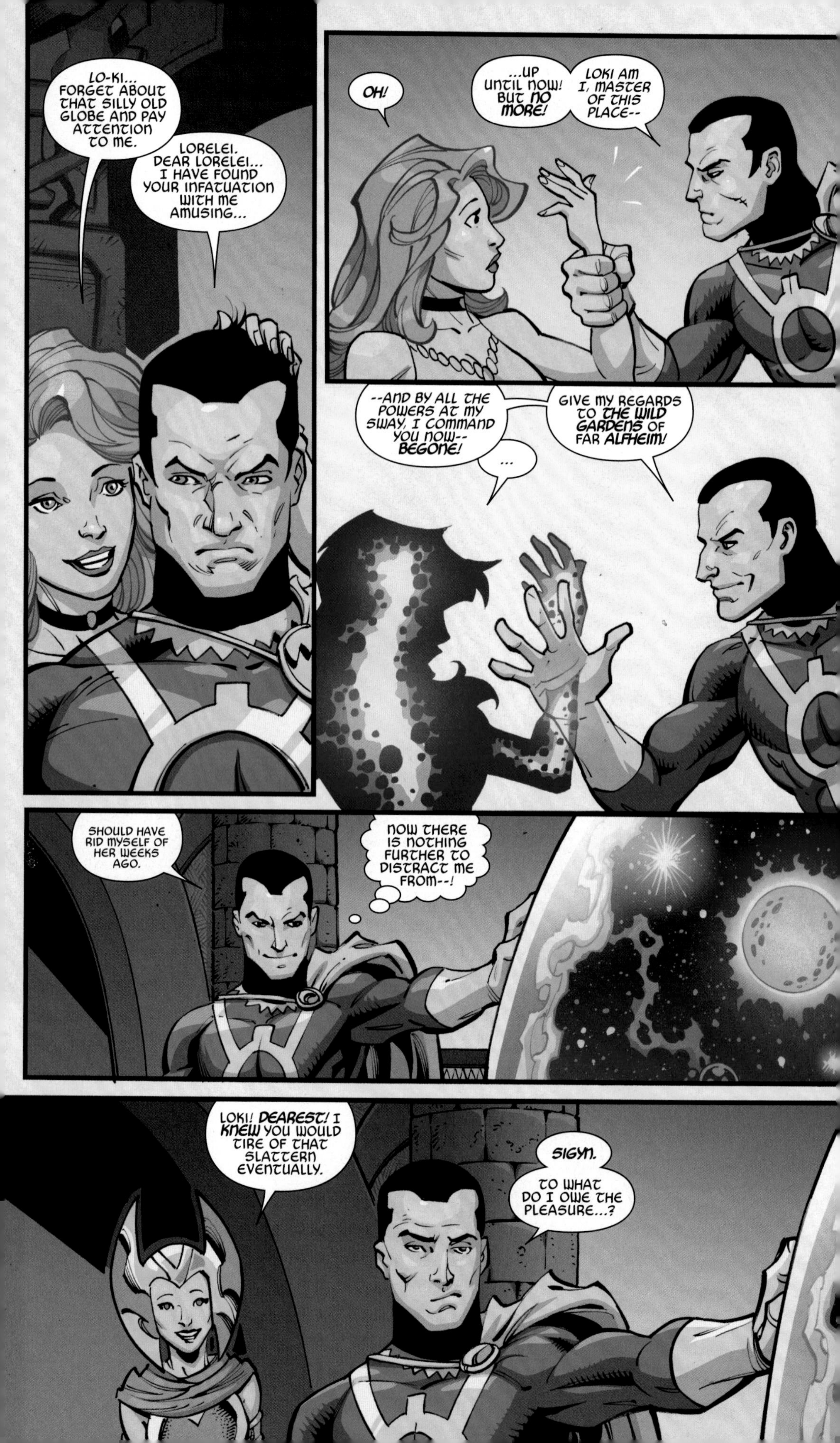
LO-KI... FORGET ABOUT THAT SILLY OLD GLOBE AND PAY ATTENTION TO ME.
LORELEI. DEAR LORELEI... I HAVE FOUND YOUR INFATUATION WITH ME AMUSING...
OH!
...UP UNTIL NOW! BUT NO MORE!
LOKI AM I, MASTER OF THIS PLACE--
--AND BY ALL THE POWERS AT MY SWAY, I COMMAND YOU NOW--BEGONE!
GIVE MY REGARDS TO THE WILD GARDENS OF FAR ALFHEIM!
...
SHOULD HAVE RID MYSELF OF HER WEEKS AGO.
NOW THERE IS NOTHING FURTHER TO DISTRACT ME FROM--!
LOKI! DEAREST! I KNEW YOU WOULD TIRE OF THAT SLATTERN EVENTUALLY.
SIGYN.
TO WHAT DO I OWE THE PLEASURE...?

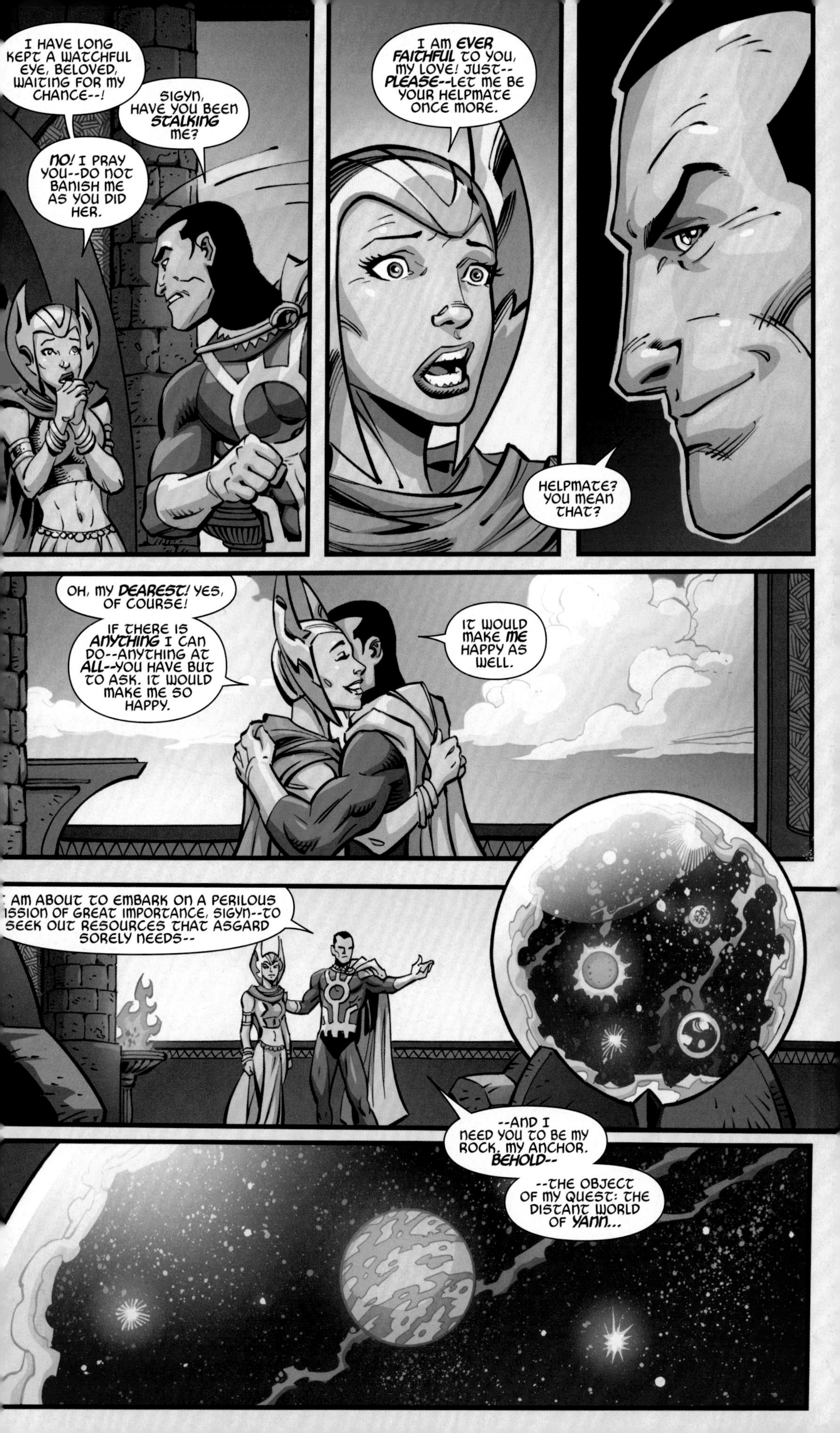

I HAVE LONG KEPT A WATCHFUL EYE, BELOVED, WAITING FOR MY CHANCE--!
SIGYN, HAVE YOU BEEN STALKING ME?
NO! I PRAY YOU--DO NOT BANISH ME AS YOU DID HER.
I AM EVER FAITHFUL TO YOU, MY LOVE! JUST-- PLEASE--LET ME BE YOUR HELPMATE ONCE MORE.
HELPMATE? YOU MEAN THAT?
OH, MY DEAREST! YES, OF COURSE!
IF THERE IS ANYTHING I CAN DO--ANYTHING AT ALL--YOU HAVE BUT TO ASK. IT WOULD MAKE ME SO HAPPY.
IT WOULD MAKE ME HAPPY AS WELL.
AM ABOUT TO EMBARK ON A PERILOUS ISSION OF GREAT IMPORTANCE, SIGYN--TO SEEK OUT RESOURCES THAT ASGARD SORELY NEEDS--
--AND I NEED YOU TO BE MY ROCK, MY ANCHOR. BEHOLD--
--THE OBJECT OF MY QUEST: THE DISTANT WORLD OF YANN...

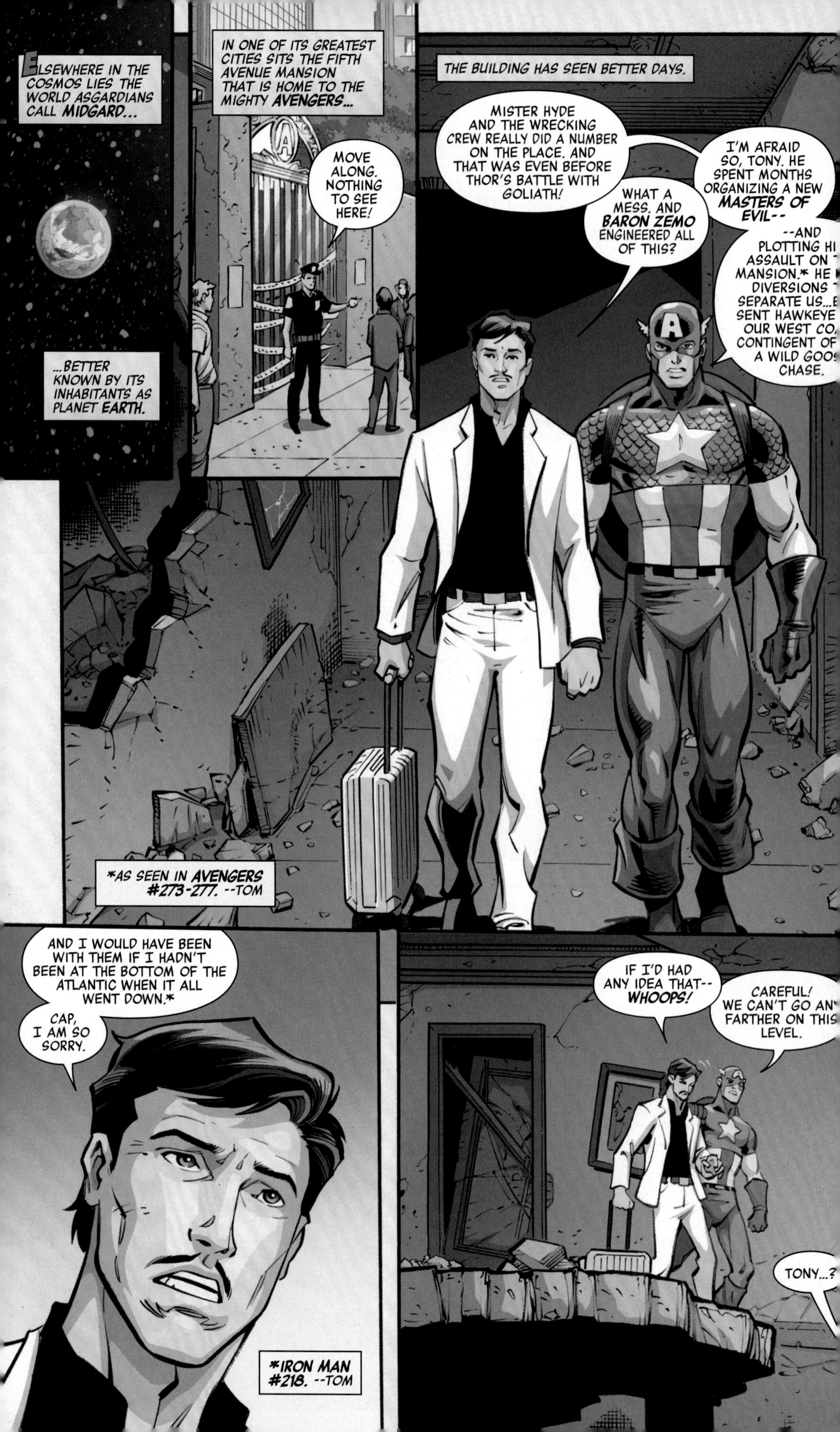
ELSEWHERE IN THE COSMOS LIES THE WORLD ASGARDIANS CALL MIDGARD...
IN ONE OF ITS GREATEST CITIES SITS THE FIFTH AVENUE MANSION THAT IS HOME TO THE MIGHTY AVENGERS...
MOVE ALONG. NOTHING TO SEE HERE!
...BETTER KNOWN BY ITS INHABITANTS AS PLANET EARTH.
THE BUILDING HAS SEEN BETTER DAYS.
MISTER HYDE AND THE WRECKING CREW REALLY DID A NUMBER ON THE PLACE. AND THAT WAS EVEN BEFORE THOR'S BATTLE WITH GOLIATH!
WHAT A MESS. AND BARON ZEMO ENGINEERED ALL OF THIS?
I'M AFRAID SO, TONY. HE SPENT MONTHS ORGANIZING A NEW MASTERS OF EVIL--
--AND PLOTTING HI ASSAULT ON T MANSION.* HE DIVERSIONS T SEPARATE US...E SENT HAWKEYE OUR WEST CO CONTINGENT OF A WILD GOO CHASE.
*AS SEEN IN AVENGERS #273-277. --TOM
AND I WOULD HAVE BEEN WITH THEM IF I HADN'T BEEN AT THE BOTTOM OF THE ATLANTIC WHEN IT ALL WENT DOWN.*
CAP, I AM SO SORRY.
*IRON MAN #218. --TOM
IF I'D HAD ANY IDEA THAT-- WHOOPS!
CAREFUL! WE CAN'T GO AN FARTHER ON THIS LEVEL.
TONY...?

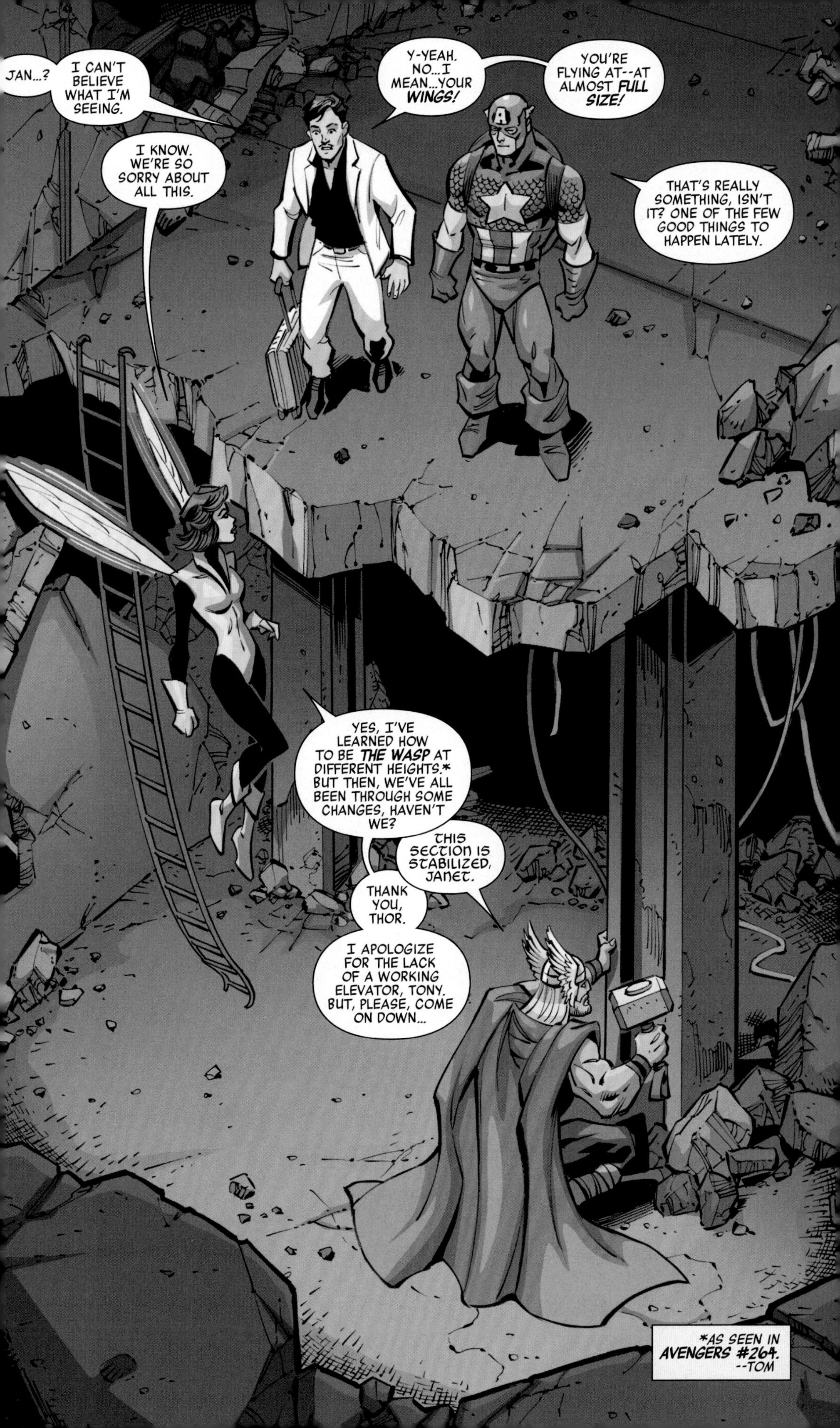
JAN...?
I CAN'T BELIEVE WHAT I'M SEEING.
Y-YEAH. NO...I MEAN...YOUR WINGS!
YOU'RE FLYING AT--AT ALMOST FULL SIZE!
I KNOW. WE'RE SO SORRY ABOUT ALL THIS.
THAT'S REALLY SOMETHING, ISN'T IT? ONE OF THE FEW GOOD THINGS TO HAPPEN LATELY.
YES, I'VE LEARNED HOW TO BE THE WASP AT DIFFERENT HEIGHTS.* BUT THEN, WE'VE ALL BEEN THROUGH SOME CHANGES, HAVEN'T WE?
THIS SECTION IS STABILIZED, JANET.
THANK YOU, THOR.
I APOLOGIZE FOR THE LACK OF A WORKING ELEVATOR, TONY. BUT, PLEASE, COME ON DOWN...
*AS SEEN IN AVENGERS #264. --TOM

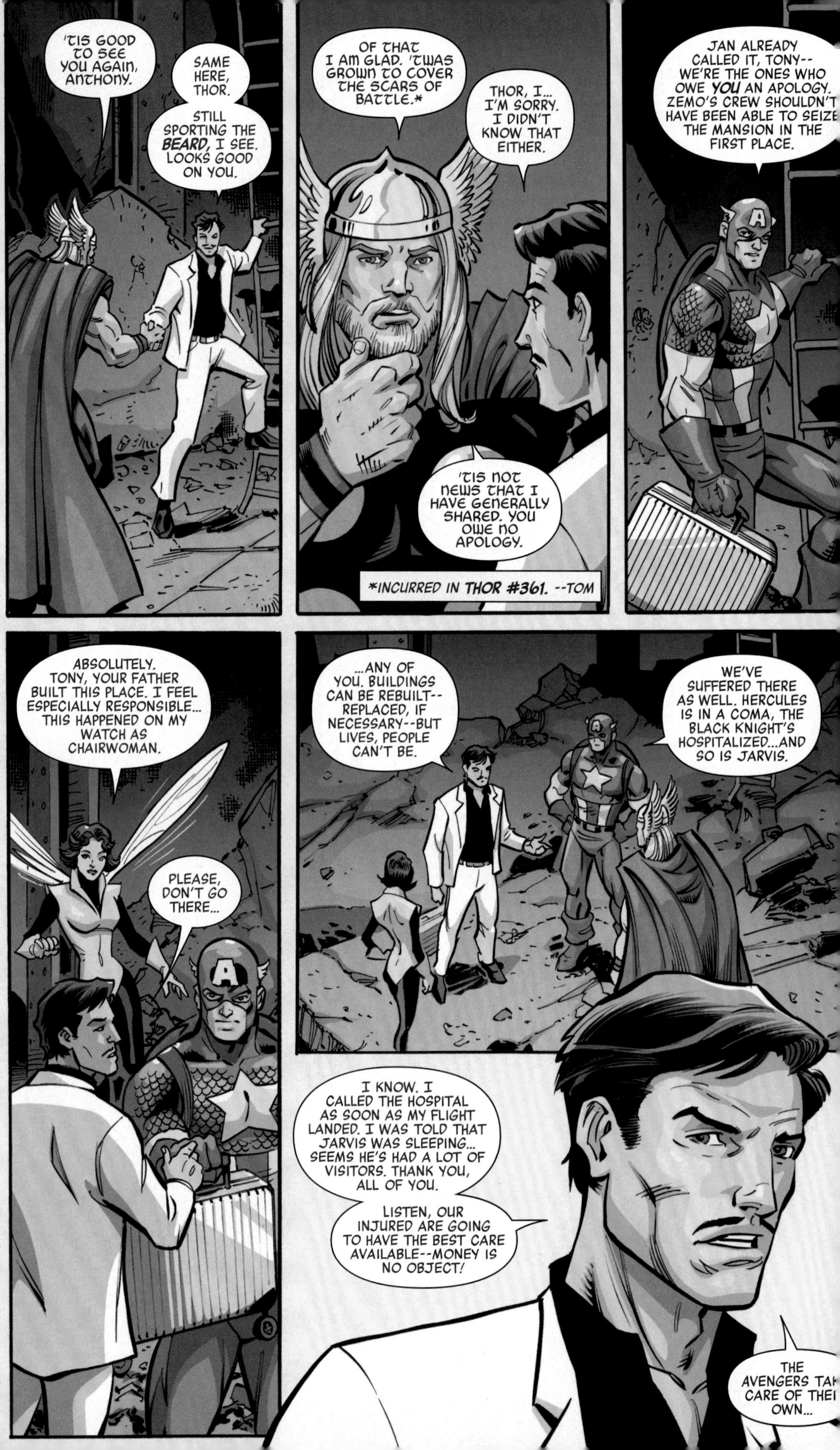
'TIS GOOD TO SEE YOU AGAIN, ANTHONY.
SAME HERE, THOR.
STILL SPORTING THE BEARD, I SEE. LOOKS GOOD ON YOU.
OF THAT I AM GLAD. 'TWAS GROWN TO COVER THE SCARS OF BATTLE.*
THOR, I... I'M SORRY. I DIDN'T KNOW THAT EITHER.
'TIS NOT NEWS THAT I HAVE GENERALLY SHARED. YOU OWE NO APOLOGY.
*INCURRED IN THOR #361. --TOM
JAN ALREADY CALLED IT, TONY-- WE'RE THE ONES WHO OWE YOU AN APOLOGY. ZEMO'S CREW SHOULDN'T HAVE BEEN ABLE TO SEIZE THE MANSION IN THE FIRST PLACE.
ABSOLUTELY. TONY, YOUR FATHER BUILT THIS PLACE. I FEEL ESPECIALLY RESPONSIBLE... THIS HAPPENED ON MY WATCH AS CHAIRWOMAN.
PLEASE, DON'T GO THERE...
...ANY OF YOU. BUILDINGS CAN BE REBUILT-- REPLACED, IF NECESSARY--BUT LIVES, PEOPLE CAN'T BE.
WE'VE SUFFERED THERE AS WELL. HERCULES IS IN A COMA, THE BLACK KNIGHT'S HOSPITALIZED...AND SO IS JARVIS.
I KNOW. I CALLED THE HOSPITAL AS SOON AS MY FLIGHT LANDED. I WAS TOLD THAT JARVIS WAS SLEEPING... SEEMS HE'S HAD A LOT OF VISITORS. THANK YOU, ALL OF YOU.
LISTEN, OUR INJURED ARE GOING TO HAVE THE BEST CARE AVAILABLE--MONEY IS NO OBJECT!
THE AVENGERS TA CARE OF THE OWN...

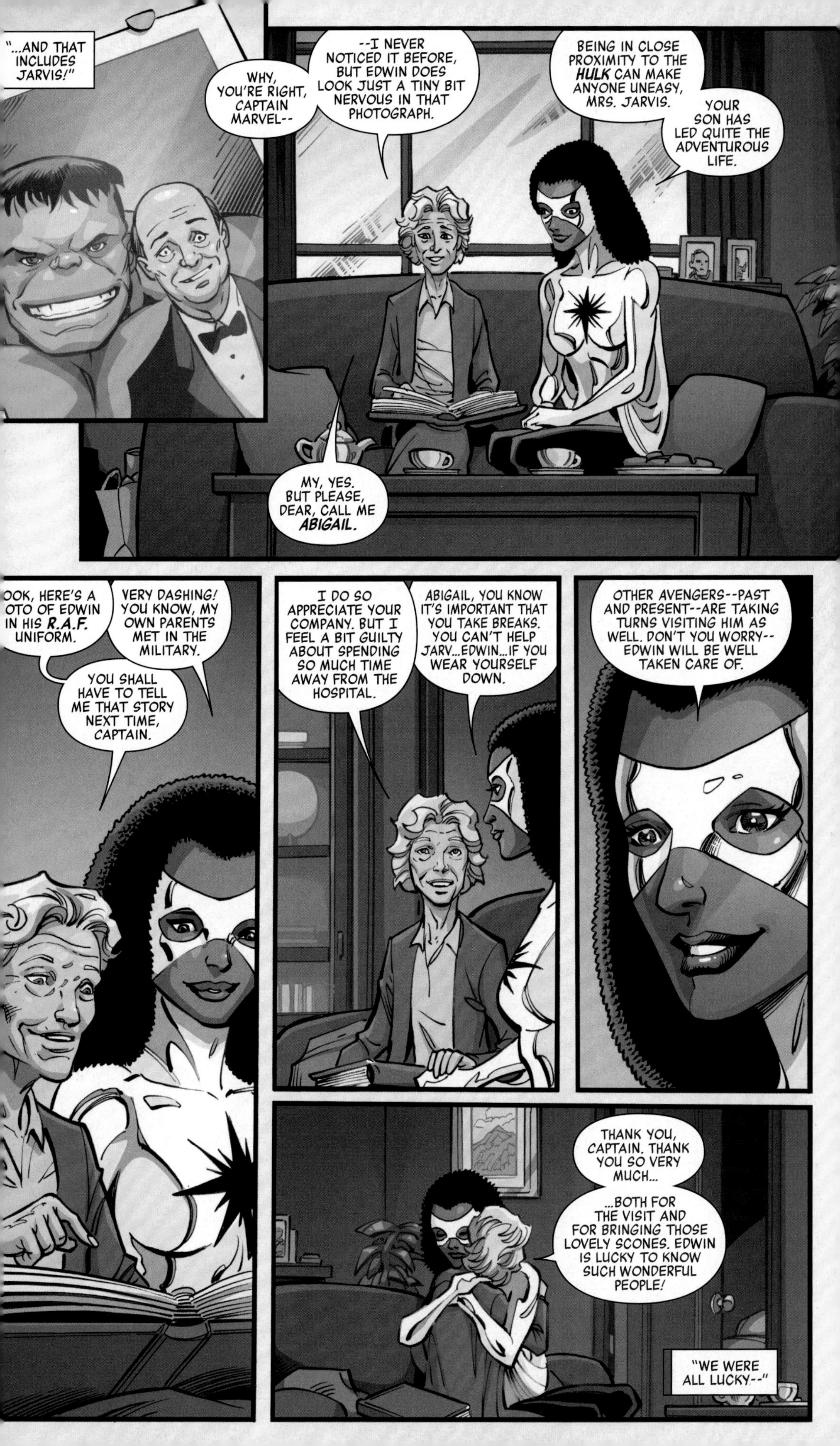
"...AND THAT INCLUDES JARVIS!"
WHY, YOU'RE RIGHT, CAPTAIN MARVEL--
--I NEVER NOTICED IT BEFORE, BUT EDWIN DOES LOOK JUST A TINY BIT NERVOUS IN THAT PHOTOGRAPH.
BEING IN CLOSE PROXIMITY TO THE HULK CAN MAKE ANYONE UNEASY, MRS. JARVIS.
YOUR SON HAS LED QUITE THE ADVENTUROUS LIFE.
MY, YES. BUT PLEASE, DEAR, CALL ME ABIGAIL.
OOK, HERE'S A OTO OF EDWIN IN HIS R.A.F. UNIFORM.
VERY DASHING! YOU KNOW, MY OWN PARENTS MET IN THE MILITARY.
YOU SHALL HAVE TO TELL ME THAT STORY NEXT TIME, CAPTAIN.
I DO SO APPRECIATE YOUR COMPANY. BUT I FEEL A BIT GUILTY ABOUT SPENDING SO MUCH TIME AWAY FROM THE HOSPITAL.
ABIGAIL, YOU KNOW IT'S IMPORTANT THAT YOU TAKE BREAKS. YOU CAN'T HELP JARV...EDWIN...IF YOU WEAR YOURSELF DOWN.
OTHER AVENGERS--PAST AND PRESENT--ARE TAKING TURNS VISITING HIM AS WELL. DON'T YOU WORRY-- EDWIN WILL BE WELL TAKEN CARE OF.
THANK YOU, CAPTAIN. THANK YOU SO VERY MUCH...
...BOTH FOR THE VISIT AND FOR BRINGING THOSE LOVELY SCONES. EDWIN IS LUCKY TO KNOW SUCH WONDERFUL PEOPLE!
"WE WERE ALL LUCKY--"

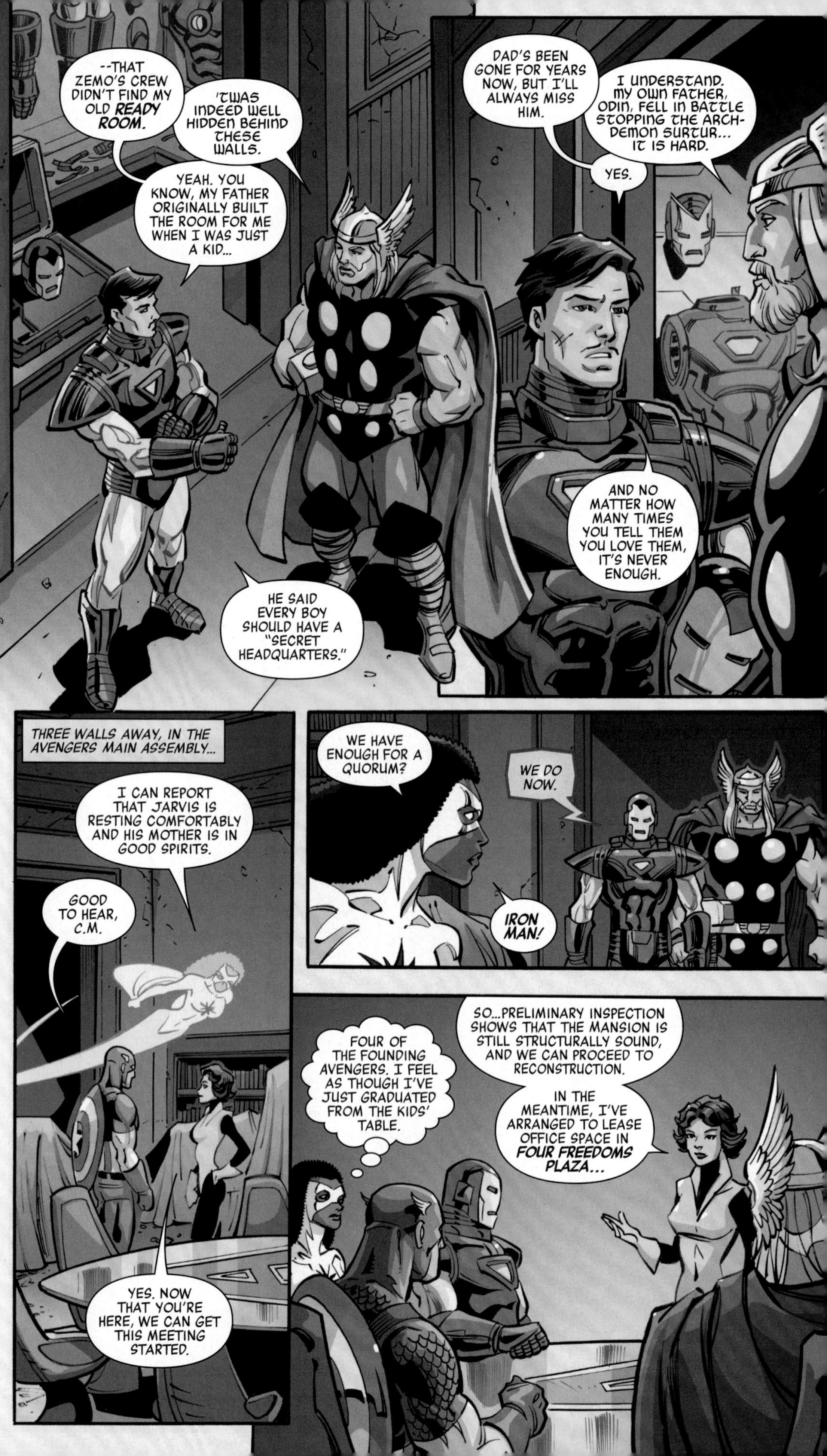
--THAT ZEMO'S CREW DIDN'T FIND MY OLD READY ROOM.
'TWAS INDEED WELL HIDDEN BEHIND THESE WALLS.
YEAH. YOU KNOW, MY FATHER ORIGINALLY BUILT THE ROOM FOR ME WHEN I WAS JUST A KID...
HE SAID EVERY BOY SHOULD HAVE A "SECRET HEADQUARTERS."
DAD'S BEEN GONE FOR YEARS NOW, BUT I'LL ALWAYS MISS HIM.
I UNDERSTAND. MY OWN FATHER, ODIN, FELL IN BATTLE STOPPING THE ARCH-DEMON SURTUR... IT IS HARD.
YES.
AND NO MATTER HOW MANY TIMES YOU TELL THEM YOU LOVE THEM, IT'S NEVER ENOUGH.
THREE WALLS AWAY, IN THE AVENGERS MAIN ASSEMBLY...
I CAN REPORT THAT JARVIS IS RESTING COMFORTABLY AND HIS MOTHER IS IN GOOD SPIRITS.
GOOD TO HEAR, C.M.
YES. NOW THAT YOU'RE HERE, WE CAN GET THIS MEETING STARTED.
WE HAVE ENOUGH FOR A QUORUM?
WE DO NOW.
IRON MAN!
FOUR OF THE FOUNDING AVENGERS. I FEEL AS THOUGH I'VE JUST GRADUATED FROM THE KIDS' TABLE.
SO...PRELIMINARY INSPECTION SHOWS THAT THE MANSION IS STILL STRUCTURALLY SOUND, AND WE CAN PROCEED TO RECONSTRUCTION.
IN THE MEANTIME, I'VE ARRANGED TO LEASE OFFICE SPACE IN FOUR FREEDOMS PLAZA...

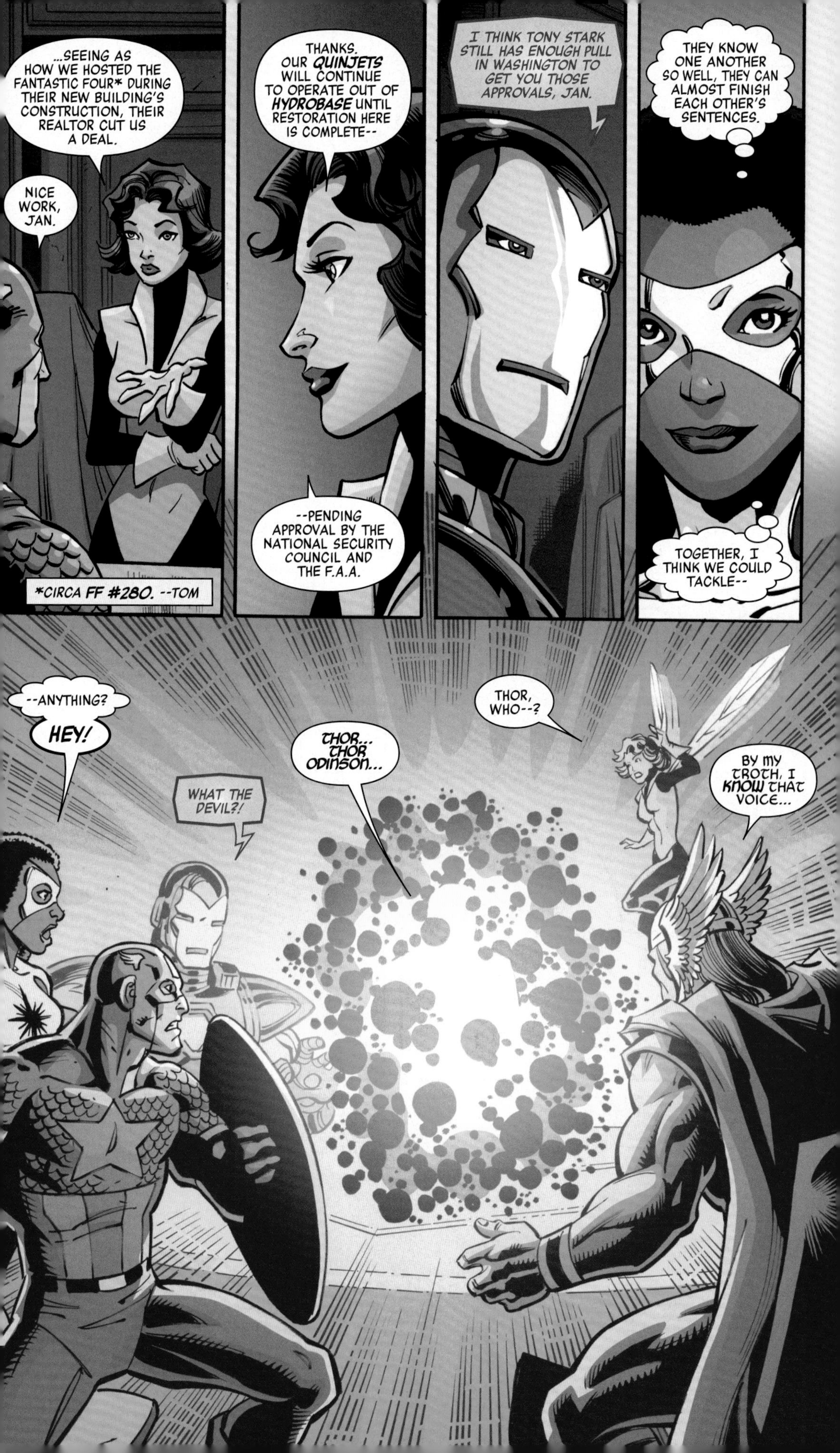
...SEEING AS HOW WE HOSTED THE FANTASTIC FOUR* DURING THEIR NEW BUILDING'S CONSTRUCTION, THEIR REALTOR CUT US A DEAL.
NICE WORK, JAN.
*CIRCA FF #280. --TOM
THANKS. OUR QUINJETS WILL CONTINUE TO OPERATE OUT OF HYDROBASE UNTIL RESTORATION HERE IS COMPLETE--
--PENDING APPROVAL BY THE NATIONAL SECURITY COUNCIL AND THE F.A.A.
I THINK TONY STARK STILL HAS ENOUGH PULL IN WASHINGTON TO GET YOU THOSE APPROVALS, JAN.
THEY KNOW ONE ANOTHER SO WELL, THEY CAN ALMOST FINISH EACH OTHER'S SENTENCES.
TOGETHER, I THINK WE COULD TACKLE--
--ANYTHING?
HEY!
WHAT THE DEVIL?!
THOR... THOR ODINSON...
THOR, WHO--?
BY MY TROTH, I KNOW THAT VOICE...

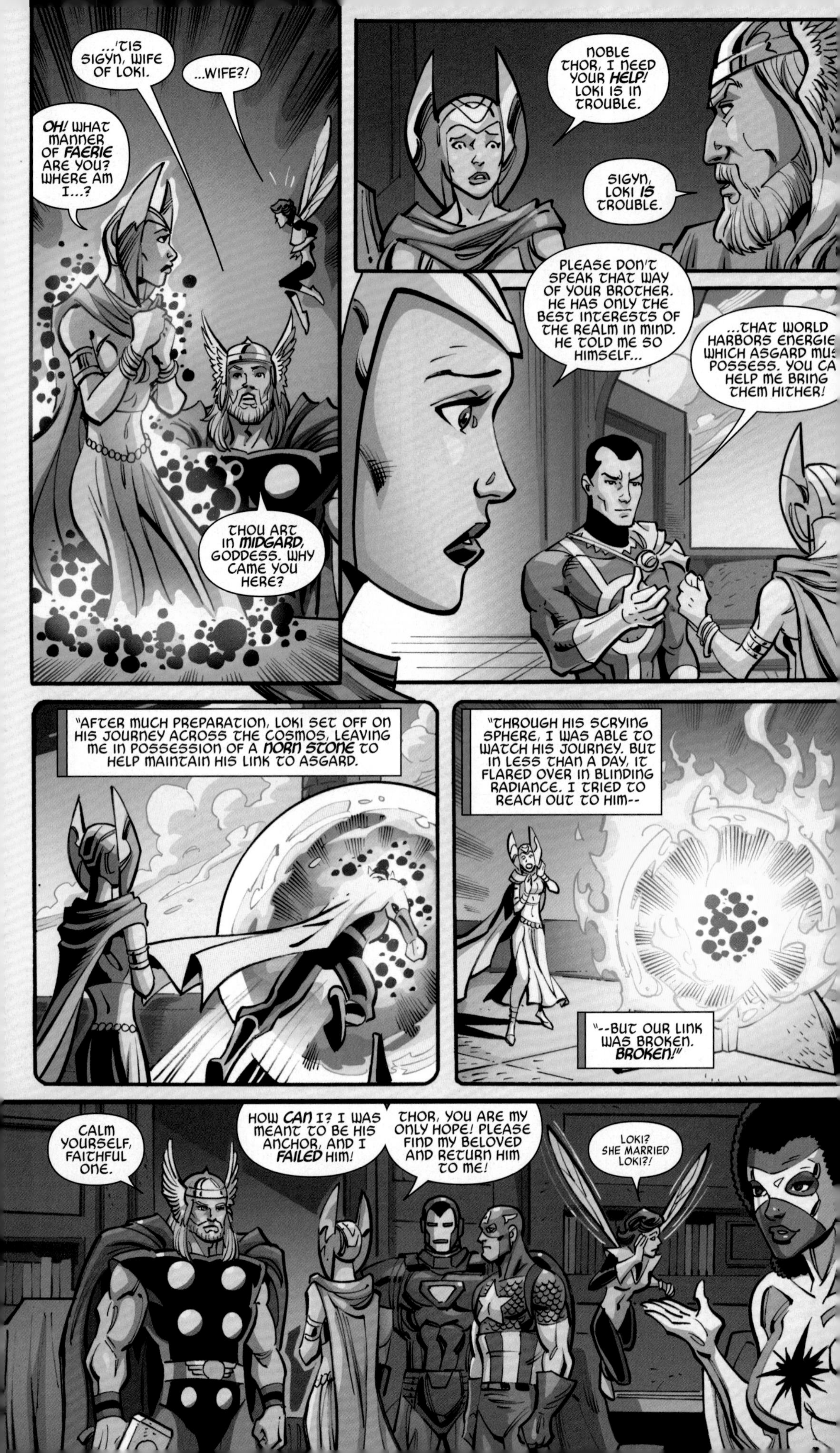

OH! WHAT MANNER OF FAERIE ARE YOU? WHERE AM I...?
...'TIS SIGYN, WIFE OF LOKI.
...WIFE?!
THOU ART IN MIDGARD, GODDESS. WHY CAME YOU HERE?
NOBLE THOR, I NEED YOUR HELP! LOKI IS IN TROUBLE.
SIGYN, LOKI IS TROUBLE.
PLEASE DON'T SPEAK THAT WAY OF YOUR BROTHER. HE HAS ONLY THE BEST INTERESTS OF THE REALM IN MIND. HE TOLD ME SO HIMSELF...
...THAT WORLD HARBORS ENERGIE WHICH ASGARD MUS POSSESS. YOU CA HELP ME BRING THEM HITHER!
"AFTER MUCH PREPARATION, LOKI SET OFF ON HIS JOURNEY ACROSS THE COSMOS, LEAVING ME IN POSSESSION OF A NORN STONE TO HELP MAINTAIN HIS LINK TO ASGARD.
"THROUGH HIS SCRYING SPHERE, I WAS ABLE TO WATCH HIS JOURNEY. BUT IN LESS THAN A DAY, IT FLARED OVER IN BLINDING RADIANCE. I TRIED TO REACH OUT TO HIM--
"--BUT OUR LINK WAS BROKEN. BROKEN!"
CALM YOURSELF, FAITHFUL ONE.
HOW CAN I? I WAS MEANT TO BE HIS ANCHOR, AND I FAILED HIM!
THOR, YOU ARE MY ONLY HOPE! PLEASE FIND MY BELOVED AND RETURN HIM TO ME!
LOKI? SHE MARRIED LOKI?!

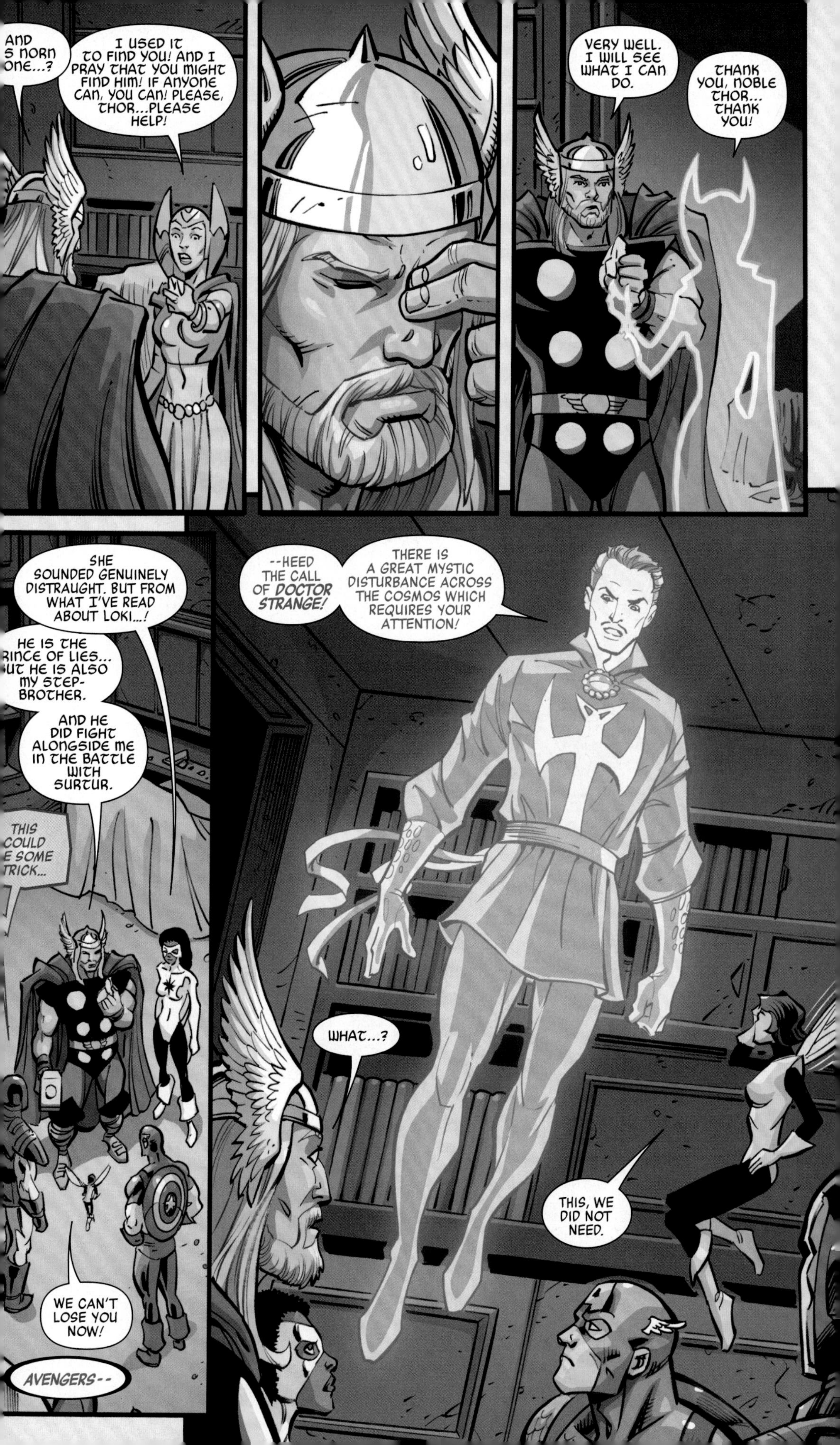
AND
S NORN
ONE...?
I USED IT TO FIND YOU! AND I PRAY THAT YOU MIGHT FIND HIM! IF ANYONE CAN, YOU CAN! PLEASE, THOR...PLEASE HELP!
VERY WELL. I WILL SEE WHAT I CAN DO.
THANK YOU, NOBLE THOR... THANK YOU!
SHE SOUNDED GENUINELY DISTRAUGHT. BUT FROM WHAT I'VE READ ABOUT LOKI...!
HE IS THE
RINCE OF LIES...
UT HE IS ALSO MY STEP-BROTHER.
AND HE DID FIGHT ALONGSIDE ME IN THE BATTLE WITH SURTUR.
THIS
COULD
E SOME
TRICK...
WE CAN'T LOSE YOU NOW!
AVENGERS--
--HEED THE CALL OF DOCTOR STRANGE!
THERE IS A GREAT MYSTIC DISTURBANCE ACROSS THE COSMOS WHICH REQUIRES YOUR ATTENTION!
WHAT...?
THIS, WE DID NOT NEED.

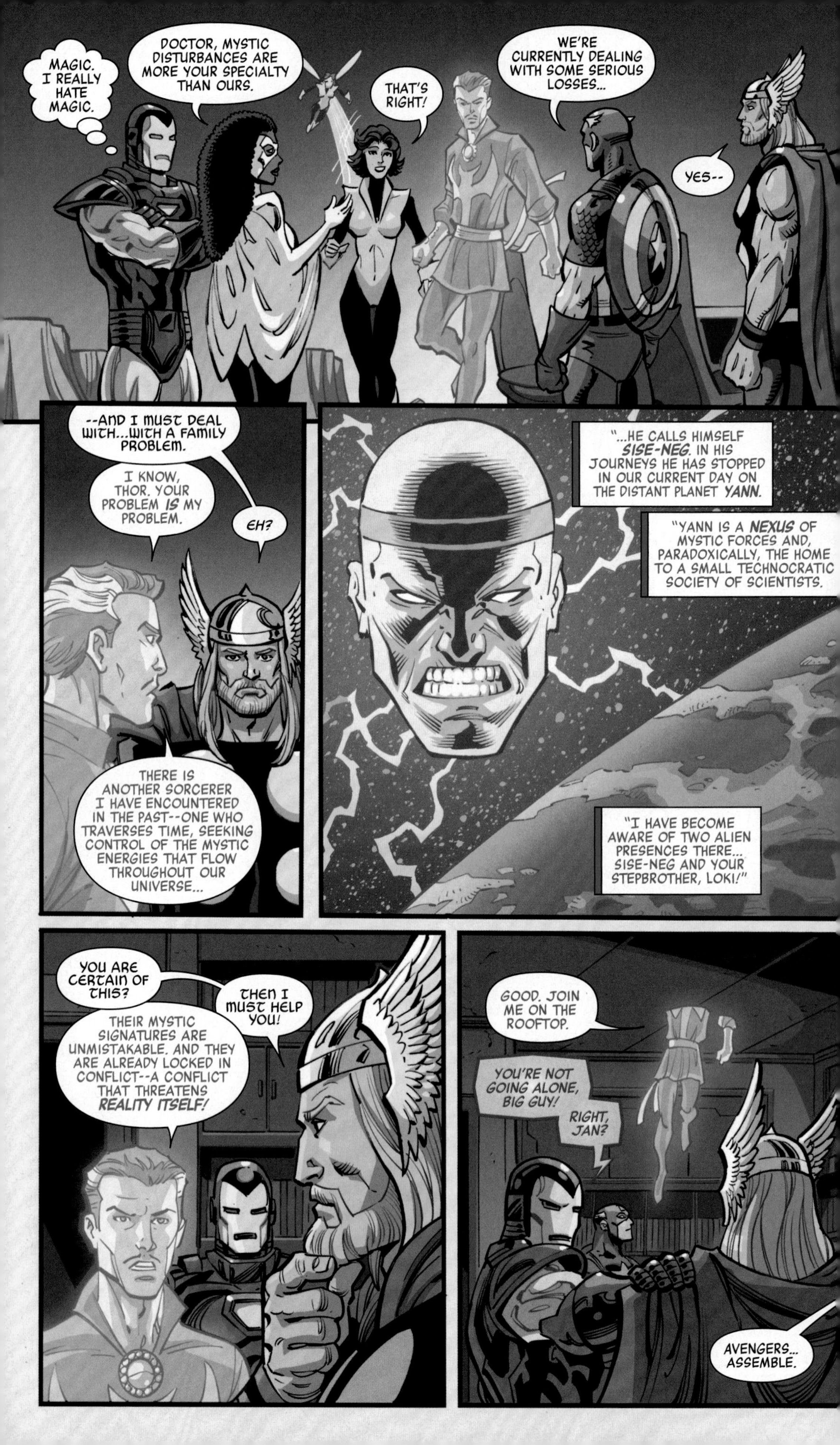
MAGIC. I REALLY HATE MAGIC.
DOCTOR, MYSTIC DISTURBANCES ARE MORE YOUR SPECIALTY THAN OURS.
THAT'S RIGHT!
WE'RE CURRENTLY DEALING WITH SOME SERIOUS LOSSES...
YES--
--AND I MUST DEAL WITH...WITH A FAMILY PROBLEM.
I KNOW, THOR. YOUR PROBLEM IS MY PROBLEM.
EH?
THERE IS ANOTHER SORCERER I HAVE ENCOUNTERED IN THE PAST--ONE WHO TRAVERSES TIME, SEEKING CONTROL OF THE MYSTIC ENERGIES THAT FLOW THROUGHOUT OUR UNIVERSE...
"...HE CALLS HIMSELF SISE-NEG. IN HIS JOURNEYS HE HAS STOPPED IN OUR CURRENT DAY ON THE DISTANT PLANET YANN.
"YANN IS A NEXUS OF MYSTIC FORCES AND, PARADOXICALLY, THE HOME TO A SMALL TECHNOCRATIC SOCIETY OF SCIENTISTS.
"I HAVE BECOME AWARE OF TWO ALIEN PRESENCES THERE... SISE-NEG AND YOUR STEPBROTHER, LOKI!"
YOU ARE CERTAIN OF THIS?
THEN I MUST HELP YOU!
THEIR MYSTIC SIGNATURES ARE UNMISTAKABLE. AND THEY ARE ALREADY LOCKED IN CONFLICT--A CONFLICT THAT THREATENS REALITY ITSELF!
GOOD. JOIN ME ON THE ROOFTOP.
YOU'RE NOT GOING ALONE, BIG GUY!
RIGHT, JAN?
AVENGERS... ASSEMBLE.

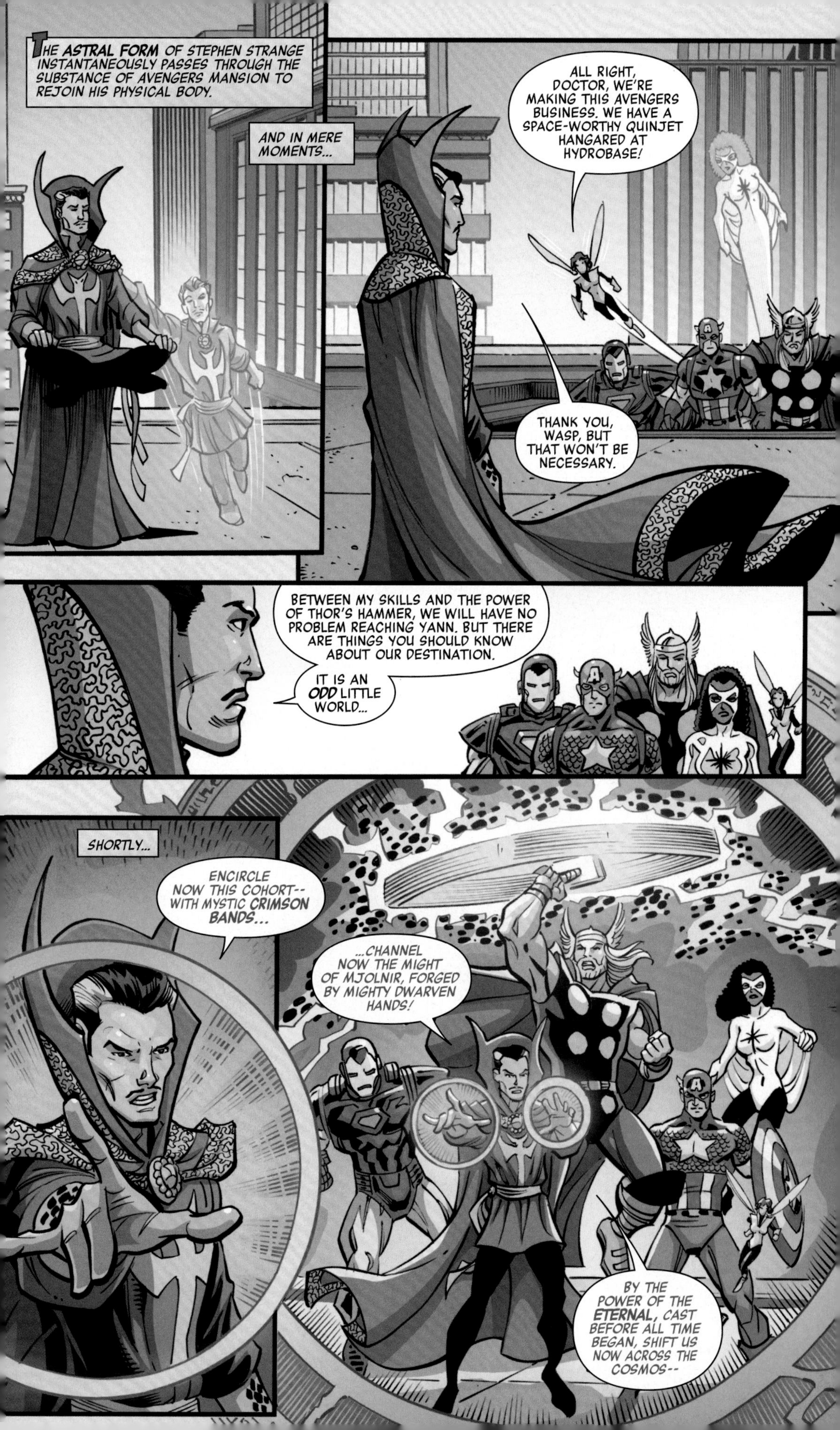
THE ASTRAL FORM OF STEPHEN STRANGE INSTANTANEOUSLY PASSES THROUGH THE SUBSTANCE OF AVENGERS MANSION TO REJOIN HIS PHYSICAL BODY.
AND IN MERE MOMENTS...
ALL RIGHT, DOCTOR, WE'RE MAKING THIS AVENGERS BUSINESS. WE HAVE A SPACE-WORTHY QUINJET HANGARED AT HYDROBASE!
THANK YOU, WASP, BUT THAT WON'T BE NECESSARY.
BETWEEN MY SKILLS AND THE POWER OF THOR'S HAMMER, WE WILL HAVE NO PROBLEM REACHING YANN. BUT THERE ARE THINGS YOU SHOULD KNOW ABOUT OUR DESTINATION.
IT IS AN ODD LITTLE WORLD...
SHORTLY...
ENCIRCLE NOW THIS COHORT-- WITH MYSTIC CRIMSON BANDS...
...CHANNEL NOW THE MIGHT OF MJOLNIR, FORGED BY MIGHTY DWARVEN HANDS!
BY THE POWER OF THE ETERNAL, CAST BEFORE ALL TIME BEGAN, SHIFT US NOW ACROSS THE COSMOS--

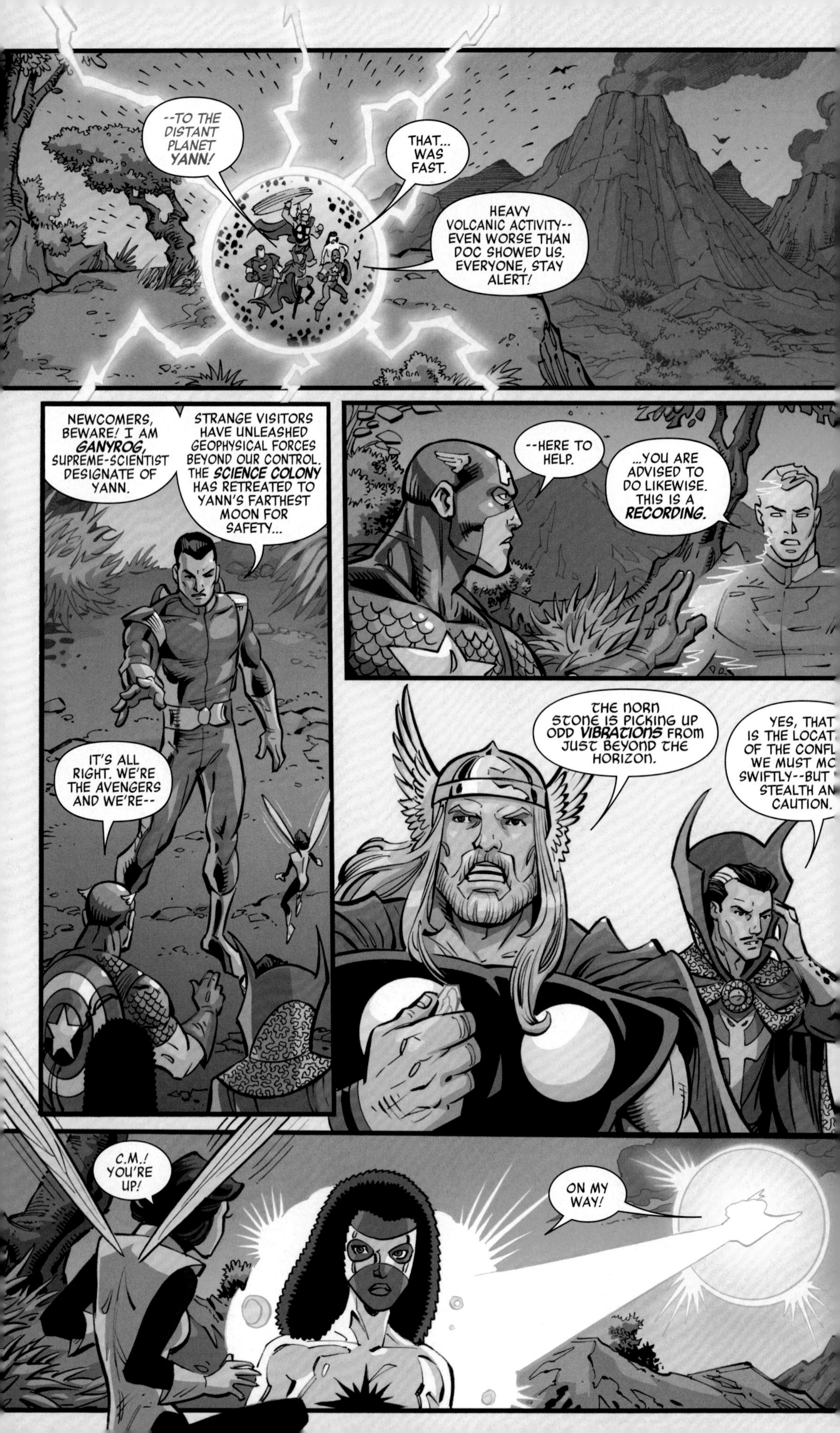
--TO THE DISTANT PLANET YANN!
THAT... WAS FAST.
HEAVY VOLCANIC ACTIVITY--EVEN WORSE THAN DOC SHOWED US. EVERYONE, STAY ALERT!
NEWCOMERS, BEWARE! I AM GANYROG, SUPREME-SCIENTIST DESIGNATE OF YANN.
STRANGE VISITORS HAVE UNLEASHED GEOPHYSICAL FORCES BEYOND OUR CONTROL. THE SCIENCE COLONY HAS RETREATED TO YANN'S FARTHEST MOON FOR SAFETY...
IT'S ALL RIGHT. WE'RE THE AVENGERS AND WE'RE--
--HERE TO HELP.
...YOU ARE ADVISED TO DO LIKEWISE. THIS IS A RECORDING.
THE NORN STONE IS PICKING UP ODD VIBRATIONS FROM JUST BEYOND THE HORIZON.
YES, THAT IS THE LOCAT OF THE CONFL WE MUST MO SWIFTLY--BUT STEALTH AN CAUTION.
C.M.! YOU'RE UP!
ON MY WAY!

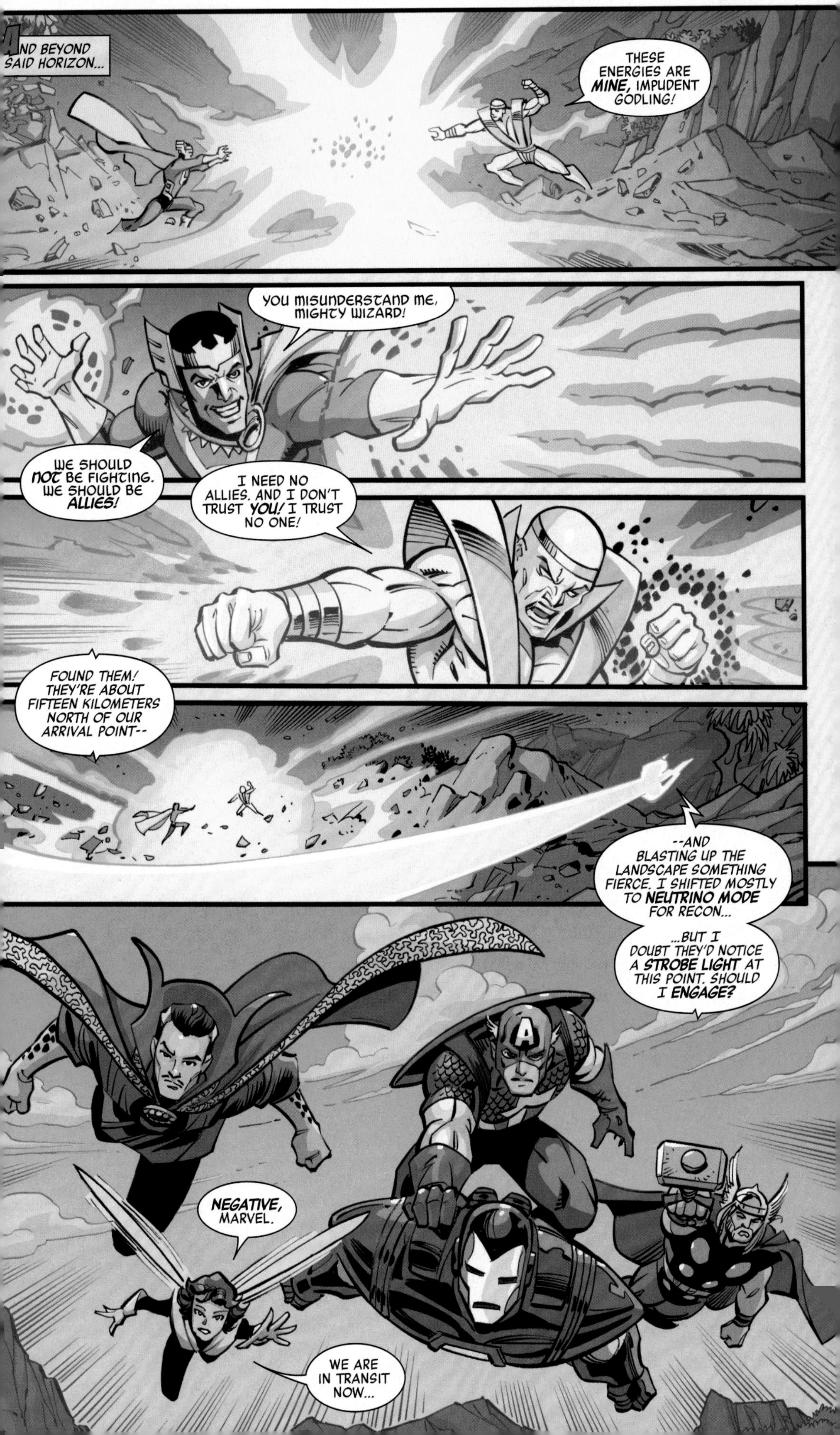
AND BEYOND SAID HORIZON...
THESE ENERGIES ARE MINE, IMPUDENT GODLING!
YOU MISUNDERSTAND ME, MIGHTY WIZARD!
WE SHOULD NOT BE FIGHTING. WE SHOULD BE ALLIES!
I NEED NO ALLIES. AND I DON'T TRUST YOU! I TRUST NO ONE!
FOUND THEM! THEY'RE ABOUT FIFTEEN KILOMETERS NORTH OF OUR ARRIVAL POINT--
--AND BLASTING UP THE LANDSCAPE SOMETHING FIERCE. I SHIFTED MOSTLY TO NEUTRINO MODE FOR RECON...
...BUT I DOUBT THEY'D NOTICE A STROBE LIGHT AT THIS POINT. SHOULD I ENGAGE?
NEGATIVE, MARVEL.
WE ARE IN TRANSIT NOW...

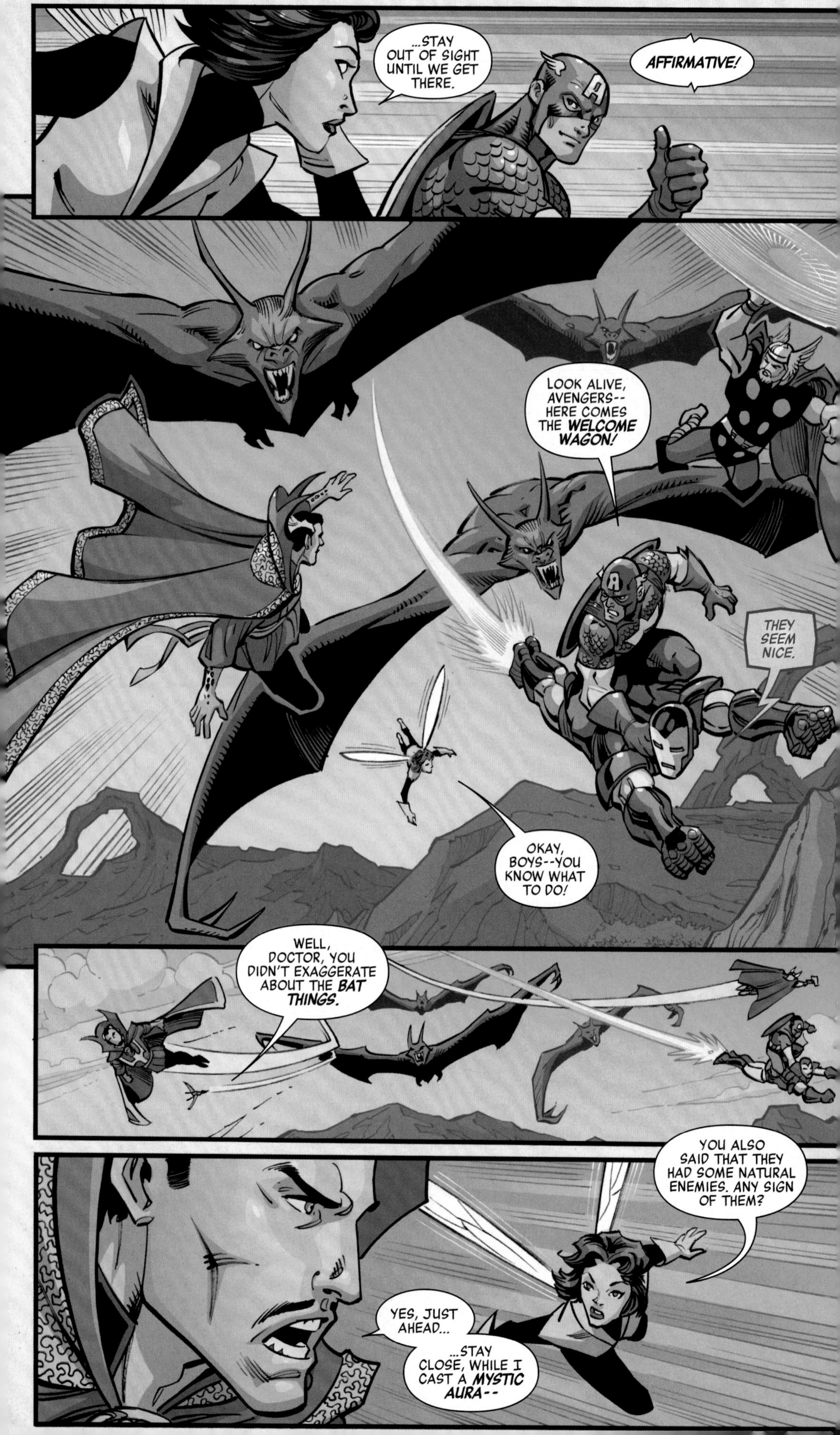
...STAY OUT OF SIGHT UNTIL WE GET THERE.
AFFIRMATIVE!
LOOK ALIVE, AVENGERS-- HERE COMES THE WELCOME WAGON!
THEY SEEM NICE.
OKAY, BOYS--YOU KNOW WHAT TO DO!
WELL, DOCTOR, YOU DIDN'T EXAGGERATE ABOUT THE BAT THINGS.
YOU ALSO SAID THAT THEY HAD SOME NATURAL ENEMIES. ANY SIGN OF THEM?
YES, JUST AHEAD...
...STAY CLOSE, WHILE I CAST A MYSTIC AURA--

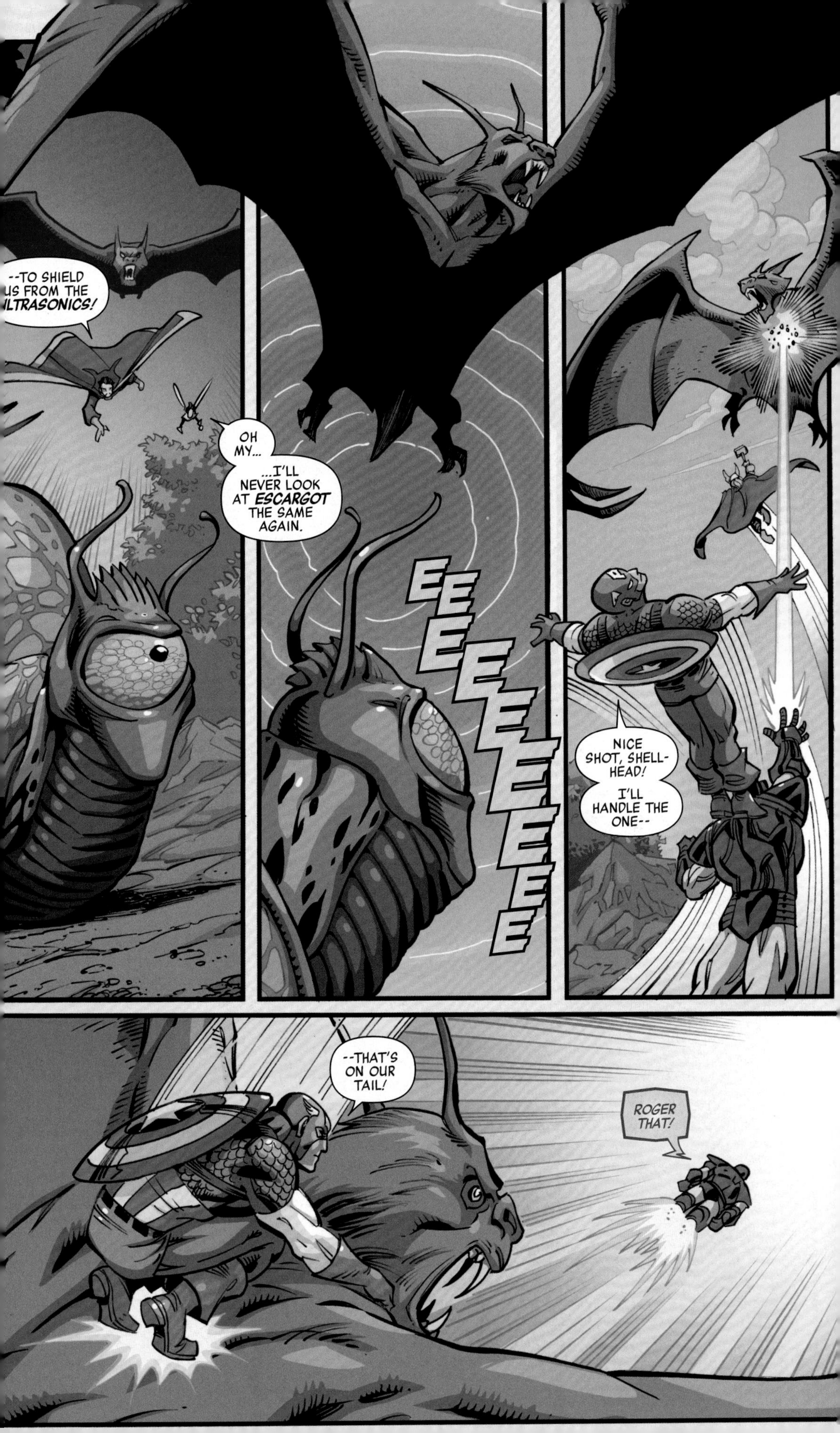
--TO SHIELD US FROM THE ULTRASONICS!
OH MY...
...I'LL NEVER LOOK AT ESCARGOT THE SAME AGAIN.
EEEEEEEEEEE
NICE SHOT, SHELL-HEAD!
I'LL HANDLE THE ONE--
--THAT'S ON OUR TAIL!
ROGER THAT!

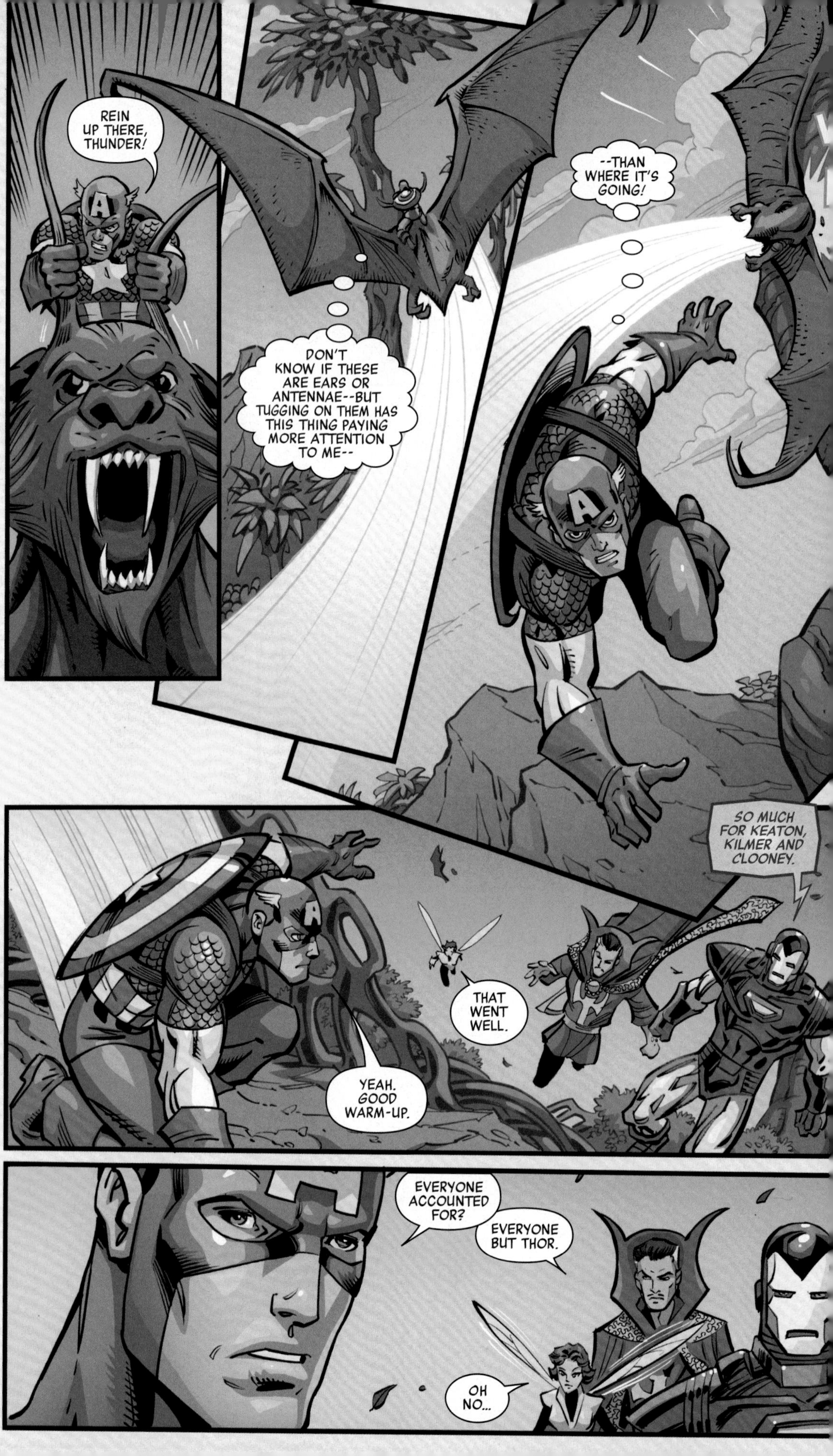
REIN UP THERE, THUNDER!
DON'T KNOW IF THESE ARE EARS OR ANTENNAE--BUT TUGGING ON THEM HAS THIS THING PAYING MORE ATTENTION TO ME--
--THAN WHERE IT'S GOING!
SO MUCH FOR KEATON, KILMER AND CLOONEY.
THAT WENT WELL.
YEAH. GOOD WARM-UP.
EVERYONE ACCOUNTED FOR?
EVERYONE BUT THOR.
OH NO...

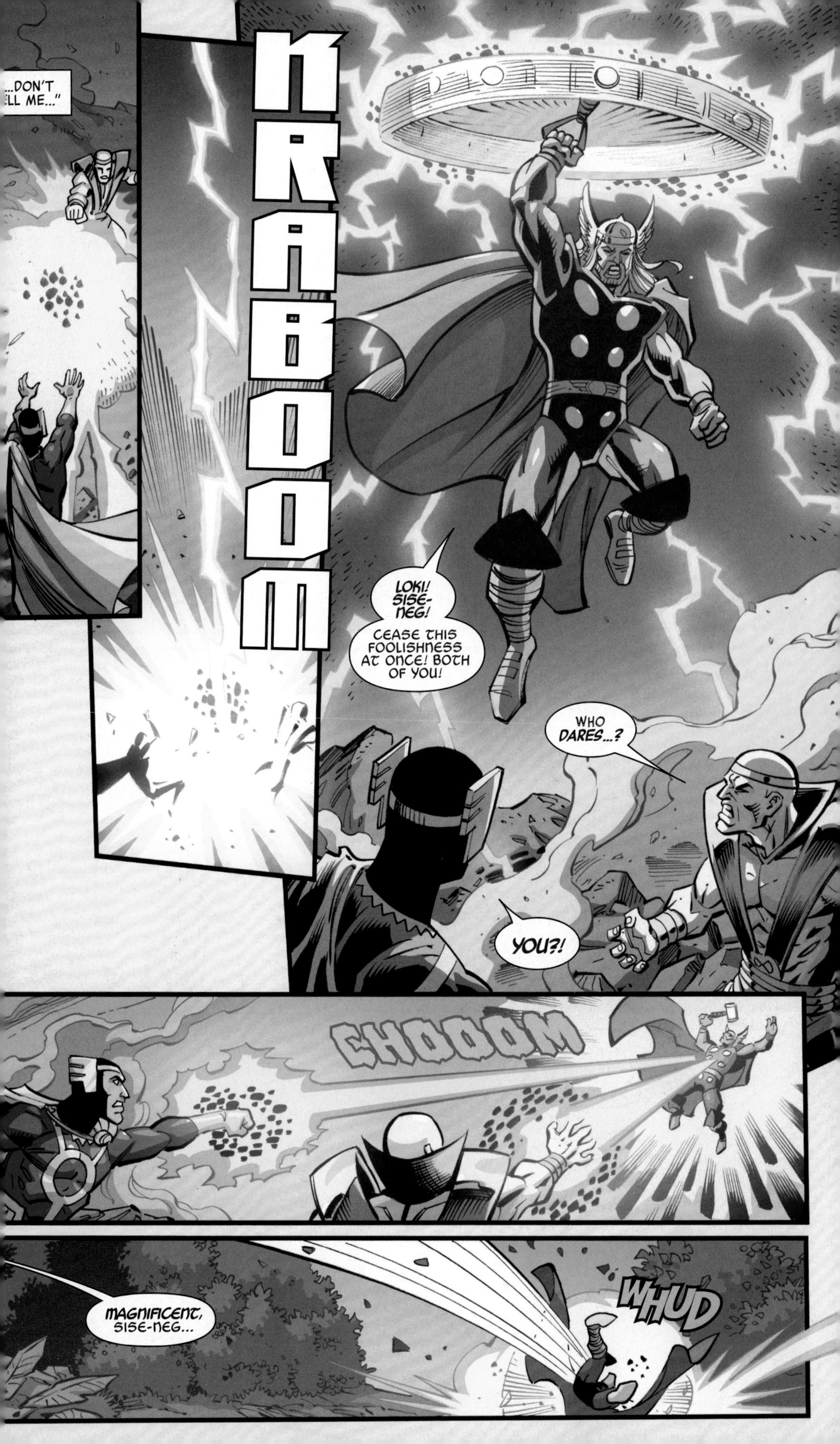
...DON'T
ELL ME..."
KRABOOM
LOKI! SISE-NEG!
CEASE THIS FOOLISHNESS AT ONCE! BOTH OF YOU!
WHO DARES...?
YOU?!
CHOOOM
MAGNIFICENT, SISE-NEG...
WHUD

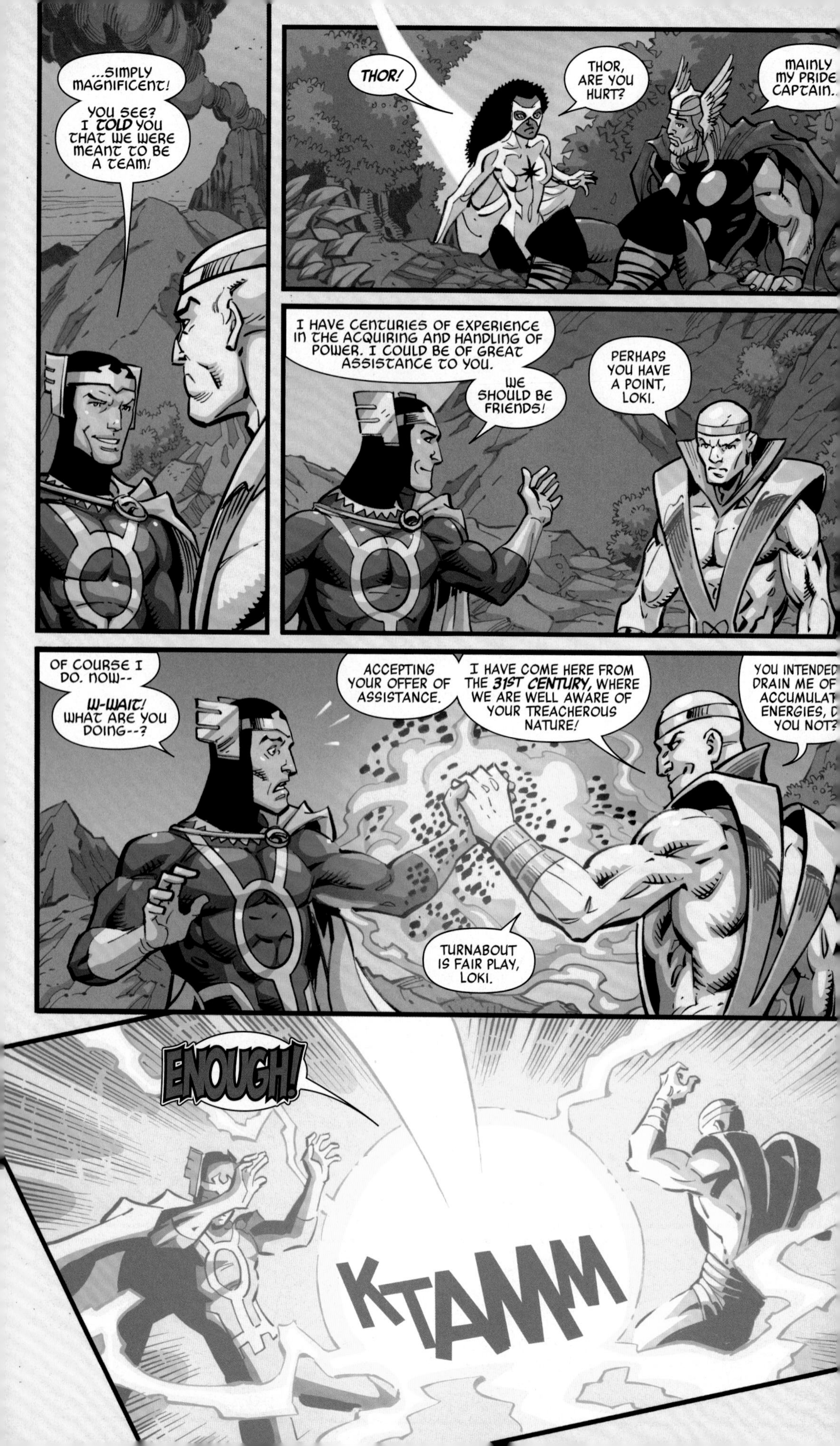
...SIMPLY MAGNIFICENT!
YOU SEE? I TOLD YOU THAT WE WERE MEANT TO BE A TEAM!
THOR!
THOR, ARE YOU HURT?
MAINLY MY PRIDE, CAPTAIN...
I HAVE CENTURIES OF EXPERIENCE IN THE ACQUIRING AND HANDLING OF POWER. I COULD BE OF GREAT ASSISTANCE TO YOU.
WE SHOULD BE FRIENDS!
PERHAPS YOU HAVE A POINT, LOKI.
OF COURSE I DO. NOW--
W-WAIT! WHAT ARE YOU DOING--?
ACCEPTING YOUR OFFER OF ASSISTANCE.
I HAVE COME HERE FROM THE 31ST CENTURY, WHERE WE ARE WELL AWARE OF YOUR TREACHEROUS NATURE!
YOU INTENDED DRAIN ME OF ACCUMULAT ENERGIES, D YOU NOT?
TURNABOUT IS FAIR PLAY, LOKI.
ENOUGH!
KTAMM

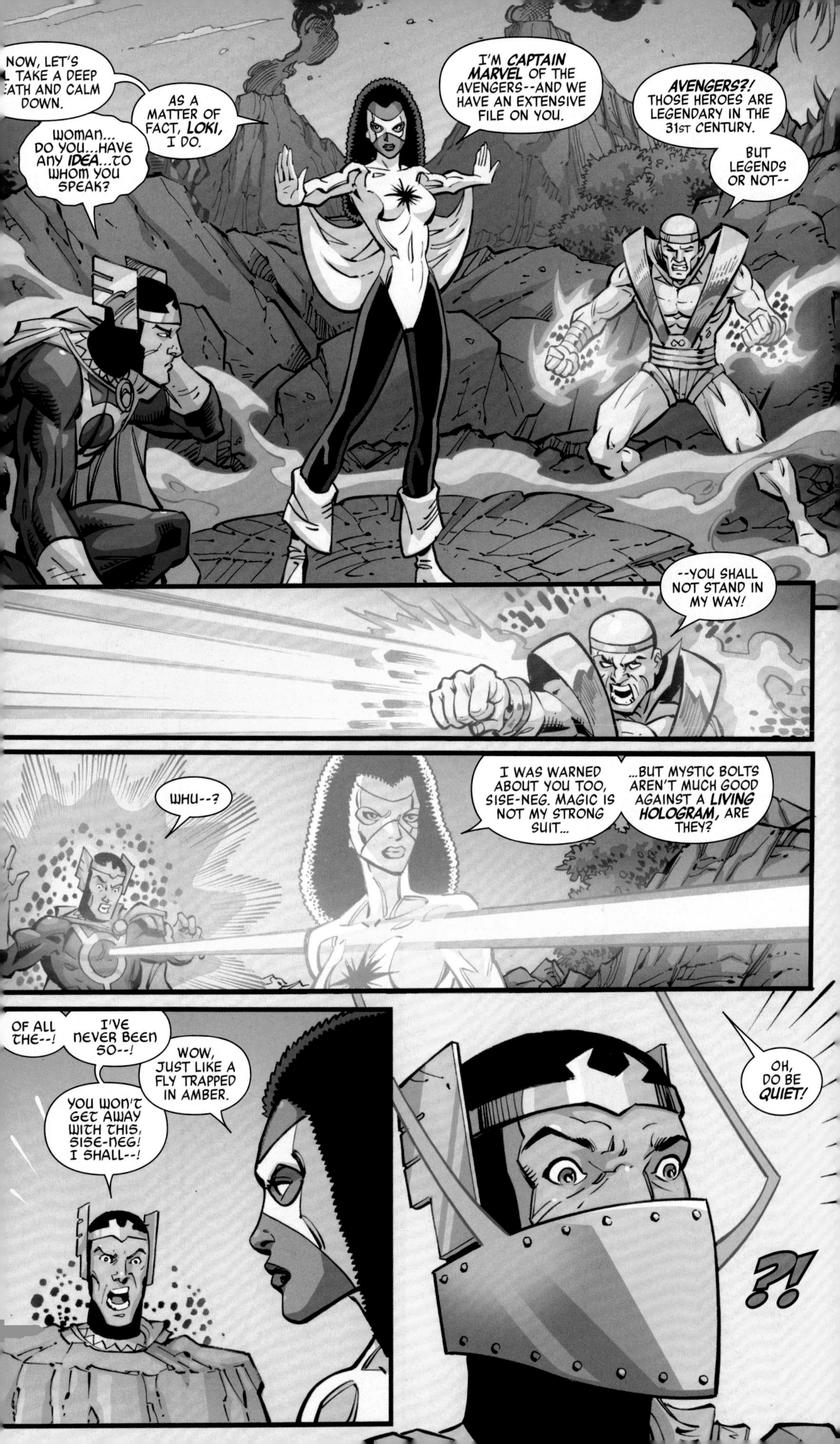
NOW, LET'S ALL TAKE A DEEP BREATH AND CALM DOWN.
WOMAN... DO YOU...HAVE ANY IDEA...TO WHOM YOU SPEAK?
AS A MATTER OF FACT, LOKI, I DO.
I'M CAPTAIN MARVEL OF THE AVENGERS--AND WE HAVE AN EXTENSIVE FILE ON YOU.
AVENGERS?! THOSE HEROES ARE LEGENDARY IN THE 31ST CENTURY.
BUT LEGENDS OR NOT--
--YOU SHALL NOT STAND IN MY WAY!
WHU--?
I WAS WARNED ABOUT YOU TOO, SISE-NEG. MAGIC IS NOT MY STRONG SUIT...
...BUT MYSTIC BOLTS AREN'T MUCH GOOD AGAINST A LIVING HOLOGRAM, ARE THEY?
OF ALL THE--!
I'VE NEVER BEEN SO--!
YOU WON'T GET AWAY WITH THIS, SISE-NEG! I SHALL--!
WOW, JUST LIKE A FLY TRAPPED IN AMBER.
OH, DO BE QUIET!
?!

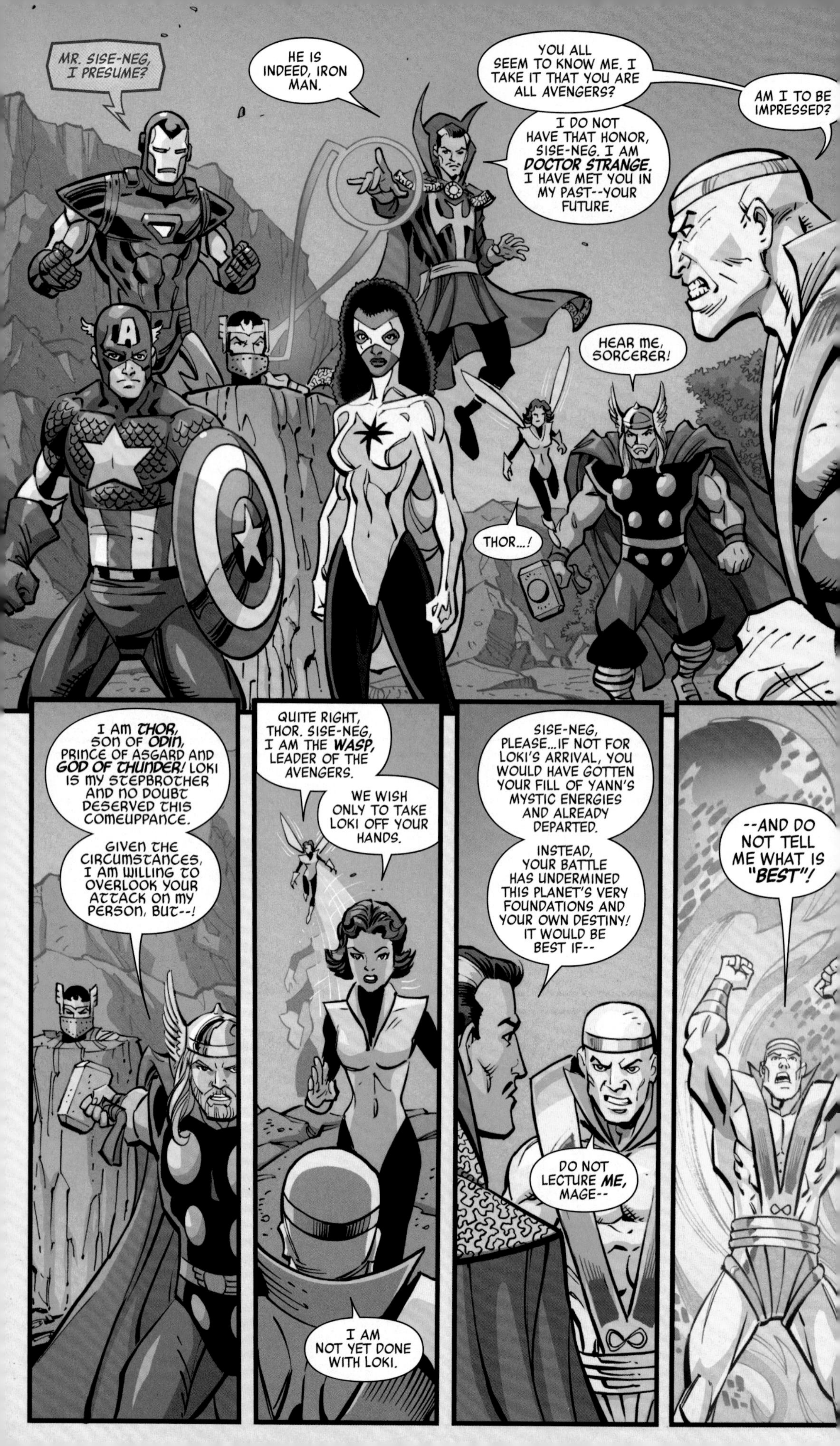
MR. SISE-NEG, I PRESUME?
HE IS INDEED, IRON MAN.
YOU ALL SEEM TO KNOW ME. I TAKE IT THAT YOU ARE ALL AVENGERS?
AM I TO BE IMPRESSED?
I DO NOT HAVE THAT HONOR, SISE-NEG. I AM DOCTOR STRANGE. I HAVE MET YOU IN MY PAST--YOUR FUTURE.
HEAR ME, SORCERER!
THOR...!
I AM THOR, SON OF ODIN, PRINCE OF ASGARD AND GOD OF THUNDER! LOKI IS MY STEPBROTHER AND NO DOUBT DESERVED THIS COMEUPPANCE.
GIVEN THE CIRCUMSTANCES, I AM WILLING TO OVERLOOK YOUR ATTACK ON MY PERSON, BUT--!
QUITE RIGHT, THOR. SISE-NEG, I AM THE WASP, LEADER OF THE AVENGERS.
WE WISH ONLY TO TAKE LOKI OFF YOUR HANDS.
I AM NOT YET DONE WITH LOKI.
SISE-NEG, PLEASE...IF NOT FOR LOKI'S ARRIVAL, YOU WOULD HAVE GOTTEN YOUR FILL OF YANN'S MYSTIC ENERGIES AND ALREADY DEPARTED.
INSTEAD, YOUR BATTLE HAS UNDERMINED THIS PLANET'S VERY FOUNDATIONS AND YOUR OWN DESTINY! IT WOULD BE BEST IF--
DO NOT LECTURE ME, MAGE--
--AND DO NOT TELL ME WHAT IS "BEST"!

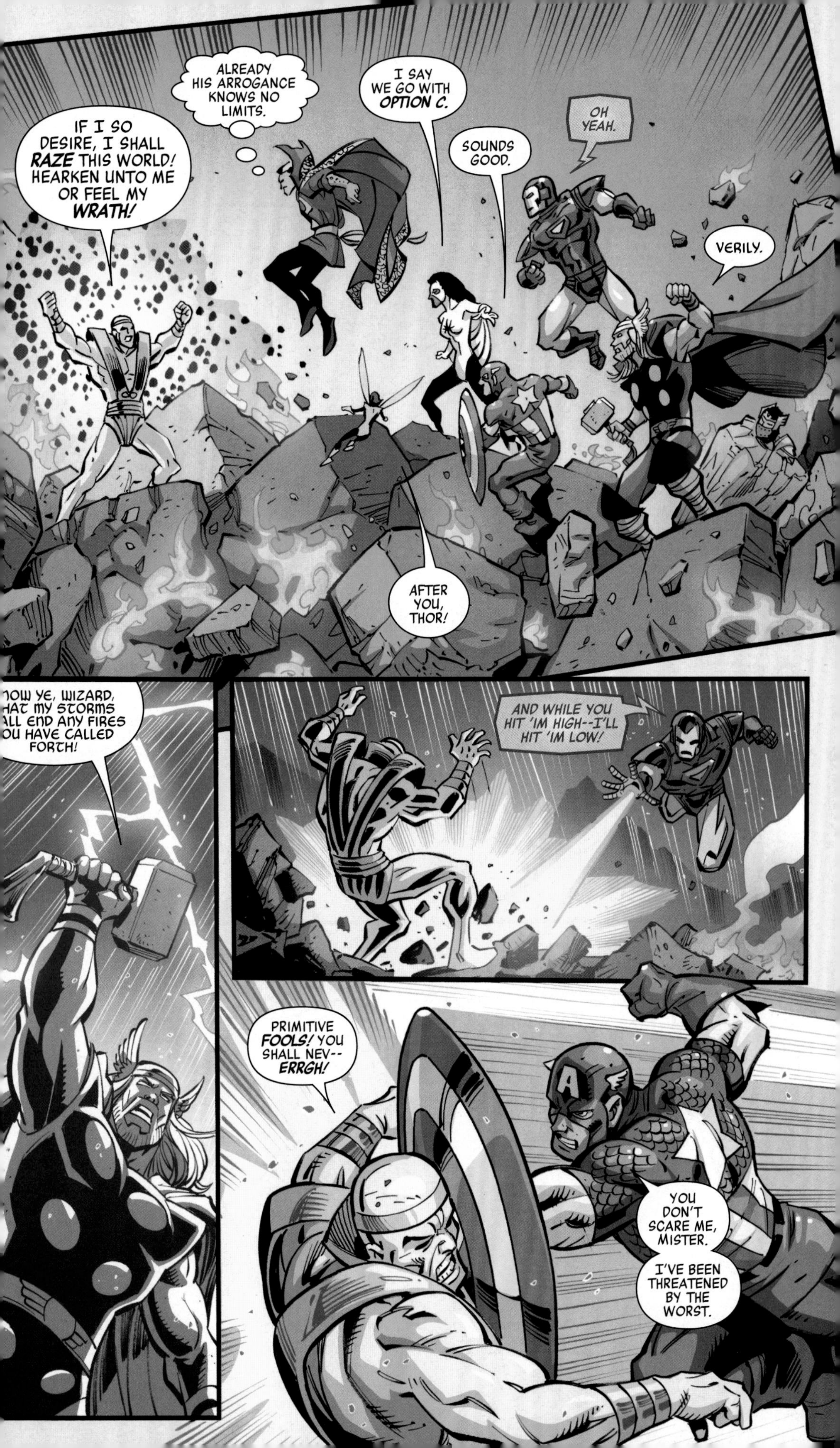

IF I SO DESIRE, I SHALL RAZE THIS WORLD! HEARKEN UNTO ME OR FEEL MY WRATH!
ALREADY HIS ARROGANCE KNOWS NO LIMITS.
I SAY WE GO WITH OPTION C.
SOUNDS GOOD.
OH YEAH.
VERILY.
AFTER YOU, THOR!
NOW YE, WIZARD, THAT MY STORMS SHALL END ANY FIRES YOU HAVE CALLED FORTH!
AND WHILE YOU HIT 'IM HIGH--I'LL HIT 'IM LOW!
PRIMITIVE FOOLS! YOU SHALL NEV-- ERRGH!
YOU DON'T SCARE ME, MISTER.
I'VE BEEN THREATENED BY THE WORST.

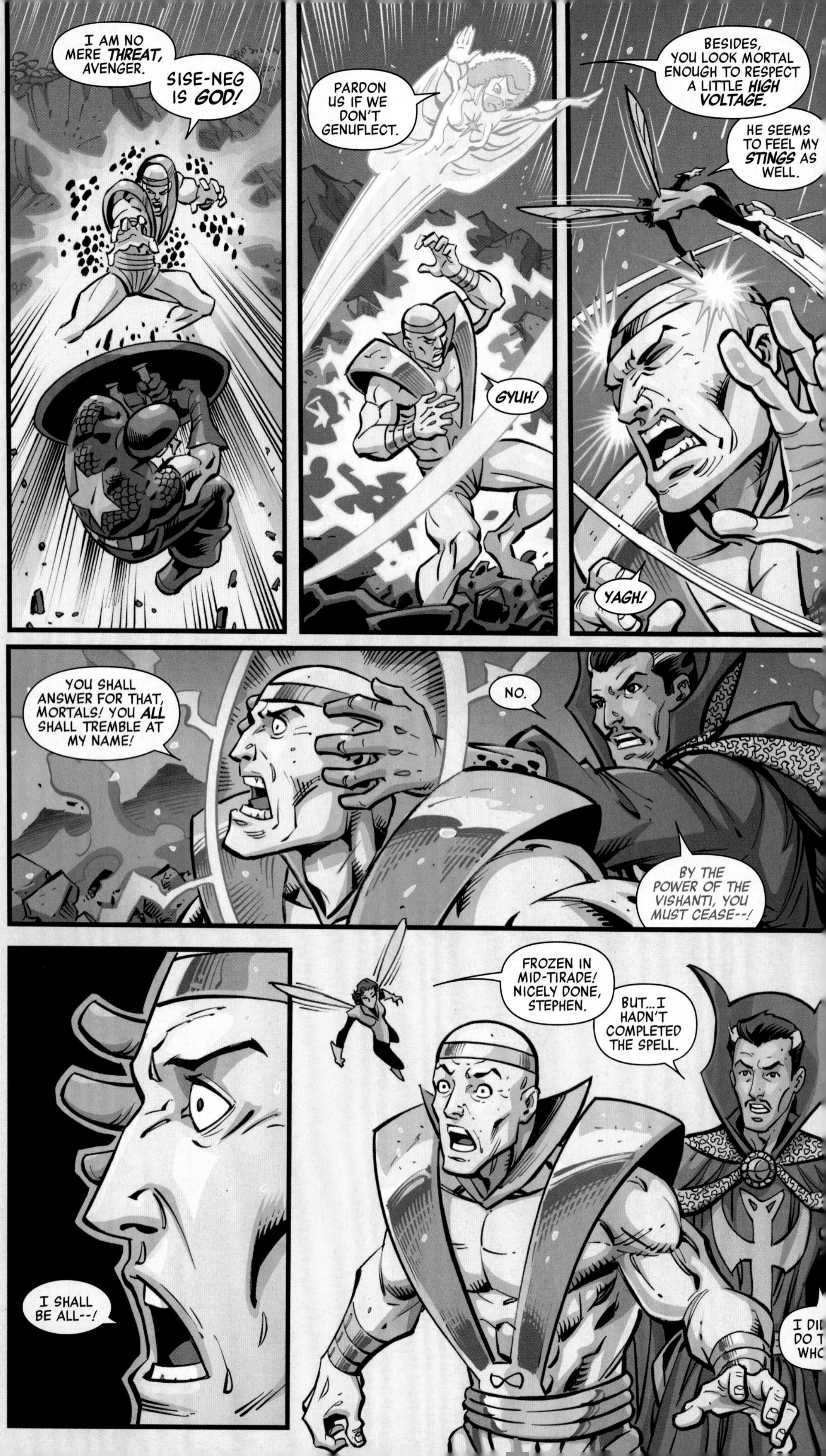

I AM NO MERE THREAT, AVENGER.
SISE-NEG IS GOD!
PARDON US IF WE DON'T GENUFLECT.
GYUH!
BESIDES, YOU LOOK MORTAL ENOUGH TO RESPECT A LITTLE HIGH VOLTAGE.
HE SEEMS TO FEEL MY STINGS AS WELL.
YAGH!
YOU SHALL ANSWER FOR THAT, MORTALS! YOU ALL SHALL TREMBLE AT MY NAME!
NO.
BY THE POWER OF THE VISHANTI, YOU MUST CEASE--!
I SHALL BE ALL--!
FROZEN IN MID-TIRADE! NICELY DONE, STEPHEN.
BUT...I HADN'T COMPLETED THE SPELL.

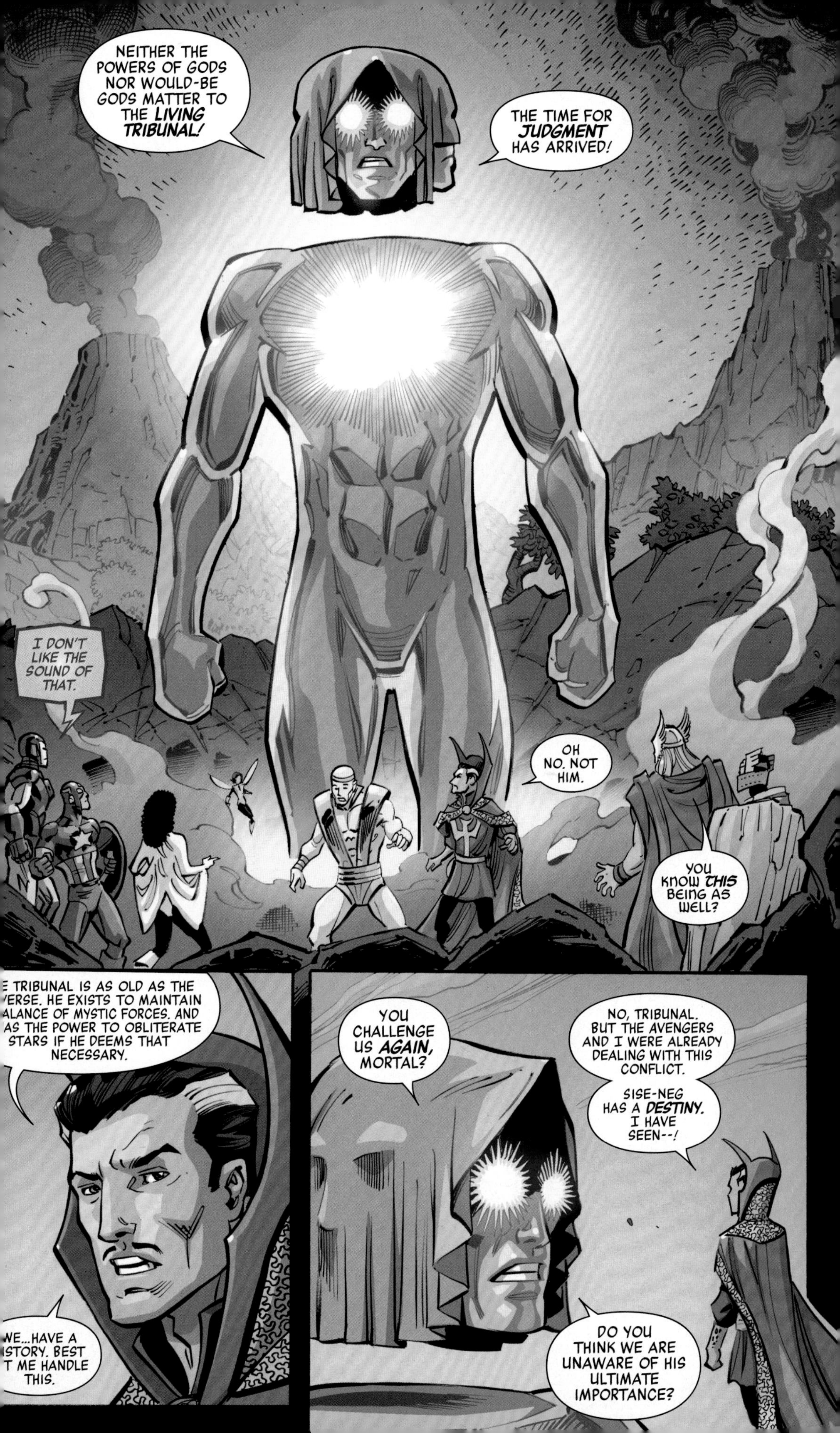
NEITHER THE POWERS OF GODS NOR WOULD-BE GODS MATTER TO THE LIVING TRIBUNAL!
THE TIME FOR JUDGMENT HAS ARRIVED!
I DON'T LIKE THE SOUND OF THAT.
OH NO. NOT HIM.
YOU KNOW THIS BEING AS WELL?
E TRIBUNAL IS AS OLD AS THE VERSE. HE EXISTS TO MAINTAIN ALANCE OF MYSTIC FORCES. AND AS THE POWER TO OBLITERATE STARS IF HE DEEMS THAT NECESSARY.
WE...HAVE A STORY. BEST T ME HANDLE THIS.
YOU CHALLENGE US AGAIN, MORTAL?
NO, TRIBUNAL. BUT THE AVENGERS AND I WERE ALREADY DEALING WITH THIS CONFLICT.
SISE-NEG HAS A DESTINY. I HAVE SEEN--!
DO YOU THINK WE ARE UNAWARE OF HIS ULTIMATE IMPORTANCE?

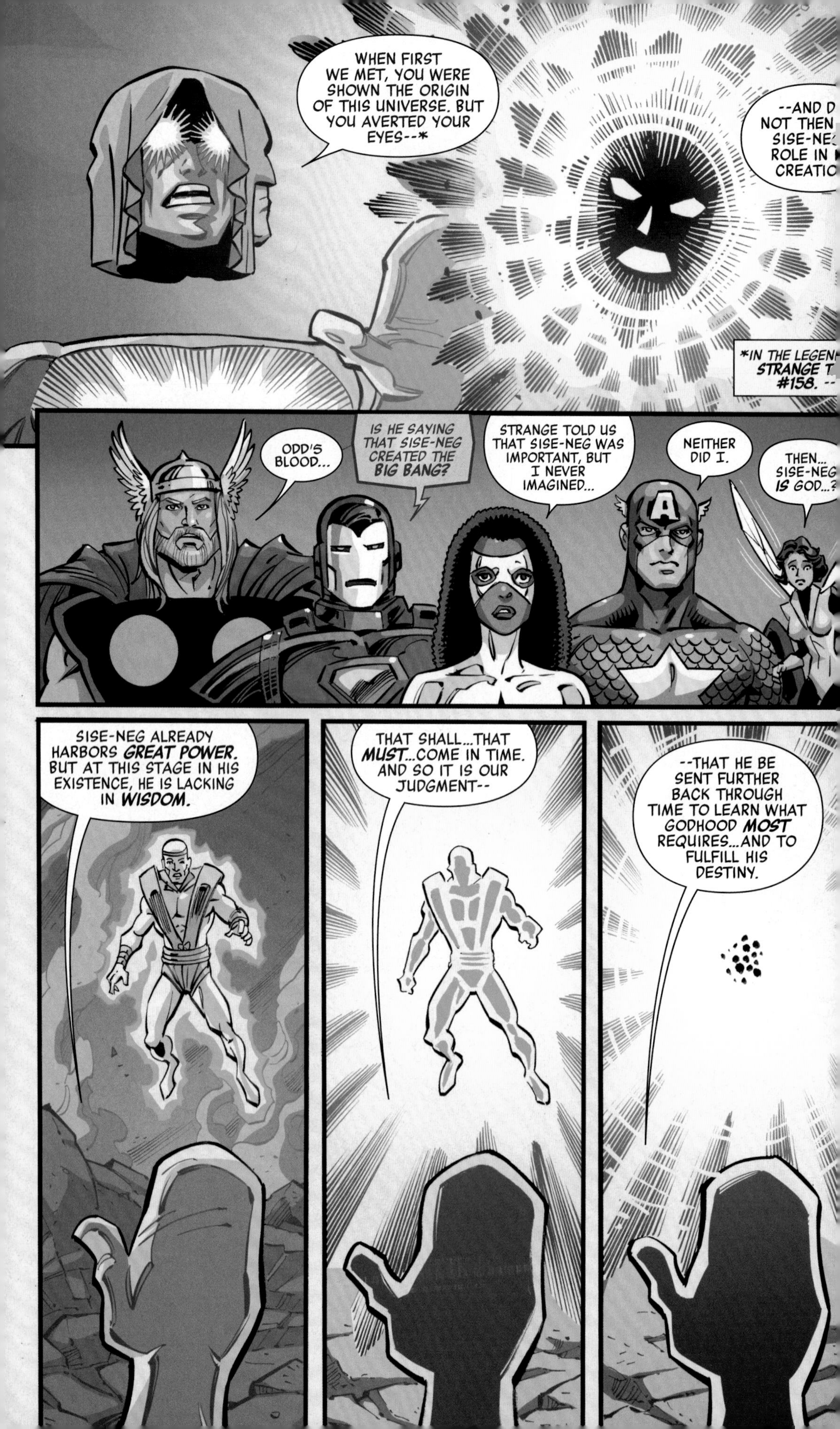
WHEN FIRST WE MET, YOU WERE SHOWN THE ORIGIN OF THIS UNIVERSE. BUT YOU AVERTED YOUR EYES--*
--AND D NOT THEN SISE-NE ROLE IN CREATIO
*IN THE LEGEN STRANGE T #158. --
ODD'S BLOOD...
IS HE SAYING THAT SISE-NEG CREATED THE BIG BANG?
STRANGE TOLD US THAT SISE-NEG WAS IMPORTANT, BUT I NEVER IMAGINED...
NEITHER DID I.
THEN... SISE-NEG IS GOD...?
SISE-NEG ALREADY HARBORS GREAT POWER. BUT AT THIS STAGE IN HIS EXISTENCE, HE IS LACKING IN WISDOM.
THAT SHALL...THAT MUST...COME IN TIME. AND SO IT IS OUR JUDGMENT--
--THAT HE BE SENT FURTHER BACK THROUGH TIME TO LEARN WHAT GODHOOD MOST REQUIRES...AND TO FULFILL HIS DESTINY.

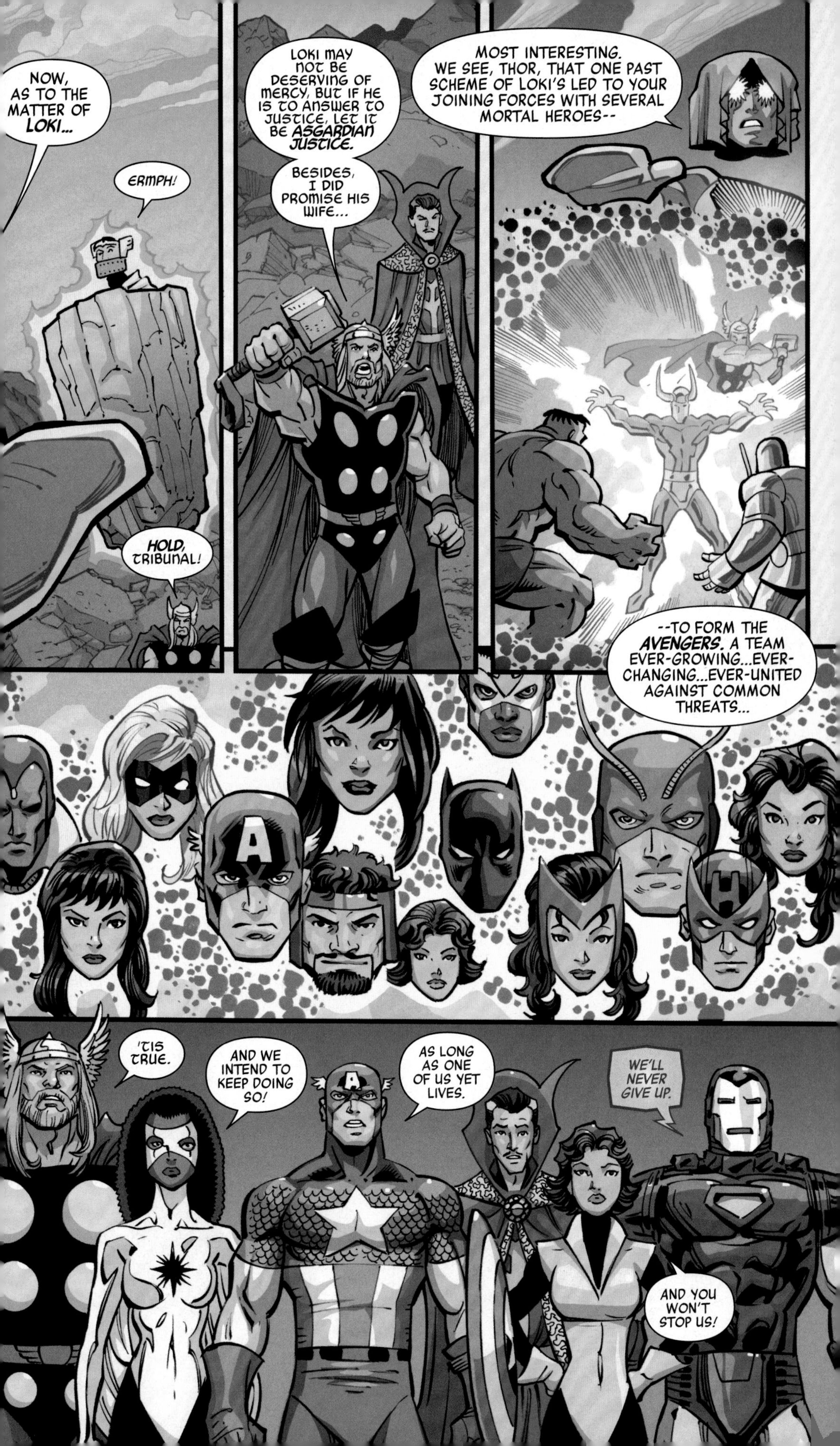
NOW, AS TO THE MATTER OF LOKI...
ERMPH!
HOLD, TRIBUNAL!
LOKI MAY NOT BE DESERVING OF MERCY, BUT IF HE IS TO ANSWER TO JUSTICE, LET IT BE ASGARDIAN JUSTICE.
BESIDES, I DID PROMISE HIS WIFE...
MOST INTERESTING. WE SEE, THOR, THAT ONE PAST SCHEME OF LOKI'S LED TO YOUR JOINING FORCES WITH SEVERAL MORTAL HEROES--
--TO FORM THE AVENGERS. A TEAM EVER-GROWING...EVER-CHANGING...EVER-UNITED AGAINST COMMON THREATS...
'TIS TRUE.
AND WE INTEND TO KEEP DOING SO!
AS LONG AS ONE OF US YET LIVES.
WE'LL NEVER GIVE UP.
AND YOU WON'T STOP US!

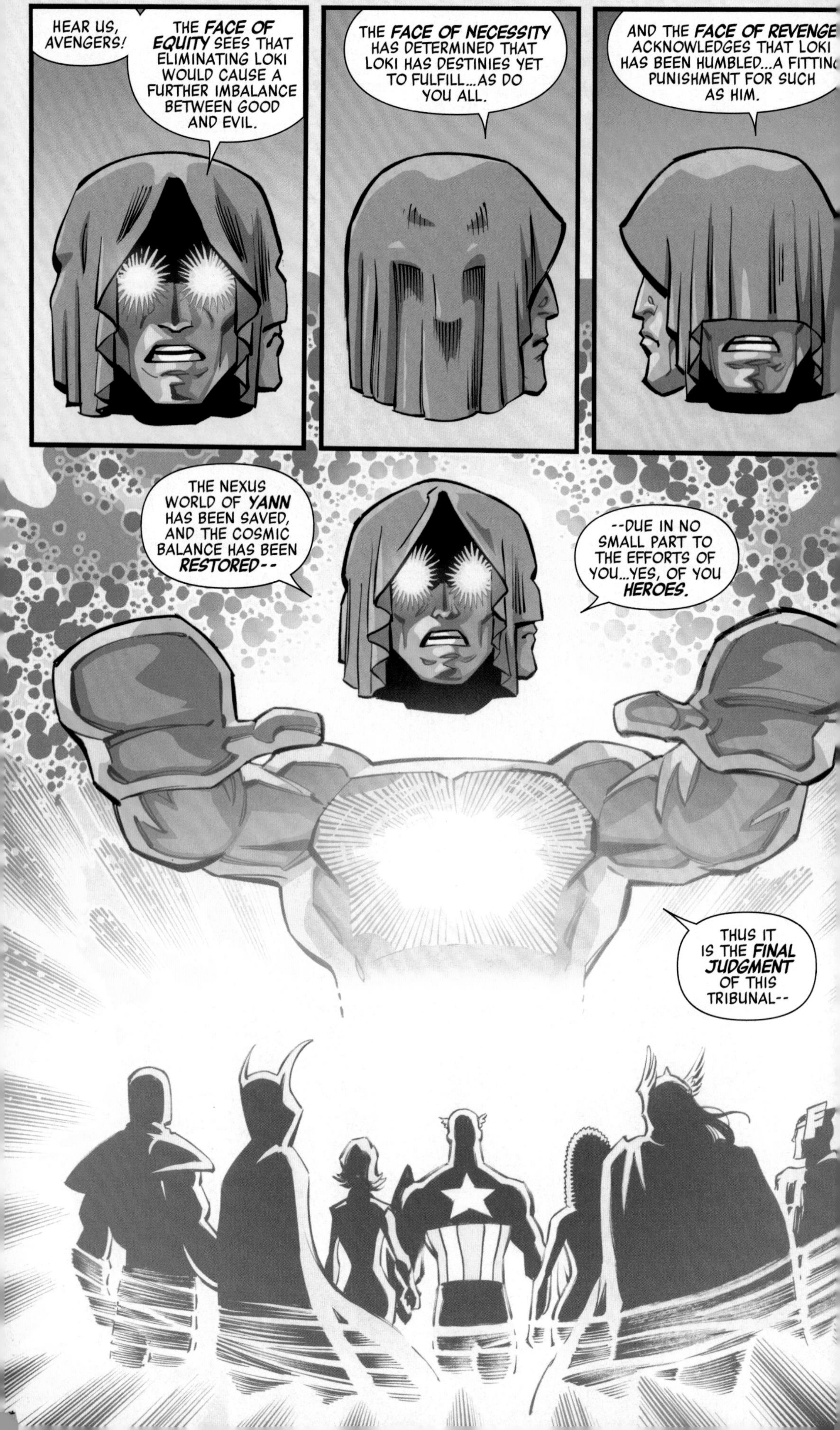
HEAR US, AVENGERS!
THE FACE OF EQUITY SEES THAT ELIMINATING LOKI WOULD CAUSE A FURTHER IMBALANCE BETWEEN GOOD AND EVIL.
THE FACE OF NECESSITY HAS DETERMINED THAT LOKI HAS DESTINIES YET TO FULFILL...AS DO YOU ALL.
AND THE FACE OF REVENGE ACKNOWLEDGES THAT LOKI HAS BEEN HUMBLED...A FITTING PUNISHMENT FOR SUCH AS HIM.
THE NEXUS WORLD OF YANN HAS BEEN SAVED, AND THE COSMIC BALANCE HAS BEEN RESTORED--
--DUE IN NO SMALL PART TO THE EFFORTS OF YOU...YES, OF YOU HEROES.
THUS IT IS THE FINAL JUDGMENT OF THIS TRIBUNAL--

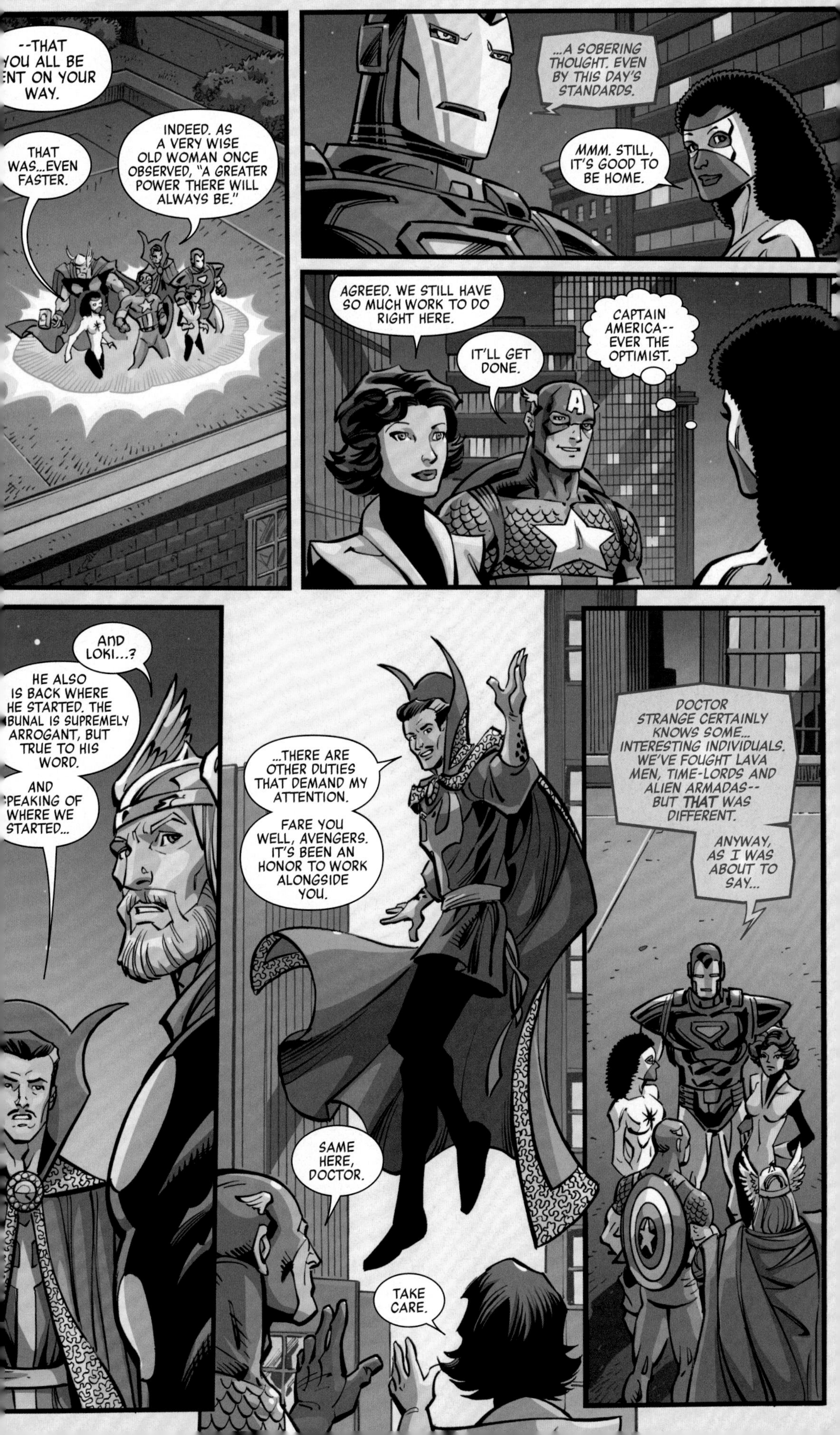
--THAT
YOU ALL BE
ENT ON YOUR
WAY.
THAT
WAS...EVEN
FASTER.
INDEED. AS
A VERY WISE
OLD WOMAN ONCE
OBSERVED, "A GREATER
POWER THERE WILL
ALWAYS BE."
...A SOBERING
THOUGHT. EVEN
BY THIS DAY'S
STANDARDS.
MMM. STILL,
IT'S GOOD TO
BE HOME.
AGREED. WE STILL HAVE
SO MUCH WORK TO DO
RIGHT HERE.
IT'LL GET
DONE.
CAPTAIN
AMERICA--
EVER THE
OPTIMIST.
AND
LOKI...?
HE ALSO
IS BACK WHERE
HE STARTED. THE
IBUNAL IS SUPREMELY
ARROGANT, BUT
TRUE TO HIS
WORD.
AND
SPEAKING OF
WHERE WE
STARTED...
...THERE ARE
OTHER DUTIES
THAT DEMAND MY
ATTENTION.
FARE YOU
WELL, AVENGERS.
IT'S BEEN AN
HONOR TO WORK
ALONGSIDE
YOU.
SAME
HERE,
DOCTOR.
TAKE
CARE.
DOCTOR
STRANGE CERTAINLY
KNOWS SOME...
INTERESTING INDIVIDUALS.
WE'VE FOUGHT LAVA
MEN, TIME-LORDS AND
ALIEN ARMADAS--
BUT THAT WAS
DIFFERENT.
ANYWAY,
AS I WAS
ABOUT TO
SAY...

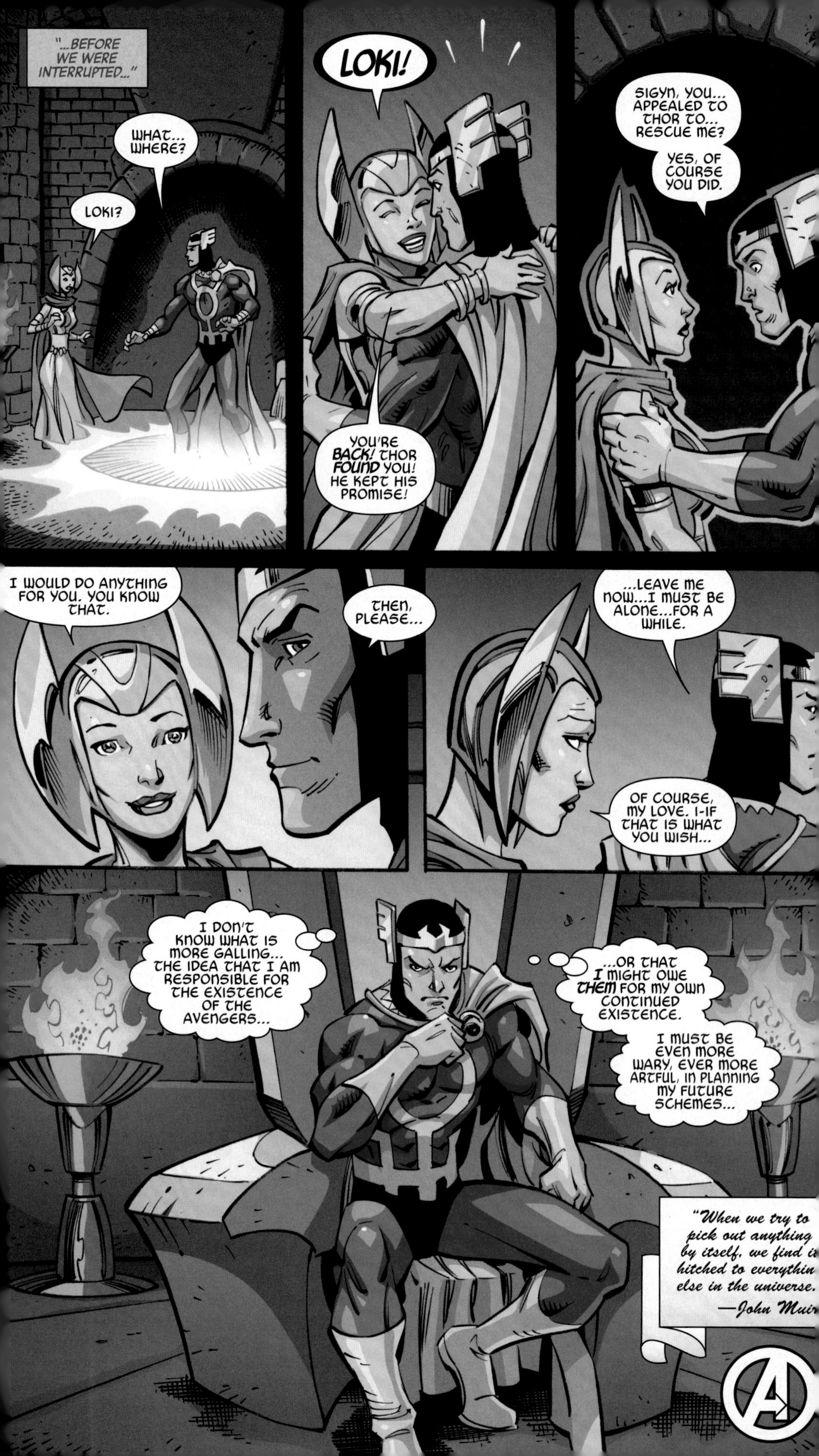

"...BEFORE WE WERE INTERRUPTED..."
WHAT... WHERE?
LOKI?
LOKI!
YOU'RE BACK! THOR FOUND YOU! HE KEPT HIS PROMISE!
SIGYN, YOU... APPEALED TO THOR TO... RESCUE ME?
YES, OF COURSE YOU DID.
I WOULD DO ANYTHING FOR YOU. YOU KNOW THAT.
THEN, PLEASE...
...LEAVE ME NOW...I MUST BE ALONE...FOR A WHILE.
OF COURSE, MY LOVE. I-IF THAT IS WHAT YOU WISH...
I DON'T KNOW WHAT IS MORE GALLING... THE IDEA THAT I AM RESPONSIBLE FOR THE EXISTENCE OF THE AVENGERS...
...OR THAT I MIGHT OWE THEM FOR MY OWN CONTINUED EXISTENCE.
I MUST BE EVEN MORE WARY, EVER MORE ARTFUL, IN PLANNING MY FUTURE SCHEMES...
"When we try to pick out anything by itself, we find it hitched to everythin else in the universe.
—John Muir

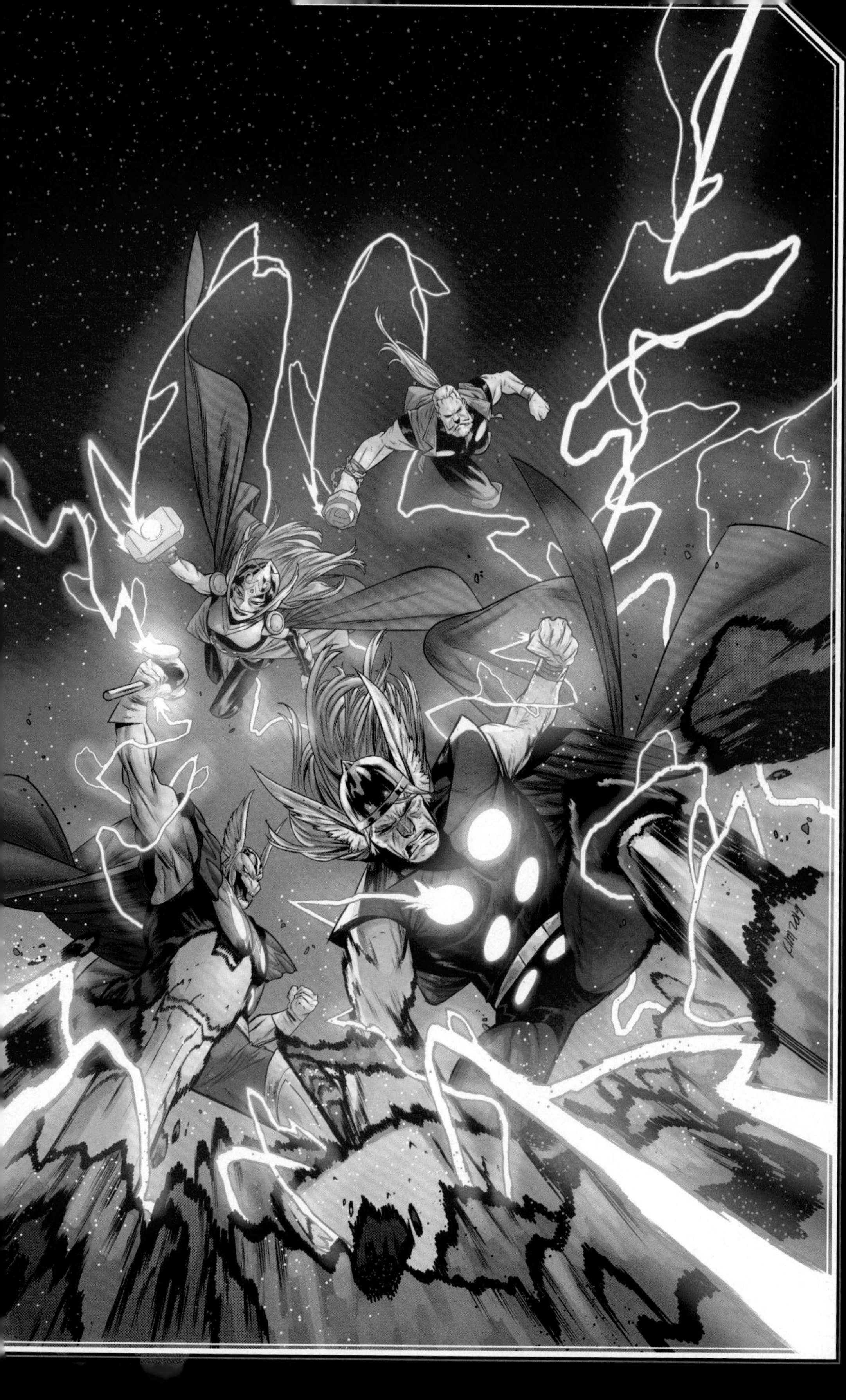

THOR ODINSON IS THE GOD OF THUNDER AND PROTECTOR OF MIDGARD. ALONG WITH ALL THE POWERS OF THE STORM, HE WIELDS MJOLNIR, A MIGHTY HAMMER FORGED OF URU THAT ONLY HE CAN LIFT — OR SO HE BELIEVED FOR MANY YEARS. OVER TIME, HE HAS WITNESSED OTHERS WHO CAN LIFT THE HAMMER. OTHERS WHO ARE...WORTHY.

"BEYOND THE FIELD WE KNOW..."

ON A QUEST TO PROTECT HIS PEOPLE, THE KORBINITES, BETA RAY BILL ONCE GOT INTO A FIGHT WITH THOR DUE TO A MISUNDERSTANDING, AND DURING THE BATTLE HE PICKED UP MJOLNIR AND WAS GRANTED THE POWER OF THOR. SO IMPRESSED WITH THE KORBINITE'S WORTHINESS WAS THOR'S FATHER, ODIN, THAT HE FORGED A NEW ENCHANTED HAMMER FOR BILL CALLED STORMBREAKER. BILL HAS BEEN AN ALLY OF ASGARD EVER SINCE, AS WELL AS AN OCCASIONAL ROMANTIC PARTNER OF THE LADY SIF.

Walter Simonson	Mike Hawthorne	Sal Buscema	Tamra Bonvillain	John Workman
WRITER	PENCILER	INKER	COLOR ARTIST	LETTERER

"HEARTS OF STONE, FEET OF CLAY"

ERIC MASTERSON WAS A MORTAL ALLY OF THOR WHO PROVED HIMSELF WORTHY OF AN ENCHANTED WEAPON OF HIS OWN AND BECAME THE HERO KNOWN AS THUNDERSTRIKE. HE WOULD EVENTUALLY DIE IN BATTLE, AND HIS SON, KEVIN, NOW CARRIES ON THE THUNDERSTRIKE LEGACY, BUT WHILE HE LIVED ERIC FOUGHT DAILY TO PROTECT MIDGARD AND REMAIN WORTHY.

Tom DeFalco & Ron Frenz	Keith Williams	Rachelle Rosenberg	VC's Clayton Cowles
SCRIPT, PLOT & PENCILS	INKER	COLOR ARTIST	LETTERER

"RULE FOR REFLECTION"

WHEN THOR BRIEFLY FOUND HIMSELF UNWORTHY TO LIFT MJOLNIR AND JANE FOSTER BECAME THE NEW THOR, INITIALLY NO ONE KNEW WHO THIS NEW GODDESS OF THUNDER WAS, NOT EVEN THOR HIMSELF. FOR A TIME, HE SUSPECTED IT MIGHT BE THE LADY SIF, AND ONE NIGHT HE CONFRONTED HER DIRECTLY WITH HIS THEORY...

Kathryn Immonen	Tom Reilly	Chris O'Halloran	VC's Clayton Cowles
WRITER	ARTIST	COLOR ARTIST	LETTERER

Kim Jacinto & Java Tartaglia
COVER ART

Sarah Brunstad
ASSOCIATE EDITOR

Wil Moss
EDITOR

Tom Brevoort
EXECUTIVE EDITOR

THOR CREATD BY Stan Lee & Jack Kirby

THOR: THE WORTHY
variant by Walter Simonson & Paul Mounts

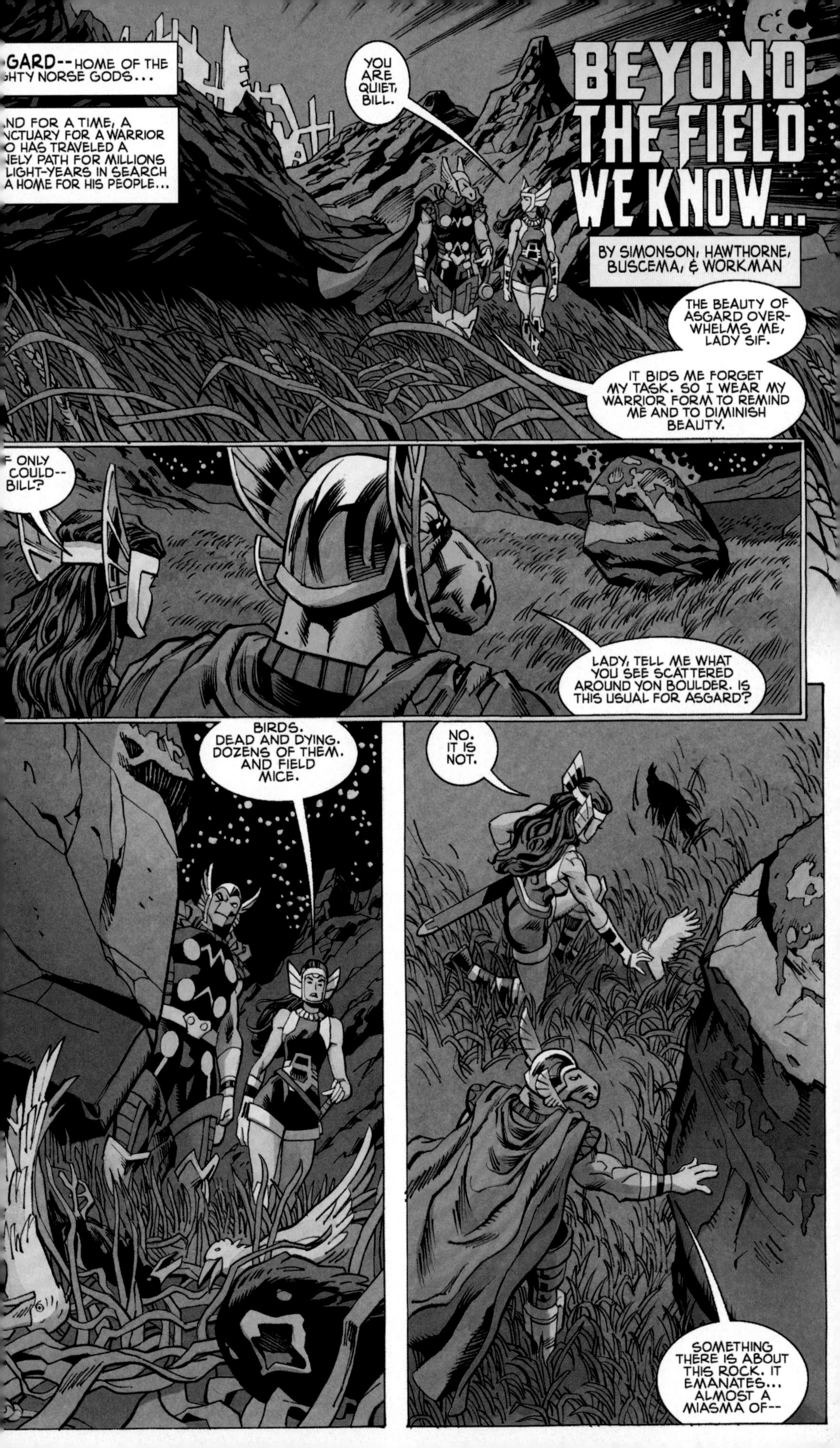

GARD--HOME OF THE
GHTY NORSE GODS...
ND FOR A TIME, A
NCTUARY FOR A WARRIOR
O HAS TRAVELED A
NELY PATH FOR MILLIONS
LIGHT-YEARS IN SEARCH
A HOME FOR HIS PEOPLE...
YOU ARE QUIET, BILL.
BEYOND THE FIELD WE KNOW...
BY SIMONSON, HAWTHORNE, BUSCEMA, & WORKMAN
THE BEAUTY OF ASGARD OVER-WHELMS ME, LADY SIF.
IT BIDS ME FORGET MY TASK. SO I WEAR MY WARRIOR FORM TO REMIND ME AND TO DIMINISH BEAUTY.
F ONLY COULD-- BILL?
LADY, TELL ME WHAT YOU SEE SCATTERED AROUND YON BOULDER. IS THIS USUAL FOR ASGARD?
BIRDS. DEAD AND DYING. DOZENS OF THEM. AND FIELD MICE.
NO. IT IS NOT.
SOMETHING THERE IS ABOUT THIS ROCK. IT EMANATES... ALMOST A MIASMA OF--

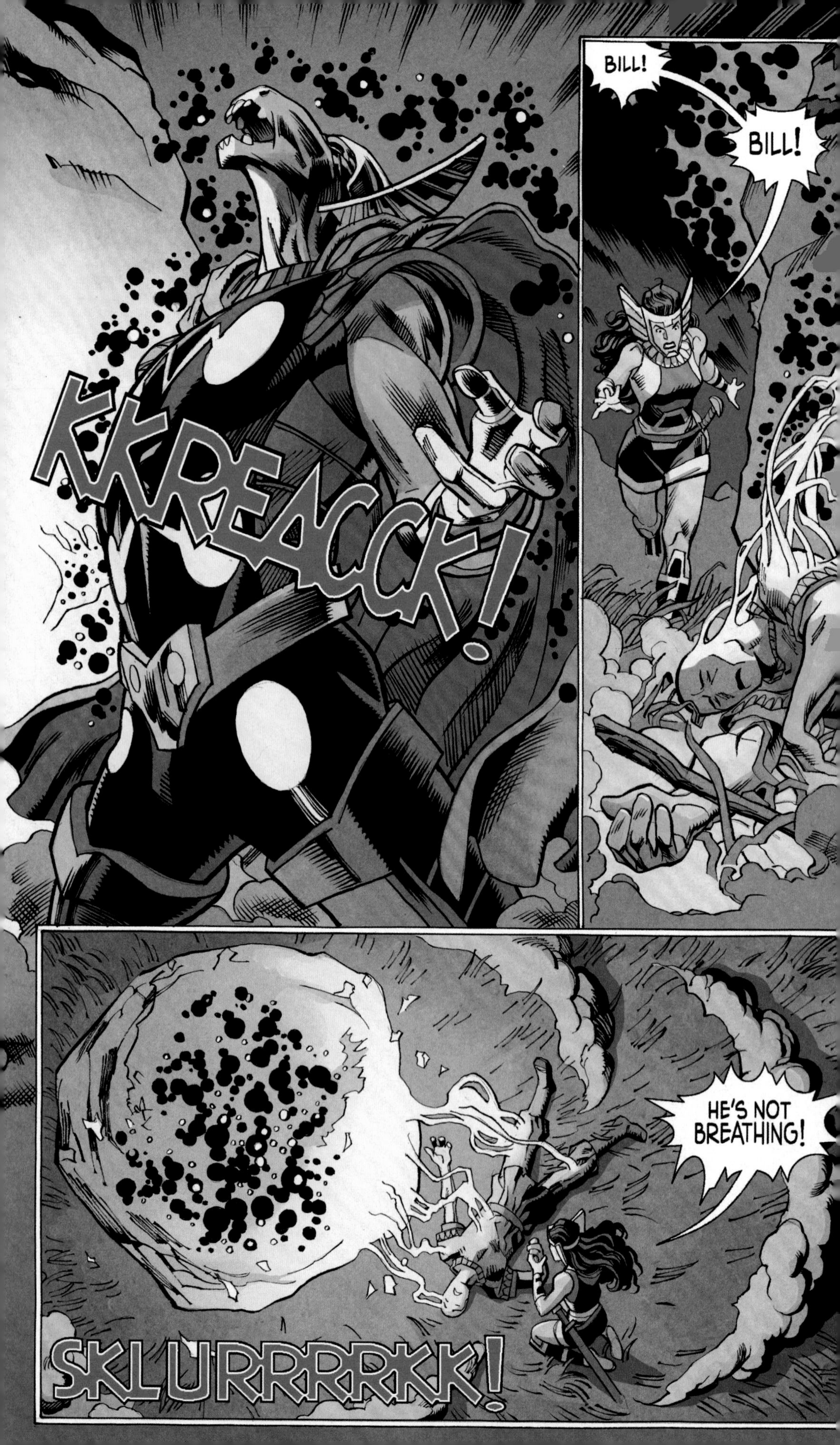
KKREACCK!
BILL!
BILL!
HE'S NOT
BREATHING!
SKLURRRRKK!

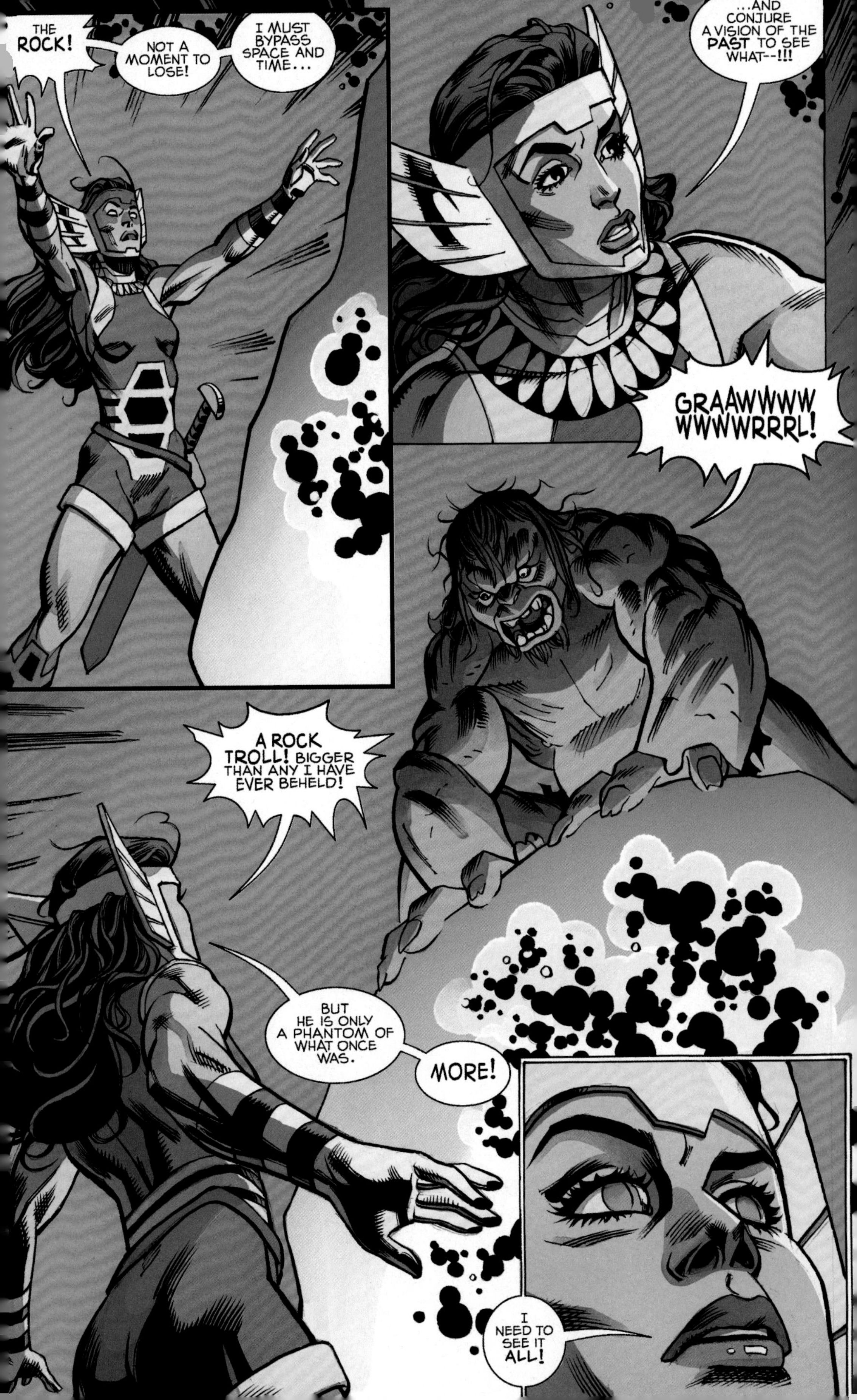
THE ROCK!
NOT A MOMENT TO LOSE!
I MUST BYPASS SPACE AND TIME...
...AND CONJURE A VISION OF THE PAST TO SEE WHAT--!!!
GRAAWWWW WWWWRRRL!
A ROCK TROLL! BIGGER THAN ANY I HAVE EVER BEHELD!
BUT HE IS ONLY A PHANTOM OF WHAT ONCE WAS.
MORE!
I NEED TO SEE IT ALL!

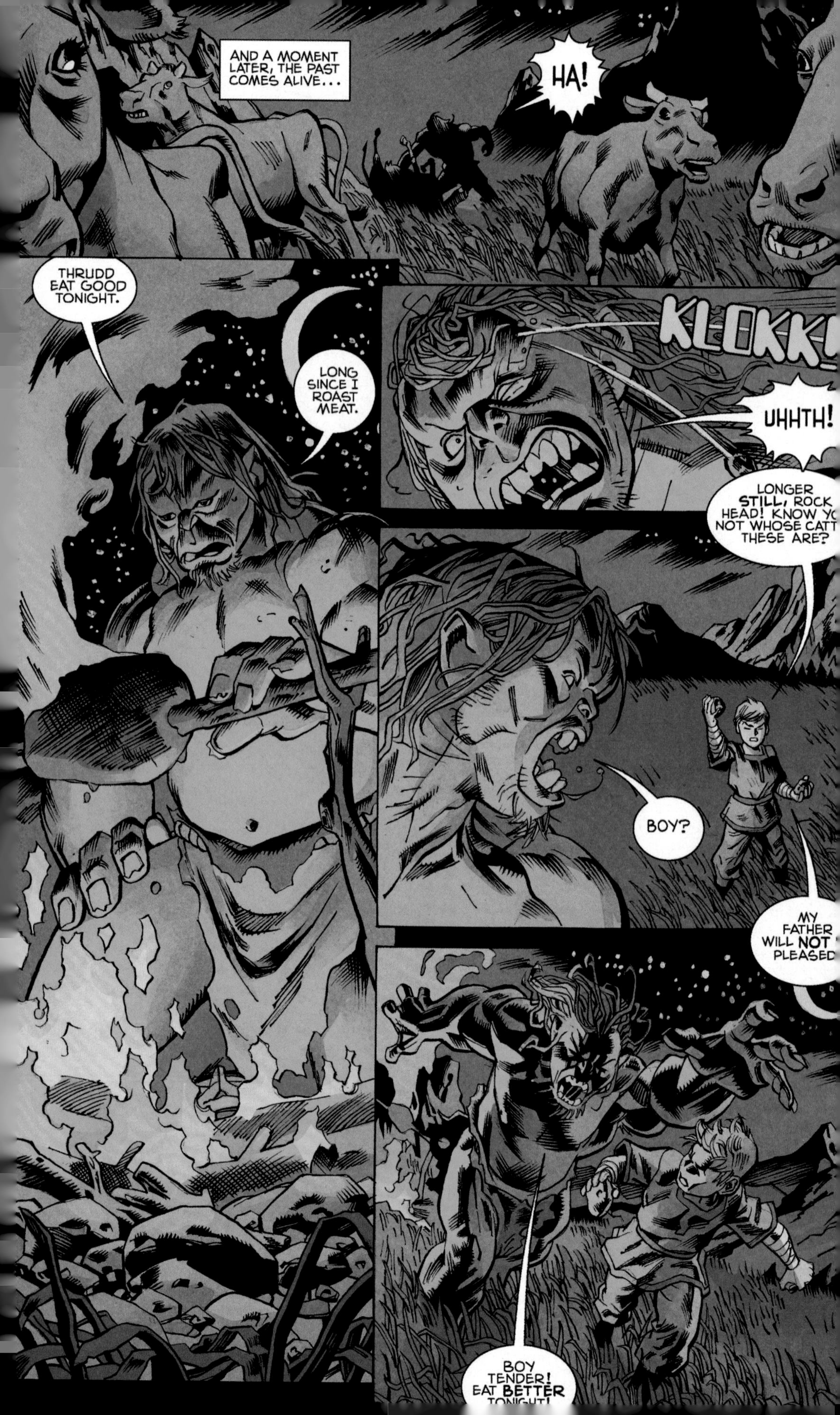

AND A MOMENT LATER, THE PAST COMES ALIVE...
HA!
THRUDD EAT GOOD TONIGHT.
LONG SINCE I ROAST MEAT.
KLOKK!
UHHTH!
LONGER STILL, ROCK HEAD! KNOW YO NOT WHOSE CATT THESE ARE?
BOY?
MY FATHER WILL NOT PLEASED
BOY TENDER! EAT BETTER

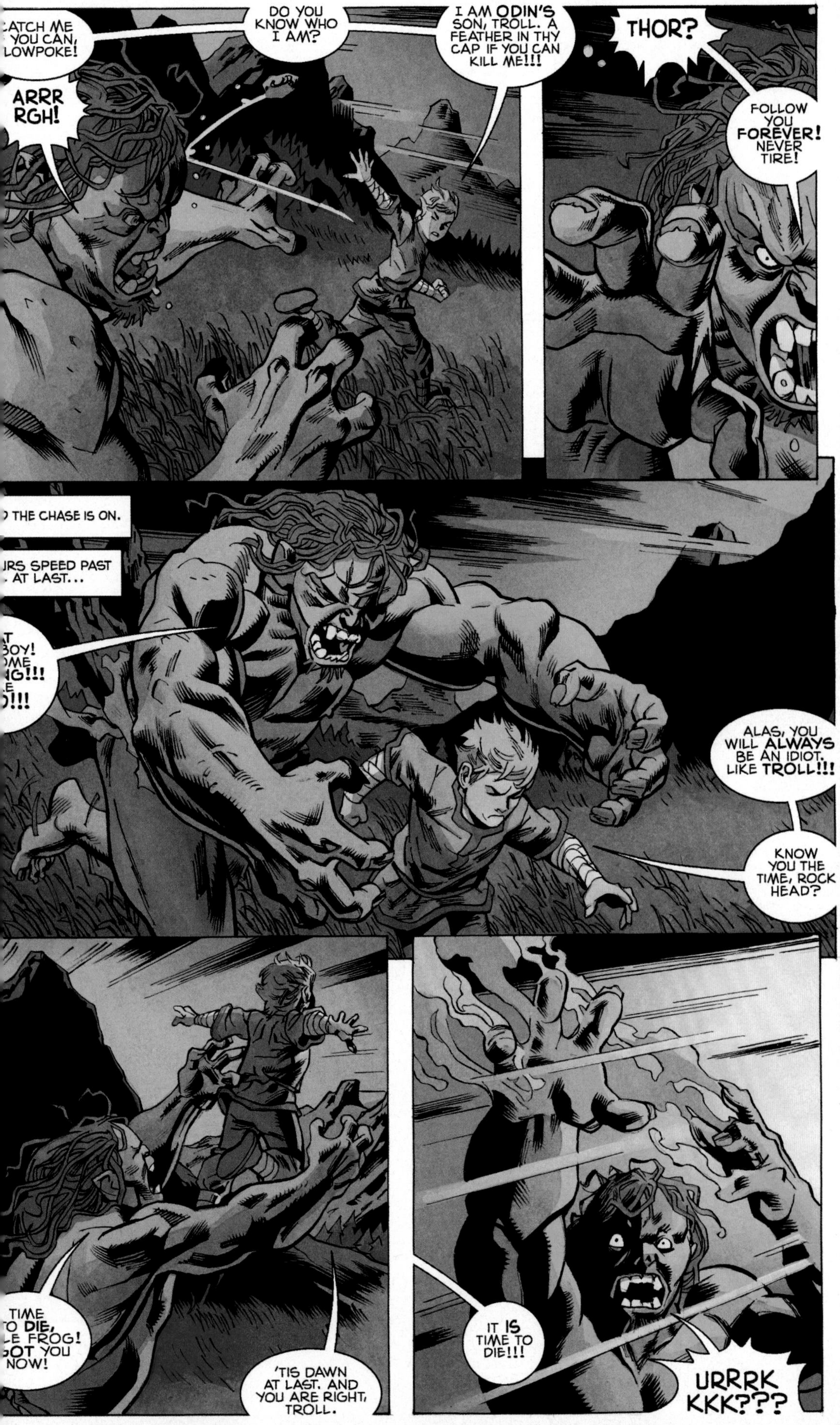

ATCH ME YOU CAN, LOWPOKE!
ARRR RGH!
DO YOU KNOW WHO I AM?
I AM ODIN'S SON, TROLL. A FEATHER IN THY CAP IF YOU CAN KILL ME!!!
THOR?
FOLLOW YOU FOREVER! NEVER TIRE!
THE CHASE IS ON.
URS SPEED PAST AT LAST...
ALAS, YOU WILL ALWAYS BE AN IDIOT. LIKE TROLL!!!
KNOW YOU THE TIME, ROCK HEAD?
TIME TO DIE, LE FROG! GOT YOU NOW!
'TIS DAWN AT LAST. AND YOU ARE RIGHT, TROLL.
IT IS TIME TO DIE!!!
URRRK KKK???

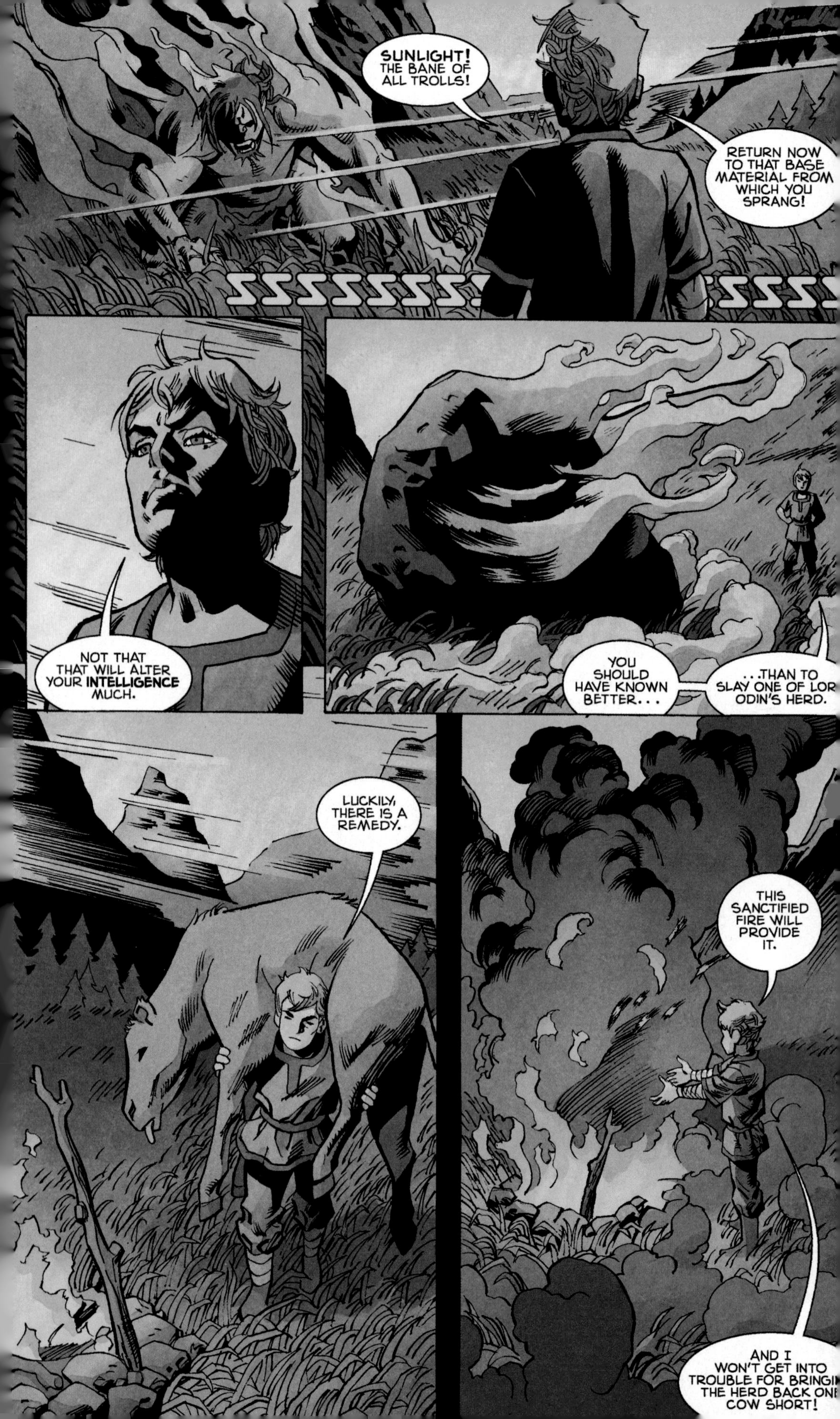
SUNLIGHT! THE BANE OF ALL TROLLS!
RETURN NOW TO THAT BASE MATERIAL FROM WHICH YOU SPRANG!
SSSSSSSS!
SSSSS
NOT THAT THAT WILL ALTER YOUR **INTELLIGENCE** MUCH.
YOU SHOULD HAVE KNOWN BETTER...
...THAN TO SLAY ONE OF LOR
ODIN'S HERD.
LUCKILY, THERE IS A REMEDY.
THIS SANCTIFIED FIRE WILL PROVIDE IT.
AND I WON'T GET INTO TROUBLE FOR BRINGI
THE HERD BACK ON
COW SHORT!

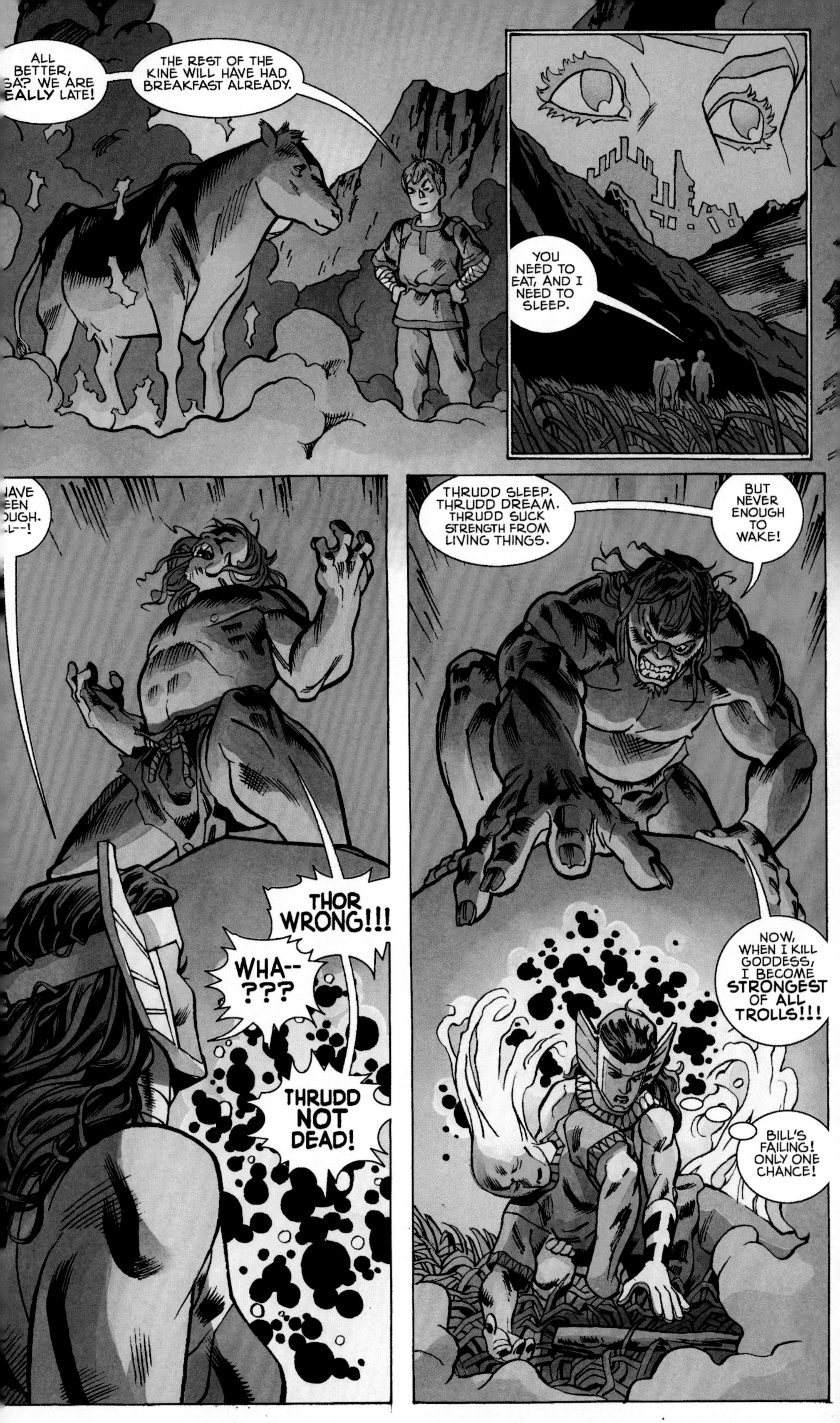
ALL BETTER, SA? WE ARE EALLY LATE!
THE REST OF THE KINE WILL HAVE HAD BREAKFAST ALREADY.
YOU NEED TO EAT, AND I NEED TO SLEEP.
THOR WRONG!!!
WHA-- ???
THRUDD NOT DEAD!
THRUDD SLEEP. THRUDD DREAM. THRUDD SUCK STRENGTH FROM LIVING THINGS.
BUT NEVER ENOUGH TO WAKE!
NOW, WHEN I KILL GODDESS, I BECOME STRONGEST OF ALL TROLLS!!!
BILL'S FAILING! ONLY ONE CHANCE!

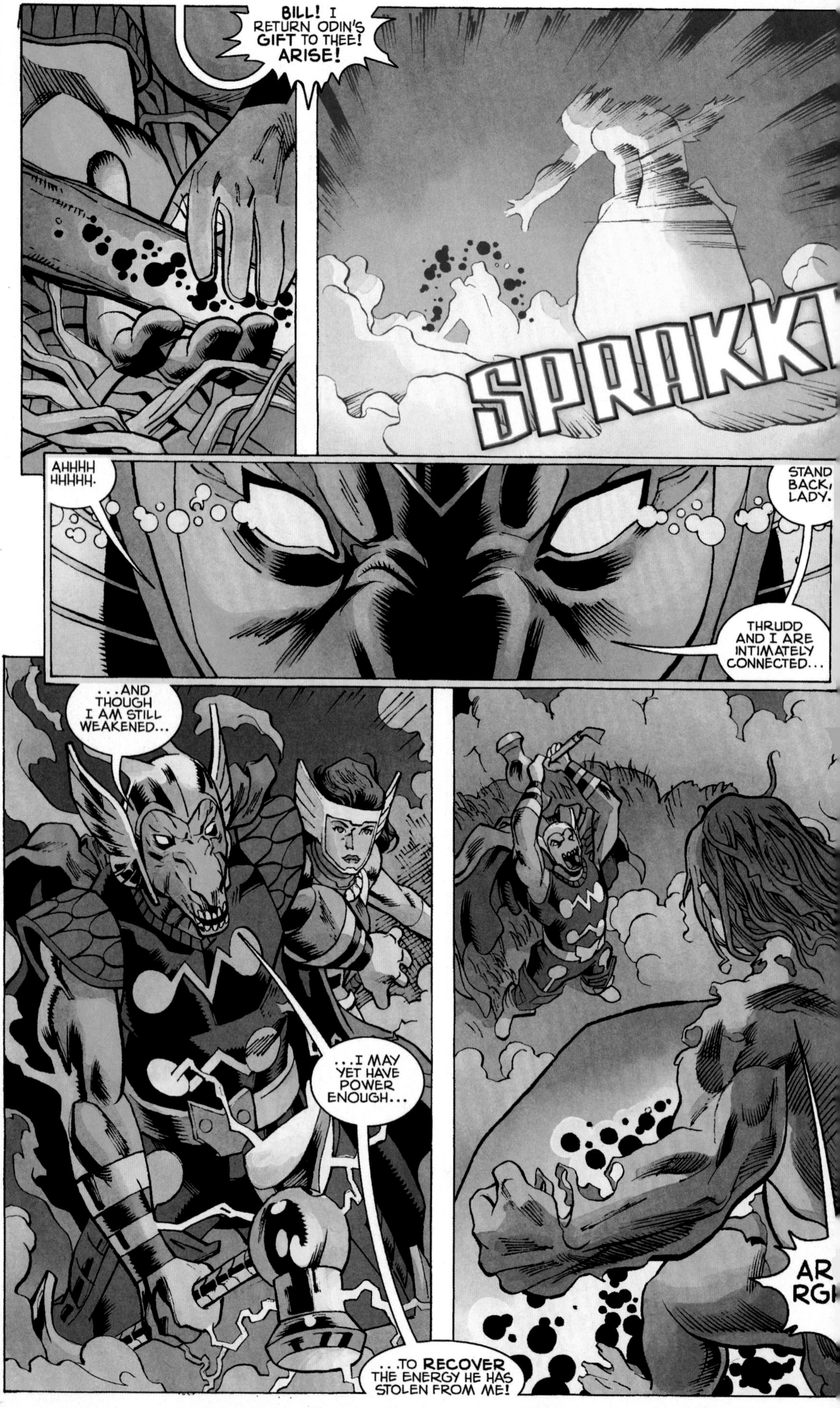

BILL! I RETURN ODIN'S GIFT TO THEE! ARISE!
SPRAKK
AHHHH HHHHH.
STAND BACK, LADY.
THRUDD AND I ARE INTIMATELY CONNECTED...
...AND THOUGH I AM STILL WEAKENED...
...I MAY YET HAVE POWER ENOUGH...
...TO RECOVER THE ENERGY HE HAS STOLEN FROM ME!
AR
RG

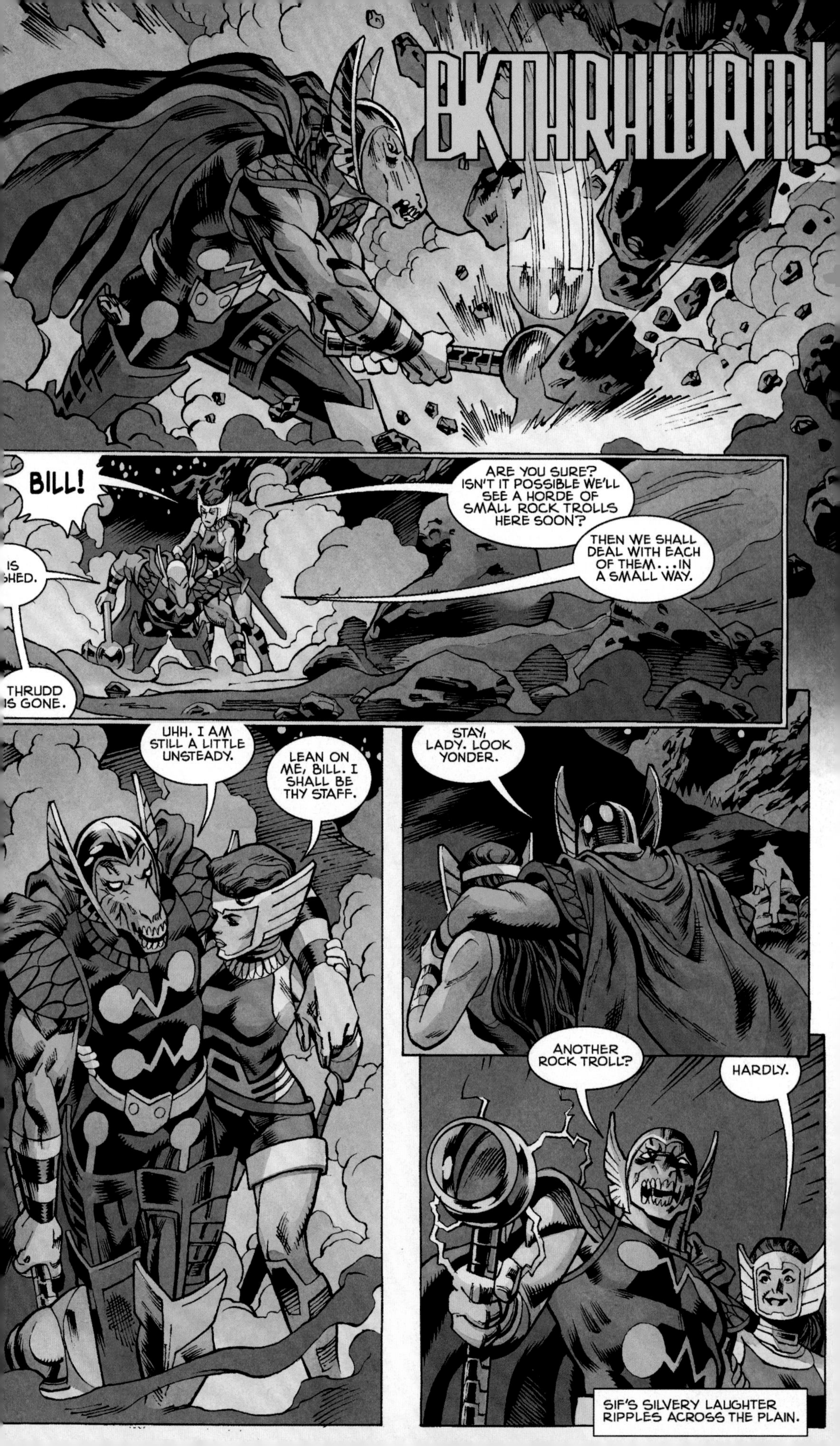

BKTHRHWRM!
BILL!
IS
SHED.
THRUDD
IS GONE.
ARE YOU SURE? ISN'T IT POSSIBLE WE'LL SEE A HORDE OF SMALL ROCK TROLLS HERE SOON?
THEN WE SHALL DEAL WITH EACH OF THEM...IN A SMALL WAY.
UHH. I AM STILL A LITTLE UNSTEADY.
LEAN ON ME, BILL. I SHALL BE THY STAFF.
STAY, LADY. LOOK YONDER.
ANOTHER ROCK TROLL?
HARDLY.
SIF'S SILVERY LAUGHTER RIPPLES ACROSS THE PLAIN.

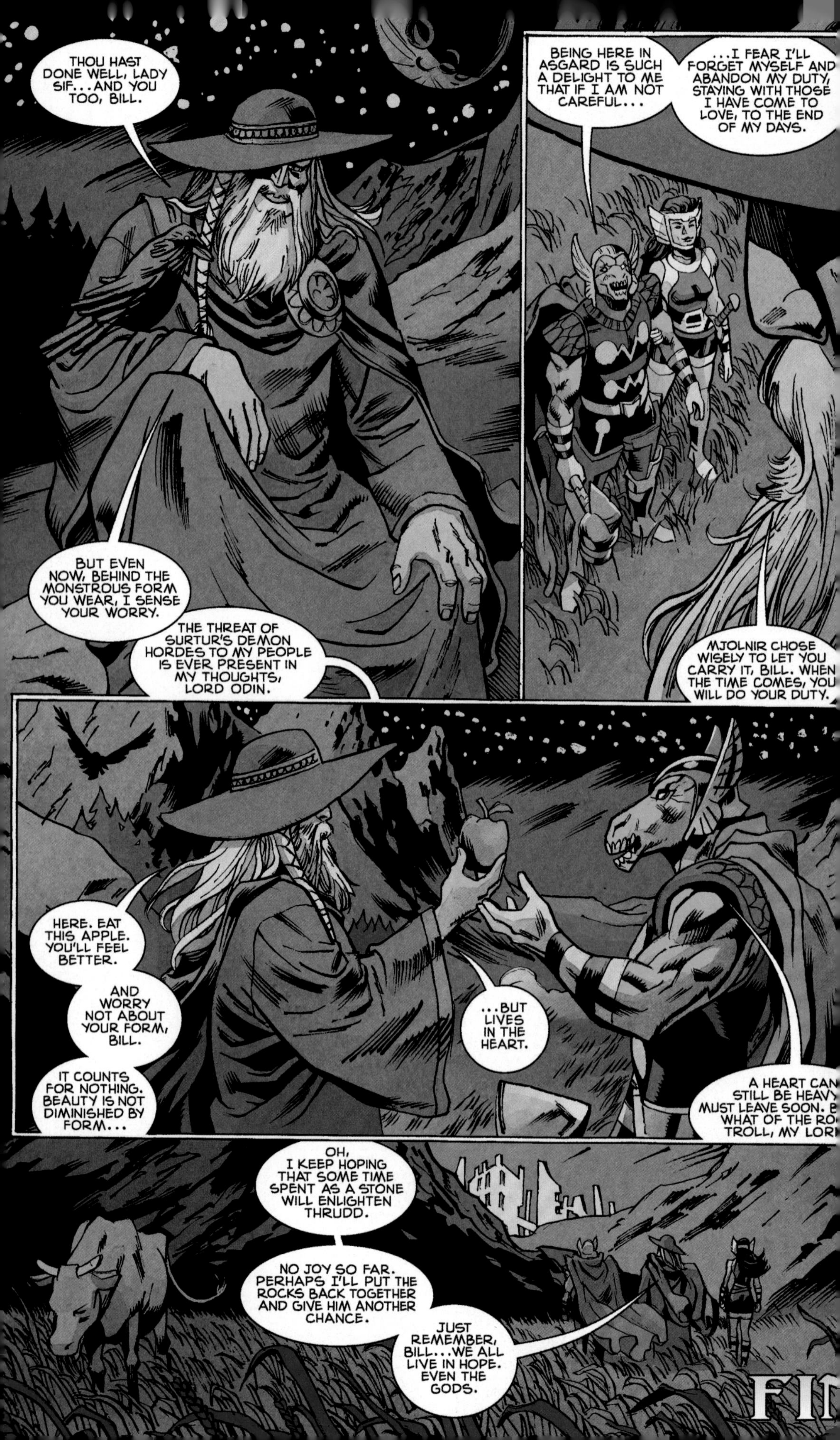
THOU HAST DONE WELL, LADY SIF...AND YOU TOO, BILL.
BUT EVEN NOW, BEHIND THE MONSTROUS FORM YOU WEAR, I SENSE YOUR WORRY.
THE THREAT OF SURTUR'S DEMON HORDES TO MY PEOPLE IS EVER PRESENT IN MY THOUGHTS, LORD ODIN.
BEING HERE IN ASGARD IS SUCH A DELIGHT TO ME THAT IF I AM NOT CAREFUL...
...I FEAR I'LL FORGET MYSELF AND ABANDON MY DUTY, STAYING WITH THOSE I HAVE COME TO LOVE, TO THE END OF MY DAYS.
MJOLNIR CHOSE WISELY TO LET YOU CARRY IT, BILL. WHEN THE TIME COMES, YOU WILL DO YOUR DUTY.
HERE. EAT THIS APPLE. YOU'LL FEEL BETTER.
AND WORRY NOT ABOUT YOUR FORM, BILL.
IT COUNTS FOR NOTHING. BEAUTY IS NOT DIMINISHED BY FORM...
...BUT LIVES IN THE HEART.
A HEART CAN STILL BE HEAVY MUST LEAVE SOON. B WHAT OF THE RO TROLL, MY LOR
OH, I KEEP HOPING THAT SOME TIME SPENT AS A STONE WILL ENLIGHTEN THRUDD.
NO JOY SO FAR. PERHAPS I'LL PUT THE ROCKS BACK TOGETHER AND GIVE HIM ANOTHER CHANCE.
JUST REMEMBER, BILL...WE ALL LIVE IN HOPE. EVEN THE GODS.
FIN

WHEN ARCHITECT **ERIC MASTERSON** STAMPS HIS WOODEN WALKING STICK UPON THE GROUND, IT IS TRANSFORMED INTO A MYSTICAL WEAPON CALLED **THUNDERSTRIKE!** ARMED WITH INCREDIBLE POWERS, MASTERSON WORKS TO PROVE THAT ONE MAN MUST MAKE A DIFFERENCE, BECAUSE THE WORLD STILL NEEDS HEROES. **MARVEL COMICS PRESENTS...**

THUNDERSTRIKE

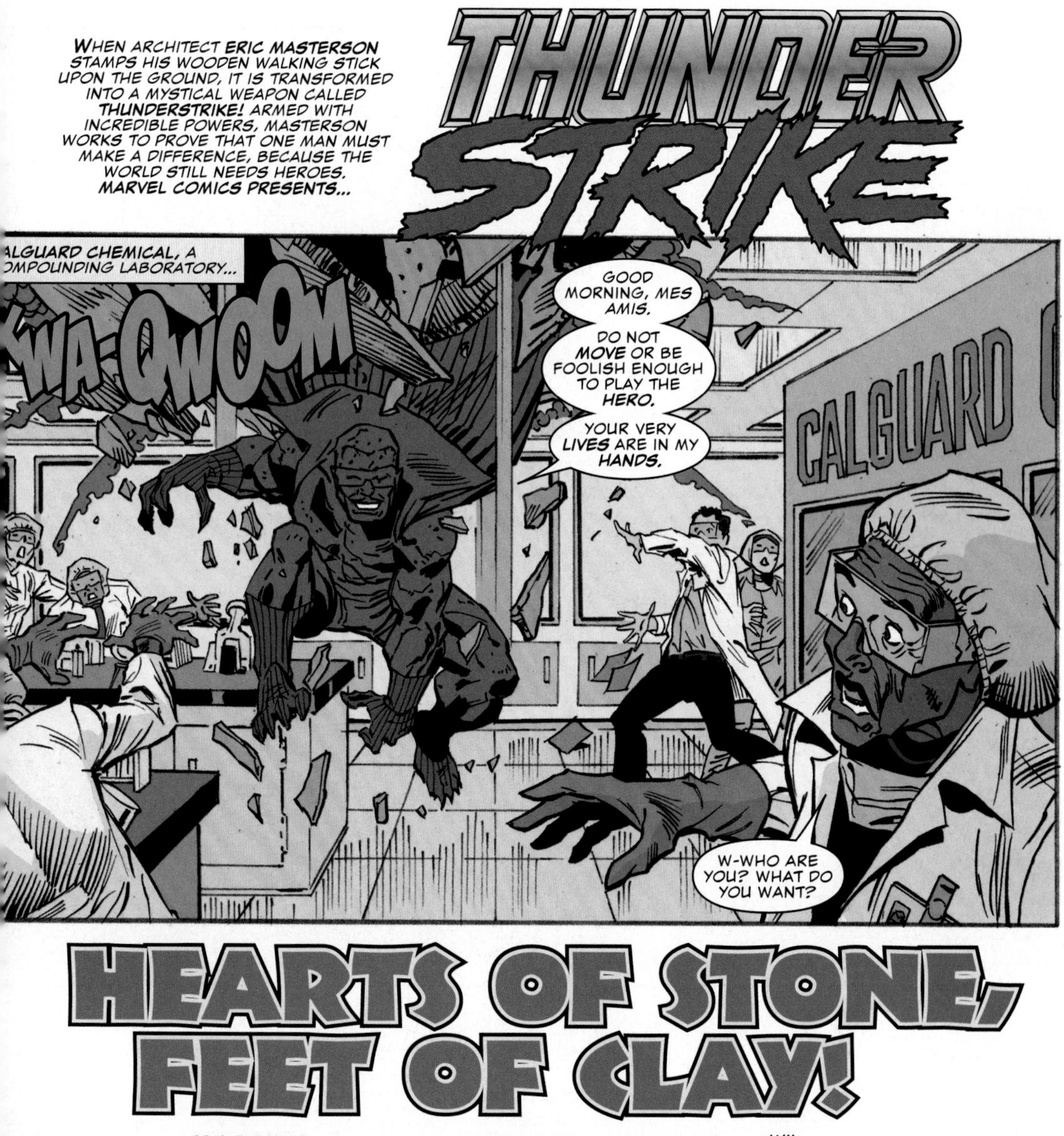

ALGUARD CHEMICAL, A OMPOUNDING LABORATORY...
KWA-QWOOM
GOOD MORNING, MES AMIS.
DO NOT MOVE OR BE FOOLISH ENOUGH TO PLAY THE HERO.
YOUR VERY LIVES ARE IN MY HANDS.
CALGUARD
W-WHO ARE YOU? WHAT DO YOU WANT?

HEARTS OF STONE, FEET OF CLAY!

TOM DEFALCO & RON FRENZ SCRIPT, PLOT & PENCILS | KEITH WILLIAMS INKS | RACHELLE ROSENBERG COLORS | VC'S CLAYTON COWLES LETTERS | WIL MOSS EDITOR

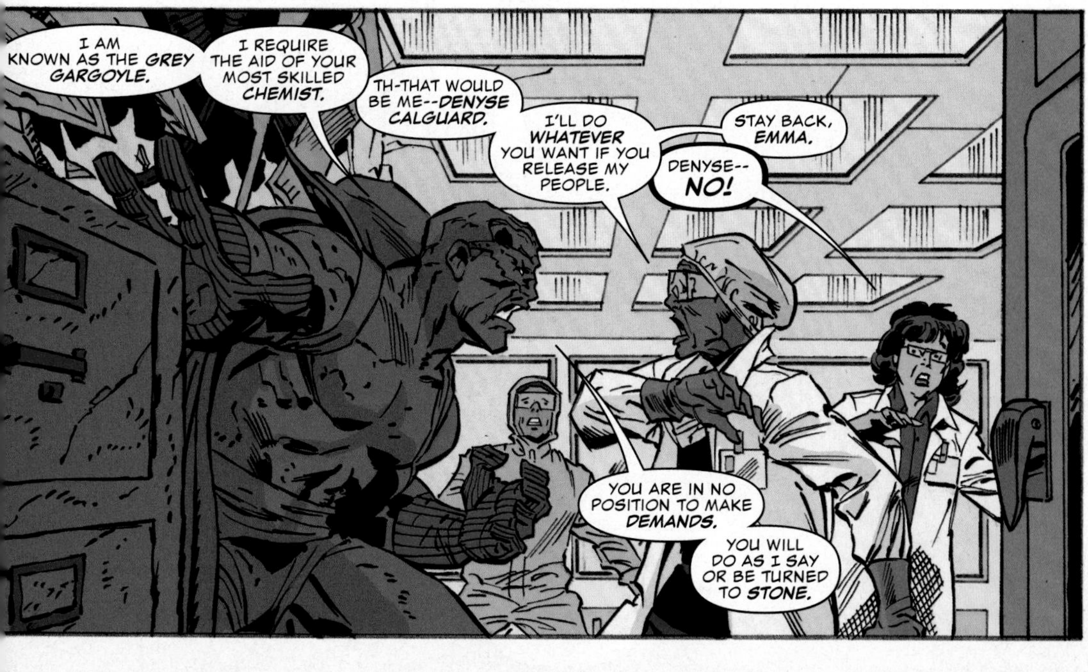

I AM KNOWN AS THE GREY GARGOYLE.
I REQUIRE THE AID OF YOUR MOST SKILLED CHEMIST.
TH-THAT WOULD BE ME--DENYSE CALGUARD.
I'LL DO WHATEVER YOU WANT IF YOU RELEASE MY PEOPLE.
STAY BACK, EMMA.
DENYSE-- NO!
YOU ARE IN NO POSITION TO MAKE DEMANDS.
YOU WILL DO AS I SAY OR BE TURNED TO STONE.

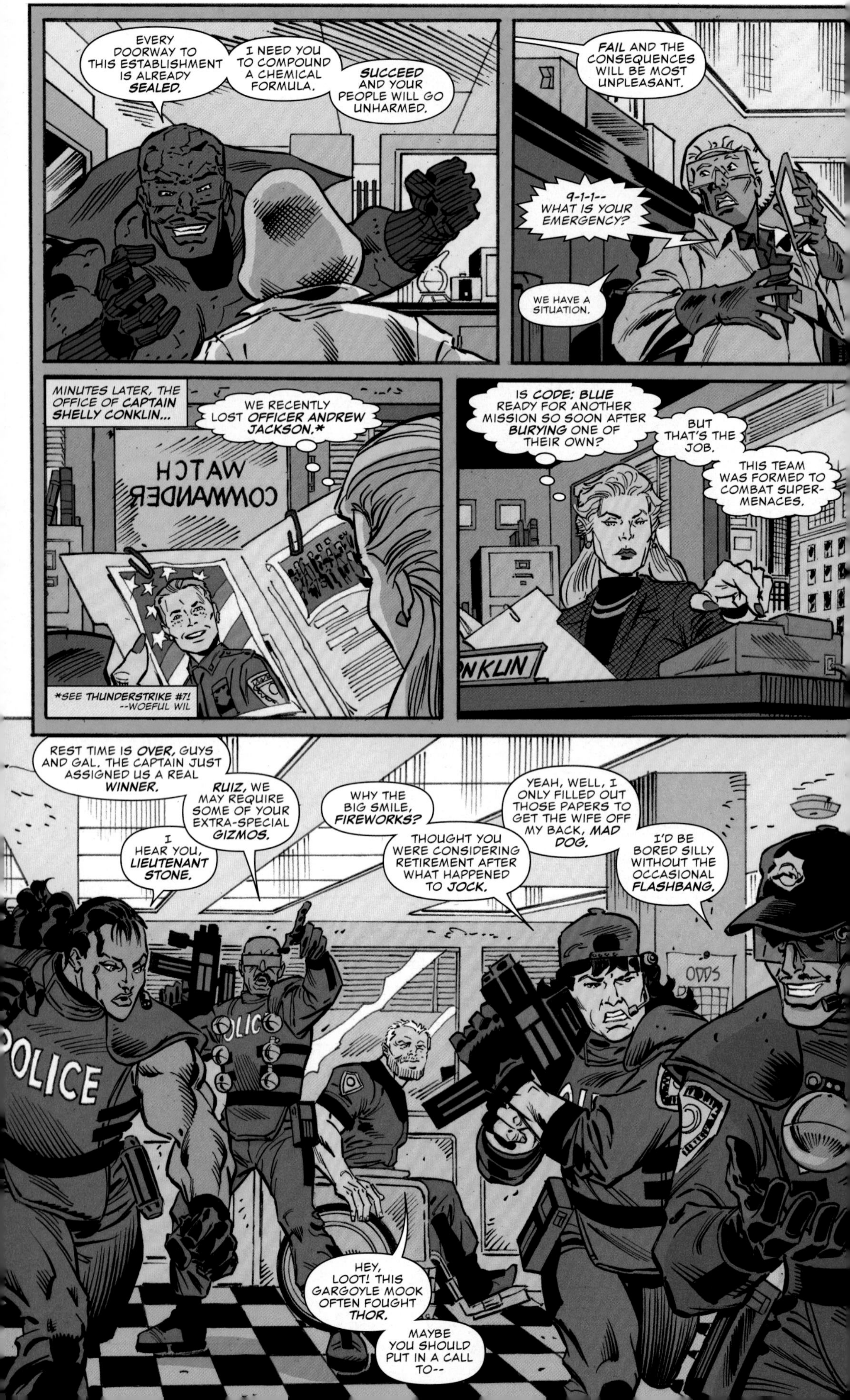
EVERY DOORWAY TO THIS ESTABLISHMENT IS ALREADY SEALED.
I NEED YOU TO COMPOUND A CHEMICAL FORMULA.
SUCCEED AND YOUR PEOPLE WILL GO UNHARMED.
FAIL AND THE CONSEQUENCES WILL BE MOST UNPLEASANT.
9-1-1-- WHAT IS YOUR EMERGENCY?
WE HAVE A SITUATION.
MINUTES LATER, THE OFFICE OF CAPTAIN SHELLY CONKLIN...
WE RECENTLY LOST OFFICER ANDREW JACKSON.*
WATCH COMMANDER
*SEE THUNDERSTRIKE #7! --WOEFUL WIL
IS CODE: BLUE READY FOR ANOTHER MISSION SO SOON AFTER BURYING ONE OF THEIR OWN?
BUT THAT'S THE JOB.
THIS TEAM WAS FORMED TO COMBAT SUPER-MENACES.
ONKLIN
REST TIME IS OVER, GUYS AND GAL. THE CAPTAIN JUST ASSIGNED US A REAL WINNER.
I HEAR YOU, LIEUTENANT STONE.
RUIZ, WE MAY REQUIRE SOME OF YOUR EXTRA-SPECIAL GIZMOS.
WHY THE BIG SMILE, FIREWORKS?
THOUGHT YOU WERE CONSIDERING RETIREMENT AFTER WHAT HAPPENED TO JOCK.
YEAH, WELL, I ONLY FILLED OUT THOSE PAPERS TO GET THE WIFE OFF MY BACK, MAD DOG.
I'D BE BORED SILLY WITHOUT THE OCCASIONAL FLASHBANG.
ODDS
POLICE
HEY, LOOT! THIS GARGOYLE MOOK OFTEN FOUGHT THOR.
MAYBE YOU SHOULD PUT IN A CALL TO--

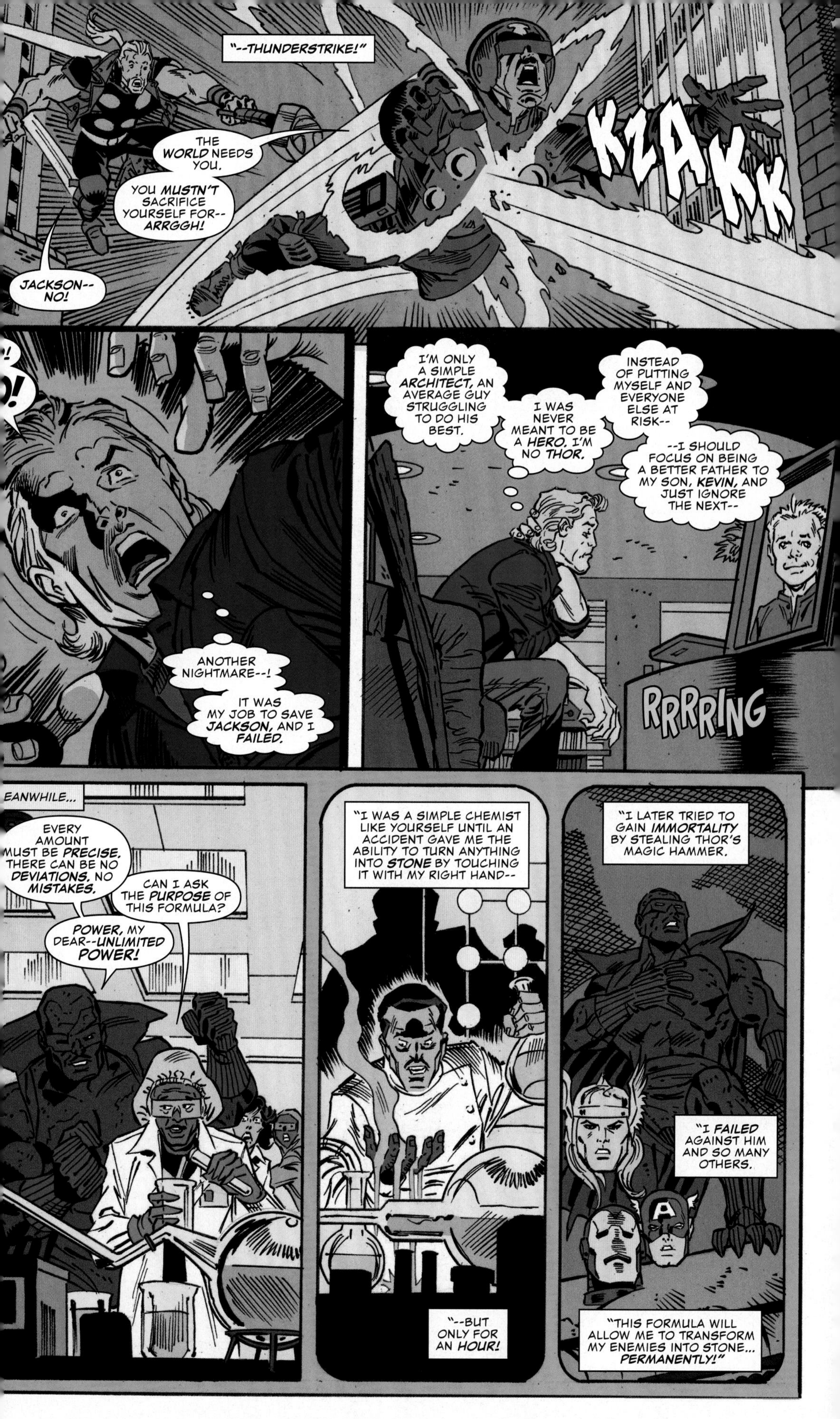
"--THUNDERSTRIKE!"
THE WORLD NEEDS YOU.
YOU MUSTN'T SACRIFICE YOURSELF FOR-- ARRGGH!
JACKSON-- NO!
KZAKKK
ANOTHER NIGHTMARE--!
IT WAS MY JOB TO SAVE JACKSON, AND I FAILED.
I'M ONLY A SIMPLE ARCHITECT, AN AVERAGE GUY STRUGGLING TO DO HIS BEST.
I WAS NEVER MEANT TO BE A HERO. I'M NO THOR.
INSTEAD OF PUTTING MYSELF AND EVERYONE ELSE AT RISK--
--I SHOULD FOCUS ON BEING A BETTER FATHER TO MY SON, KEVIN, AND JUST IGNORE THE NEXT--
RRRRING
EANWHILE...
EVERY AMOUNT MUST BE PRECISE. THERE CAN BE NO DEVIATIONS, NO MISTAKES.
CAN I ASK THE PURPOSE OF THIS FORMULA?
POWER, MY DEAR--UNLIMITED POWER!
"I WAS A SIMPLE CHEMIST LIKE YOURSELF UNTIL AN ACCIDENT GAVE ME THE ABILITY TO TURN ANYTHING INTO STONE BY TOUCHING IT WITH MY RIGHT HAND--
"--BUT ONLY FOR AN HOUR!
"I LATER TRIED TO GAIN IMMORTALITY BY STEALING THOR'S MAGIC HAMMER.
"I FAILED AGAINST HIM AND SO MANY OTHERS.
"THIS FORMULA WILL ALLOW ME TO TRANSFORM MY ENEMIES INTO STONE... PERMANENTLY!"

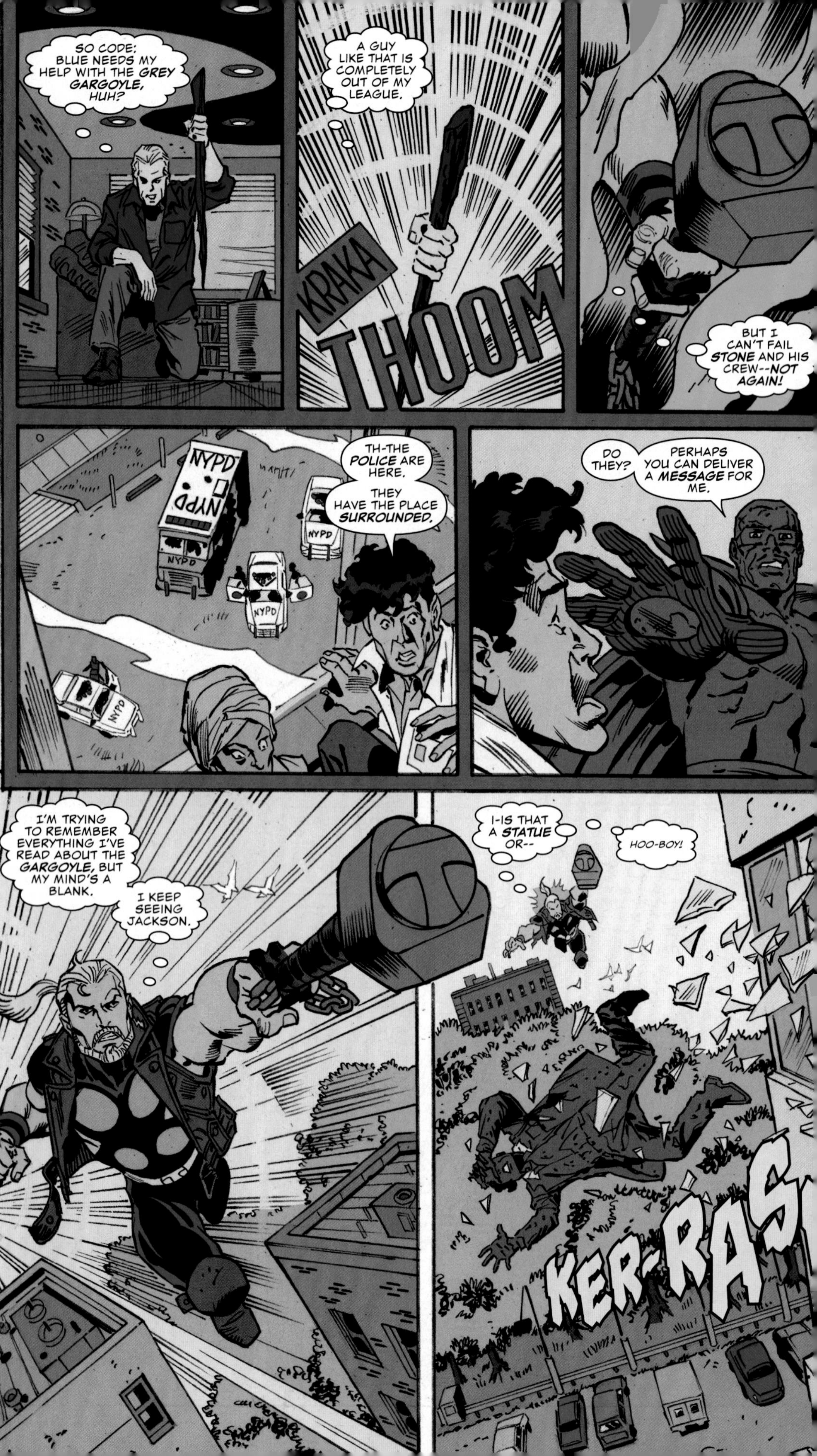

SO CODE: BLUE NEEDS MY HELP WITH THE GREY GARGOYLE, HUH?
A GUY LIKE THAT IS COMPLETELY OUT OF MY LEAGUE.
KRAKA
THOOM
BUT I CAN'T FAIL STONE AND HIS CREW--NOT AGAIN!
TH-THE POLICE ARE HERE.
THEY HAVE THE PLACE SURROUNDED.
NYPD
DO THEY?
PERHAPS YOU CAN DELIVER A MESSAGE FOR ME.
I'M TRYING TO REMEMBER EVERYTHING I'VE READ ABOUT THE GARGOYLE, BUT MY MIND'S A BLANK.
I KEEP SEEING JACKSON.
I-IS THAT A STATUE OR--
HOO-BOY!
KER-RAS

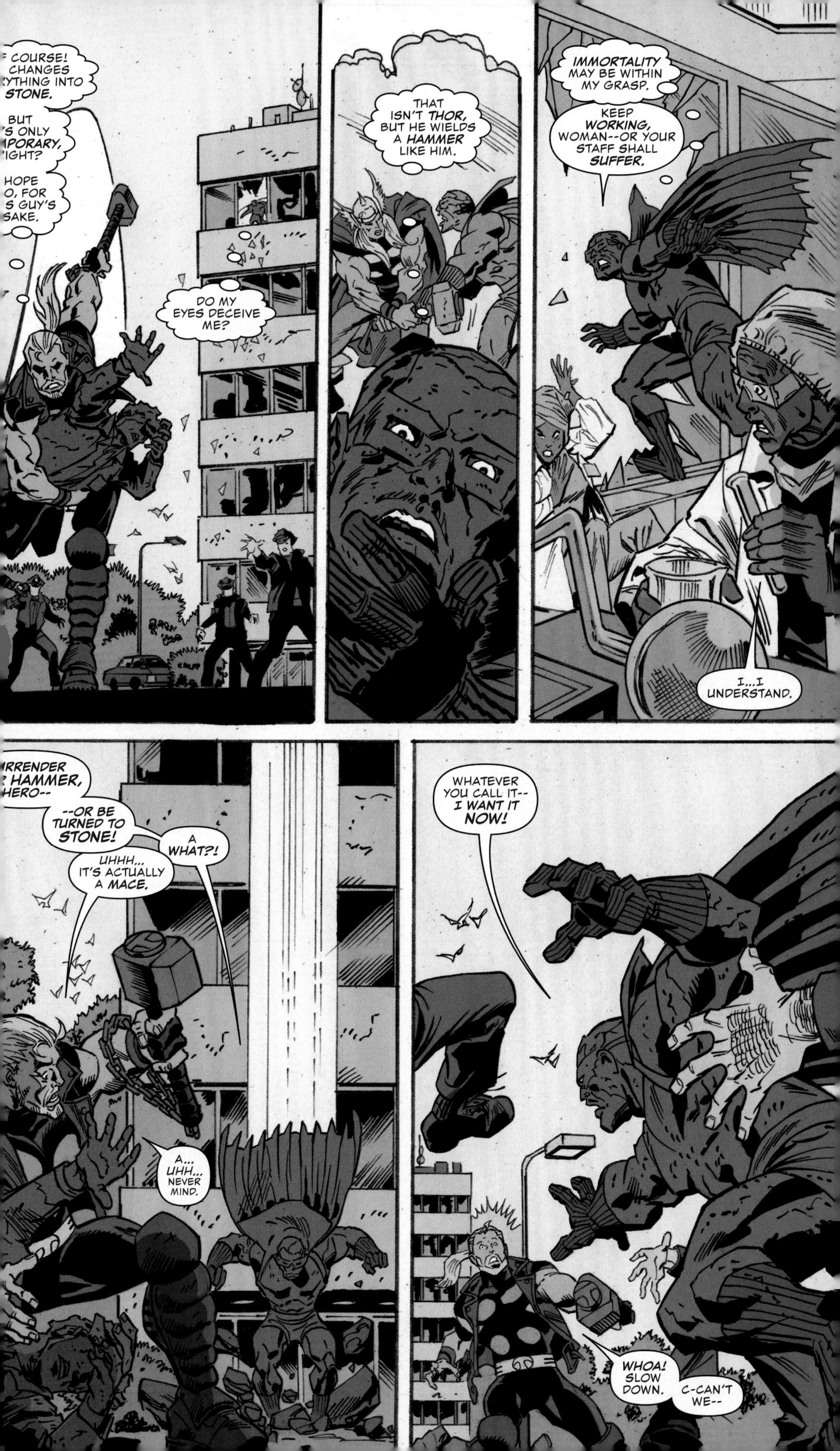
F COURSE! CHANGES RYTHING INTO STONE.
BUT 'S ONLY MPORARY, IGHT?
HOPE O, FOR S GUY'S SAKE.
DO MY EYES DECEIVE ME?
THAT ISN'T THOR, BUT HE WIELDS A HAMMER LIKE HIM.
IMMORTALITY MAY BE WITHIN MY GRASP.
KEEP WORKING, WOMAN--OR YOUR STAFF SHALL SUFFER.
I...I UNDERSTAND.
RRENDER HAMMER, HERO--
--OR BE TURNED TO STONE!
A WHAT?!
UHHH... IT'S ACTUALLY A MACE.
A... UHH... NEVER MIND.
WHATEVER YOU CALL IT-- I WANT IT NOW!
WHOA! SLOW DOWN.
C-CAN'T WE--

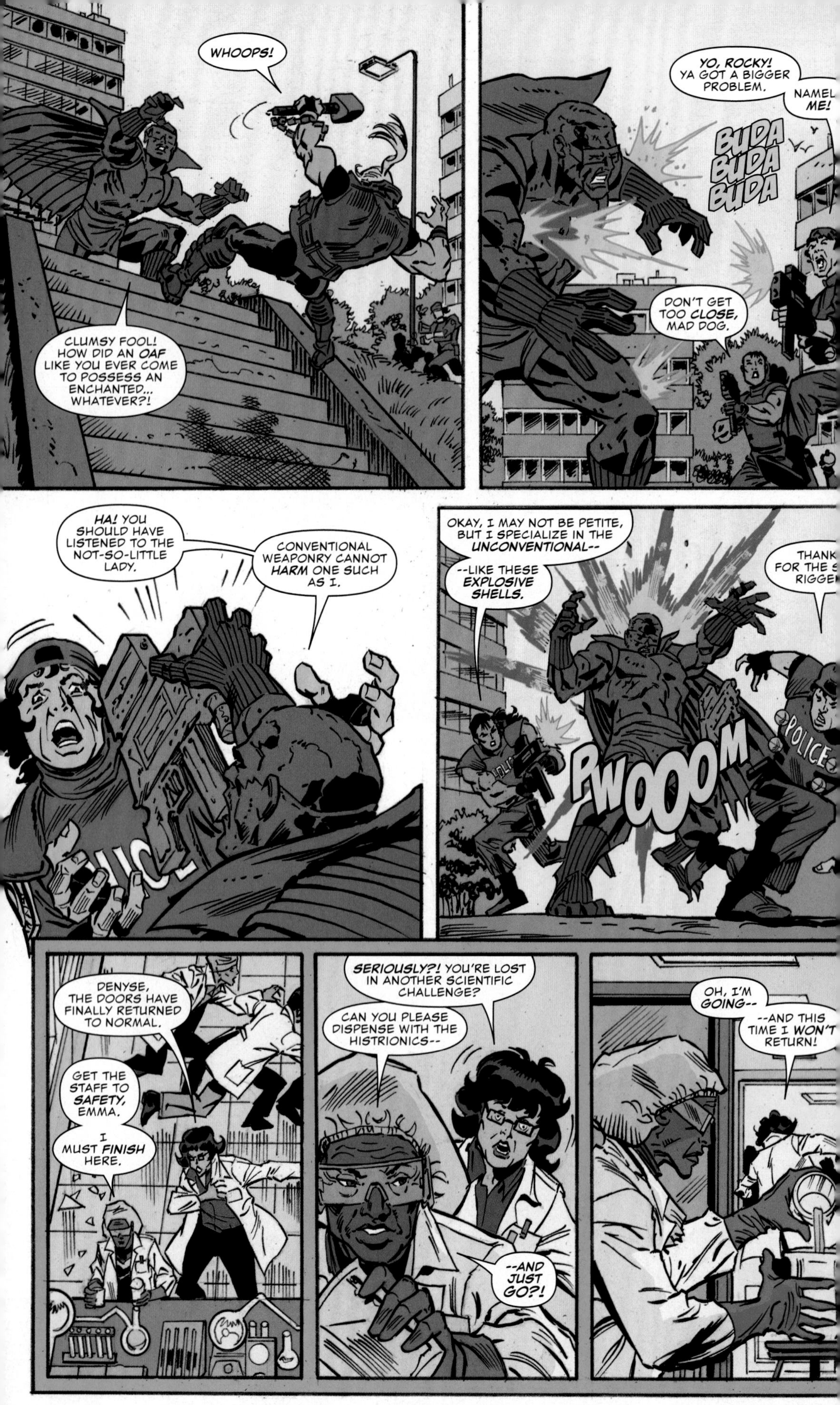
WHOOPS!
CLUMSY FOOL! HOW DID AN OAF LIKE YOU EVER COME TO POSSESS AN ENCHANTED... WHATEVER?!
YO, ROCKY! YA GOT A BIGGER PROBLEM.
NAMEL ME!
BUDA BUDA BUDA
DON'T GET TOO CLOSE, MAD DOG.
HA! YOU SHOULD HAVE LISTENED TO THE NOT-SO-LITTLE LADY.
CONVENTIONAL WEAPONRY CANNOT HARM ONE SUCH AS I.
OKAY, I MAY NOT BE PETITE, BUT I SPECIALIZE IN THE UNCONVENTIONAL--
--LIKE THESE EXPLOSIVE SHELLS.
THANK FOR THE S RIGGE
PWOOOM
DENYSE, THE DOORS HAVE FINALLY RETURNED TO NORMAL.
GET THE STAFF TO SAFETY, EMMA.
I MUST FINISH HERE.
SERIOUSLY?! YOU'RE LOST IN ANOTHER SCIENTIFIC CHALLENGE?
CAN YOU PLEASE DISPENSE WITH THE HISTRIONICS--
--AND JUST GO?!
OH, I'M GOING--
--AND THIS TIME I WON'T RETURN!

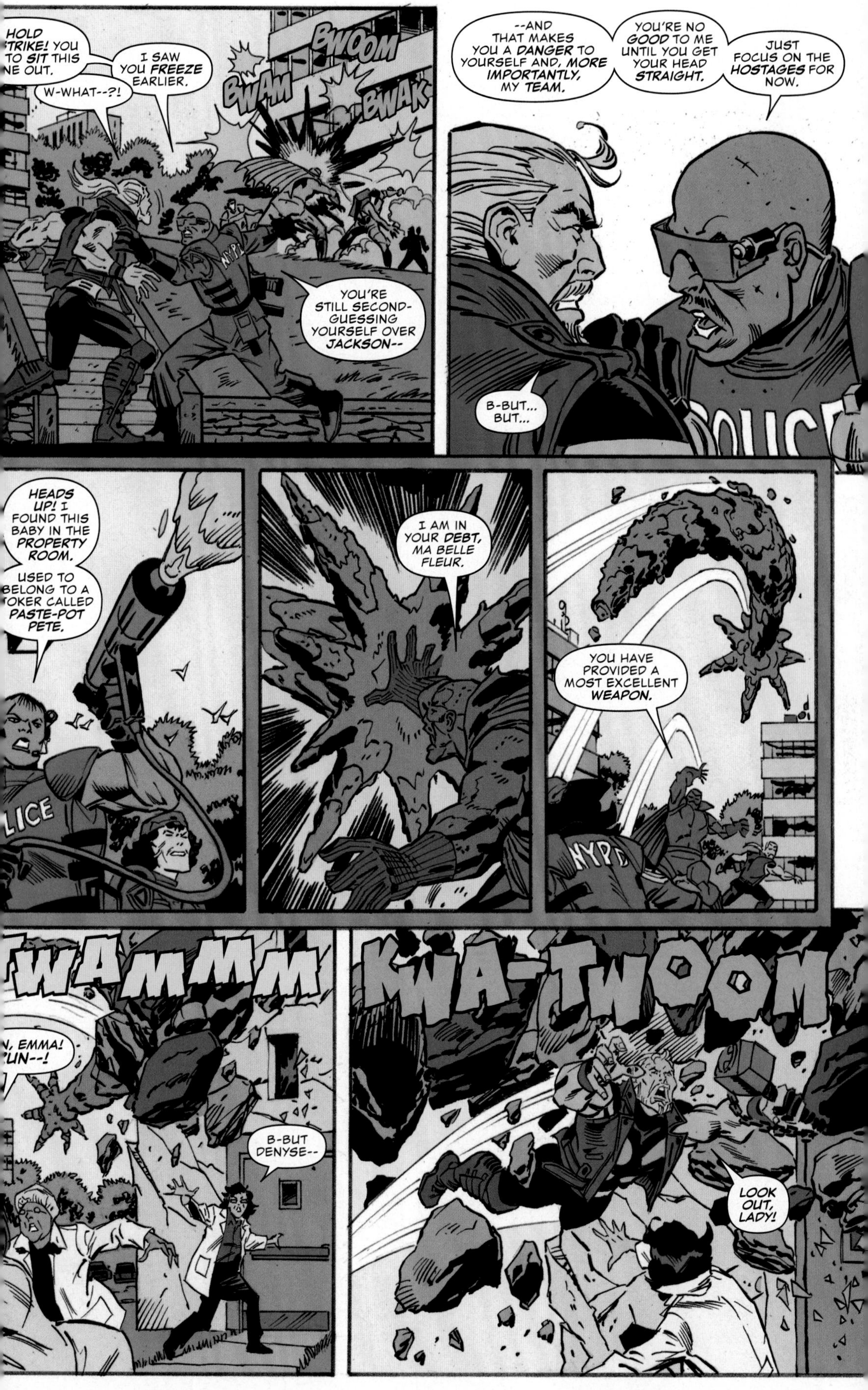

HOLD
STRIKE! YOU
TO SIT THIS
NE OUT.
I SAW YOU FREEZE EARLIER.
W-WHAT--?!
BWOOM
BWAM
BWAK
YOU'RE STILL SECOND-GUESSING YOURSELF OVER JACKSON--
--AND THAT MAKES YOU A DANGER TO YOURSELF AND, MORE IMPORTANTLY, MY TEAM.
YOU'RE NO GOOD TO ME UNTIL YOU GET YOUR HEAD STRAIGHT.
JUST FOCUS ON THE HOSTAGES FOR NOW.
B-BUT... BUT...
HEADS UP! I FOUND THIS BABY IN THE PROPERTY ROOM.
USED TO BELONG TO A JOKER CALLED PASTE-POT PETE.
I AM IN YOUR DEBT, MA BELLE FLEUR.
YOU HAVE PROVIDED A MOST EXCELLENT WEAPON.
WAMMMM
N, EMMA!
RUN--!
B-BUT DENYSE--
KWA-TWOOM
LOOK OUT, LADY!

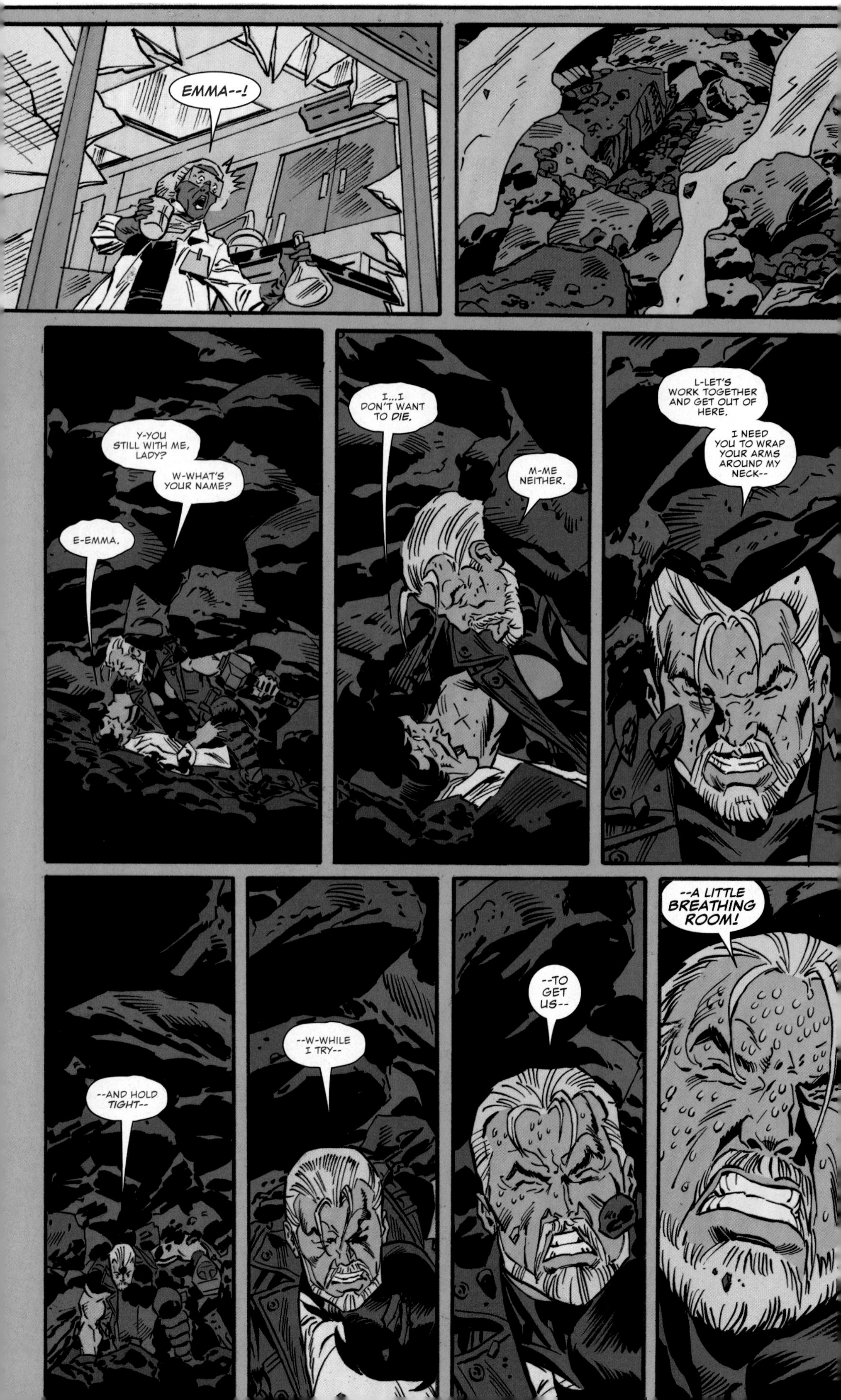
EMMA--!
Y-YOU STILL WITH ME, LADY?
W-WHAT'S YOUR NAME?
E-EMMA.
I...I DON'T WANT TO DIE.
M-ME NEITHER.
L-LET'S WORK TOGETHER AND GET OUT OF HERE.
I NEED YOU TO WRAP YOUR ARMS AROUND MY NECK--
--AND HOLD TIGHT--
--W-WHILE I TRY--
--TO GET US--
--A LITTLE BREATHING ROOM!

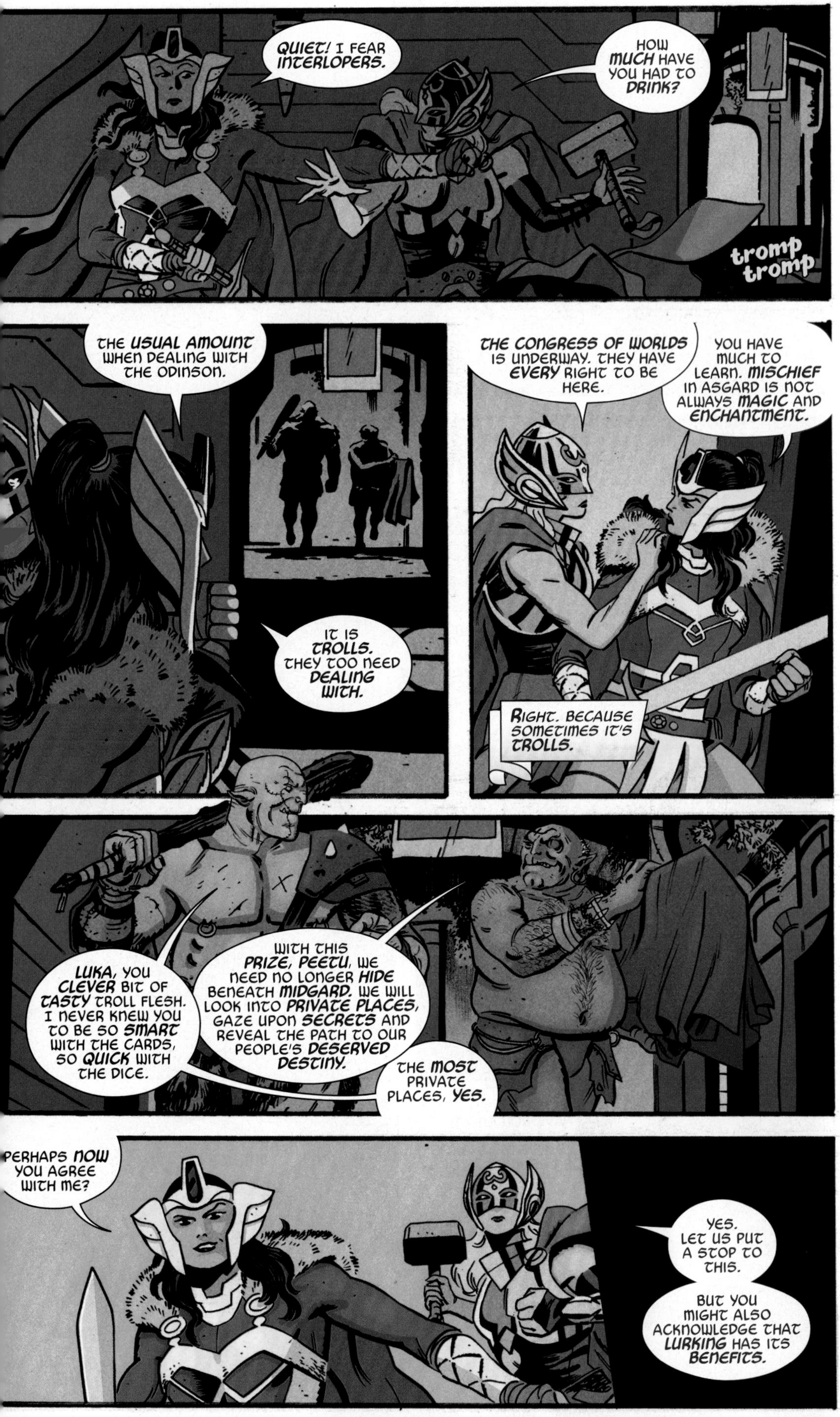
QUIET! I FEAR INTERLOPERS.
HOW MUCH HAVE YOU HAD TO DRINK?
tromp tromp
THE USUAL AMOUNT WHEN DEALING WITH THE ODINSON.
IT IS TROLLS. THEY TOO NEED DEALING WITH.
THE CONGRESS OF WORLDS IS UNDERWAY. THEY HAVE EVERY RIGHT TO BE HERE.
YOU HAVE MUCH TO LEARN. MISCHIEF IN ASGARD IS NOT ALWAYS MAGIC AND ENCHANTMENT.
RIGHT. BECAUSE SOMETIMES IT'S TROLLS.
LUKA, YOU CLEVER BIT OF TASTY TROLL FLESH. I NEVER KNEW YOU TO BE SO SMART WITH THE CARDS, SO QUICK WITH THE DICE.
WITH THIS PRIZE, PEETU, WE NEED NO LONGER HIDE BENEATH MIDGARD. WE WILL LOOK INTO PRIVATE PLACES, GAZE UPON SECRETS AND REVEAL THE PATH TO OUR PEOPLE'S DESERVED DESTINY.
THE MOST PRIVATE PLACES, YES.
PERHAPS NOW YOU AGREE WITH ME?
YES. LET US PUT A STOP TO THIS.
BUT YOU MIGHT ALSO ACKNOWLEDGE THAT LURKING HAS ITS BENEFITS.

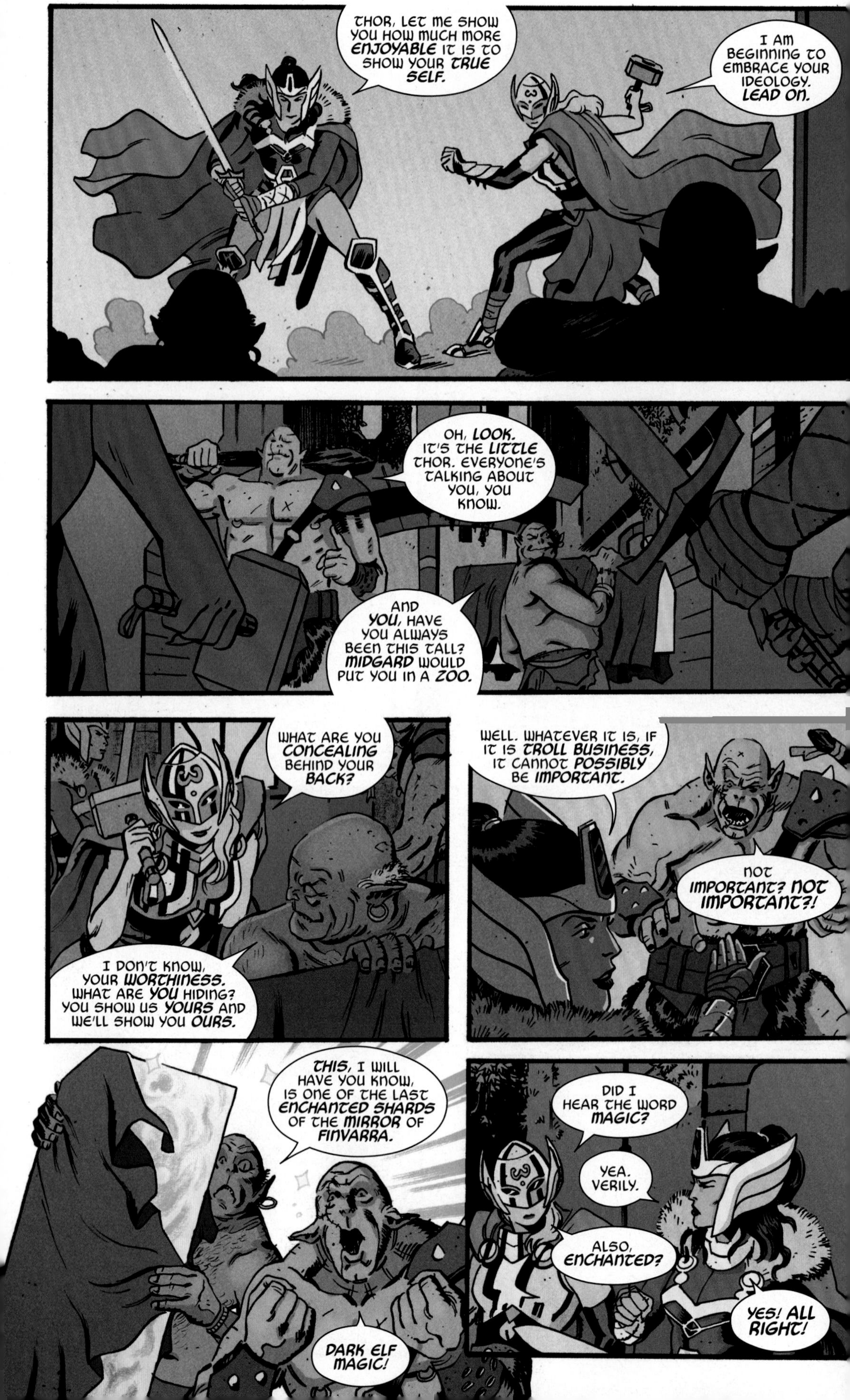
THOR, LET ME SHOW YOU HOW MUCH MORE ENJOYABLE IT IS TO SHOW YOUR TRUE SELF.
I AM BEGINNING TO EMBRACE YOUR IDEOLOGY. LEAD ON.
OH, LOOK. IT'S THE LITTLE THOR. EVERYONE'S TALKING ABOUT YOU, YOU KNOW.
AND YOU, HAVE YOU ALWAYS BEEN THIS TALL? MIDGARD WOULD PUT YOU IN A ZOO.
WHAT ARE YOU CONCEALING BEHIND YOUR BACK?
I DON'T KNOW, YOUR WORTHINESS. WHAT ARE YOU HIDING? YOU SHOW US YOURS AND WE'LL SHOW YOU OURS.
WELL. WHATEVER IT IS, IF IT IS TROLL BUSINESS, IT CANNOT POSSIBLY BE IMPORTANT.
NOT IMPORTANT? NOT IMPORTANT?!
THIS, I WILL HAVE YOU KNOW, IS ONE OF THE LAST ENCHANTED SHARDS OF THE MIRROR OF FINVARRA.
DARK ELF MAGIC!
DID I HEAR THE WORD MAGIC?
YEA. VERILY.
ALSO, ENCHANTED?
YES! ALL RIGHT!

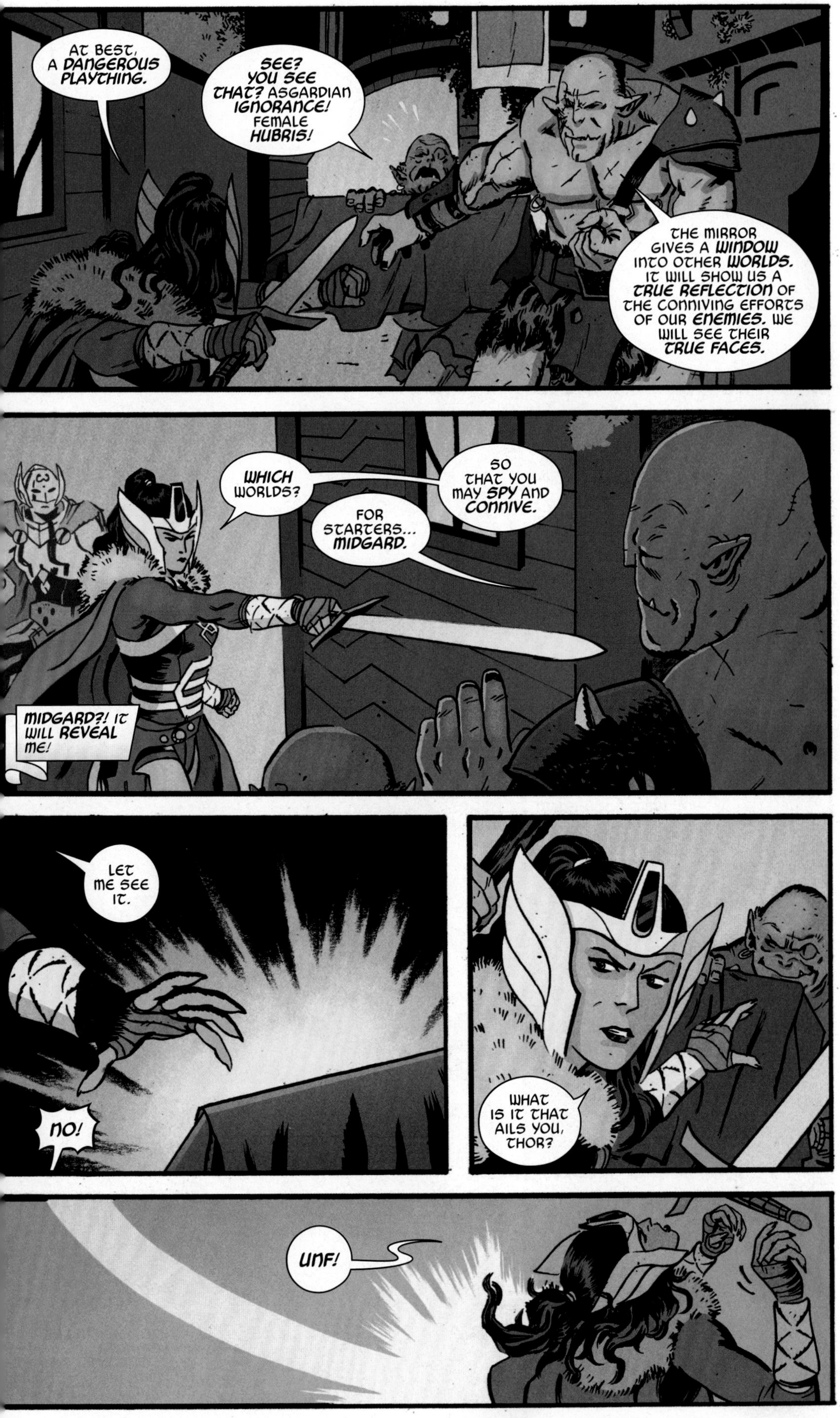
AT BEST, A DANGEROUS PLAYTHING.
SEE? YOU SEE THAT? ASGARDIAN IGNORANCE! FEMALE HUBRIS!
THE MIRROR GIVES A WINDOW INTO OTHER WORLDS. IT WILL SHOW US A TRUE REFLECTION OF THE CONNIVING EFFORTS OF OUR ENEMIES. WE WILL SEE THEIR TRUE FACES.
SO THAT YOU MAY SPY AND CONNIVE.
WHICH WORLDS?
FOR STARTERS... MIDGARD.
MIDGARD?! IT WILL REVEAL ME!
LET ME SEE IT.
NO!
WHAT IS IT THAT AILS YOU, THOR?
UNF!

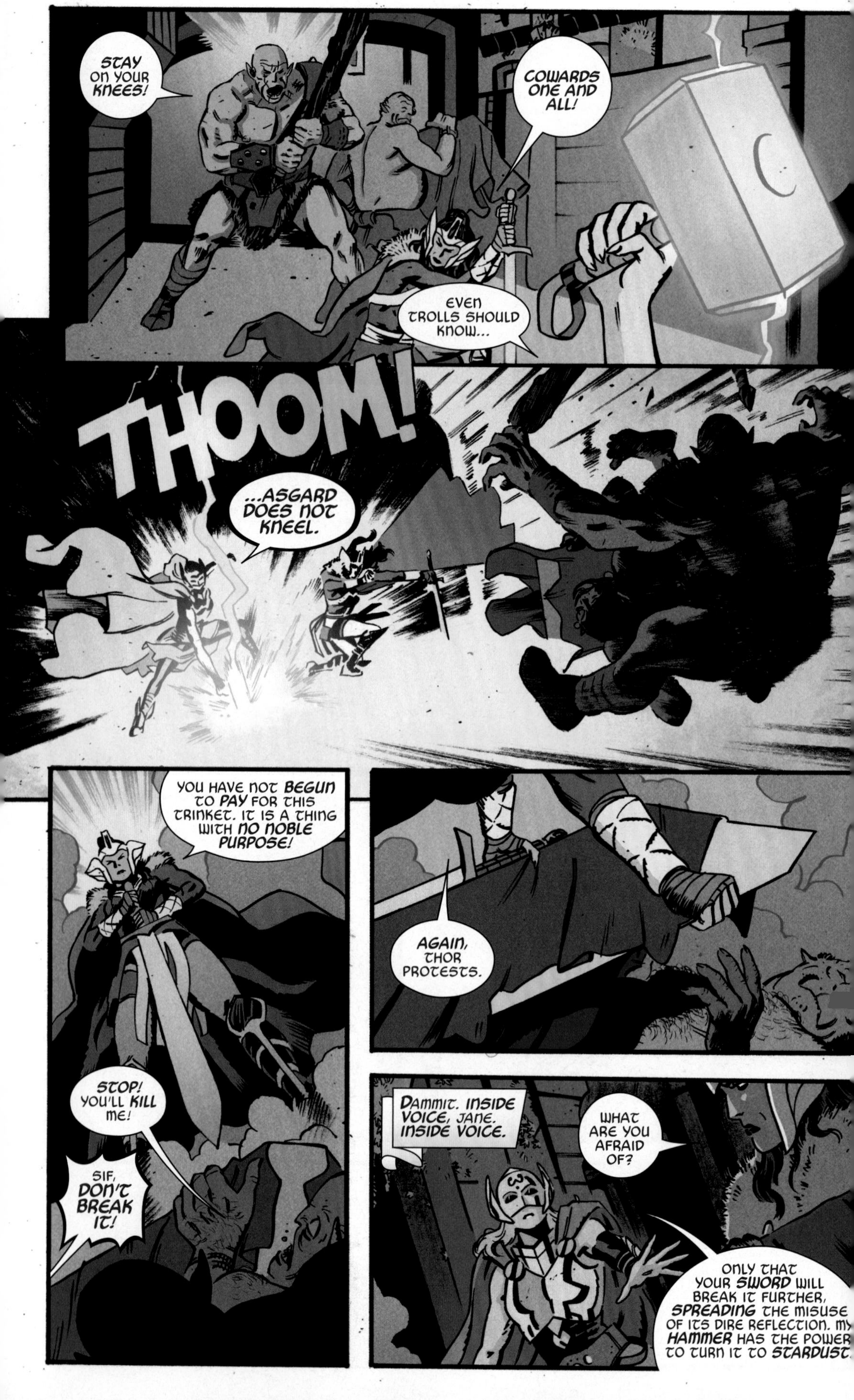
STAY ON YOUR KNEES!
COWARDS ONE AND ALL!
EVEN TROLLS SHOULD KNOW...
THOOM!
...ASGARD DOES NOT KNEEL.
YOU HAVE NOT BEGUN TO PAY FOR THIS TRINKET. IT IS A THING WITH NO NOBLE PURPOSE!
AGAIN, THOR PROTESTS.
STOP! YOU'LL KILL ME!
SIF, DON'T BREAK IT!
DAMMIT. INSIDE VOICE, JANE. INSIDE VOICE.
WHAT ARE YOU AFRAID OF?
ONLY THAT YOUR SWORD WILL BREAK IT FURTHER, SPREADING THE MISUSE OF ITS DIRE REFLECTION. MY HAMMER HAS THE POWER TO TURN IT TO STARDUST.

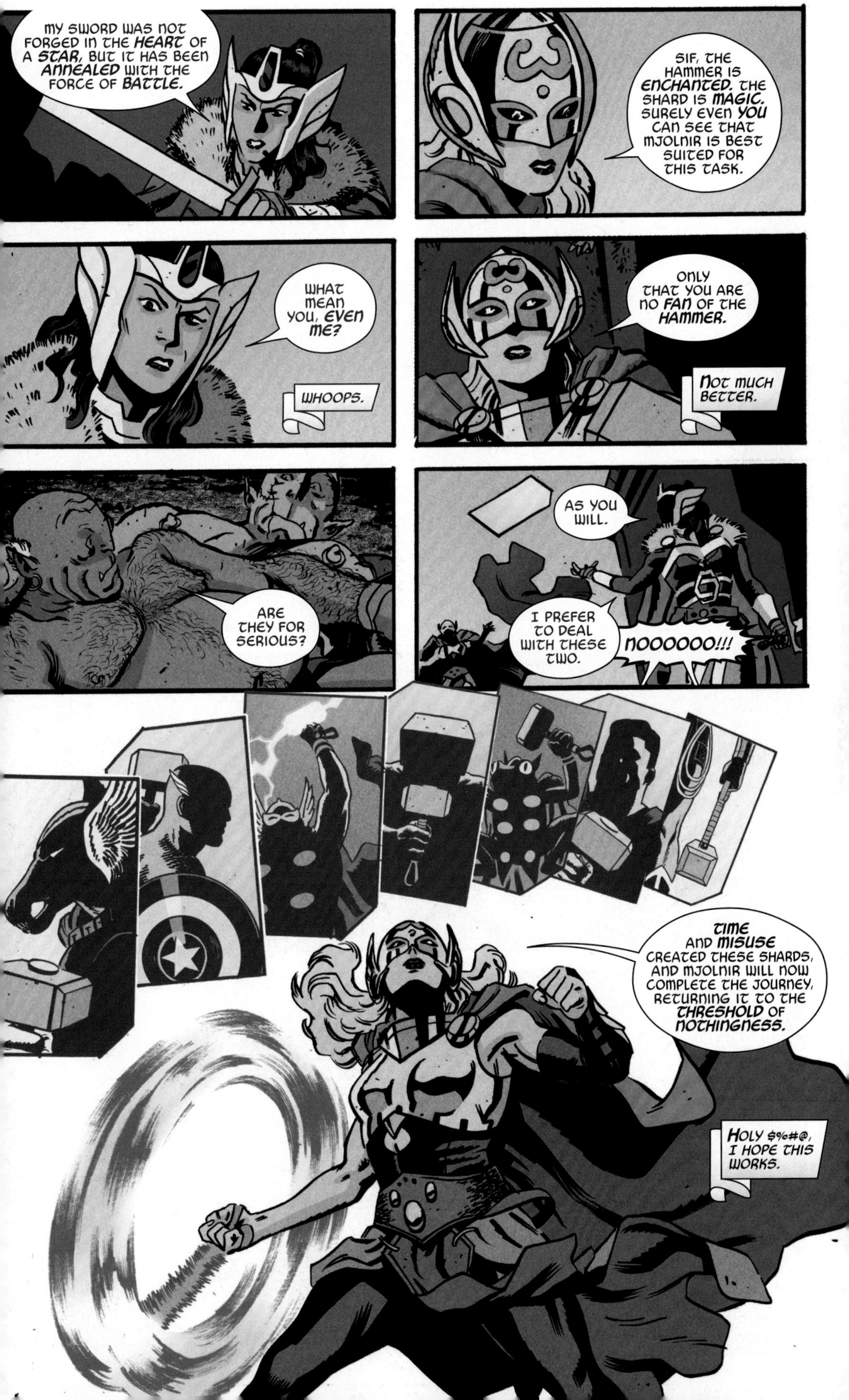
MY SWORD WAS NOT FORGED IN THE HEART OF A STAR, BUT IT HAS BEEN ANNEALED WITH THE FORCE OF BATTLE.
SIF, THE HAMMER IS ENCHANTED. THE SHARD IS MAGIC. SURELY EVEN YOU CAN SEE THAT MJOLNIR IS BEST SUITED FOR THIS TASK.
WHAT MEAN YOU, EVEN ME?
WHOOPS.
ONLY THAT YOU ARE NO FAN OF THE HAMMER.
NOT MUCH BETTER.
ARE THEY FOR SERIOUS?
AS YOU WILL.
I PREFER TO DEAL WITH THESE TWO.
NOOOOOO!!!
TIME AND MISUSE CREATED THESE SHARDS, AND MJOLNIR WILL NOW COMPLETE THE JOURNEY, RETURNING IT TO THE THRESHOLD OF NOTHINGNESS.
HOLY $%#@, I HOPE THIS WORKS.

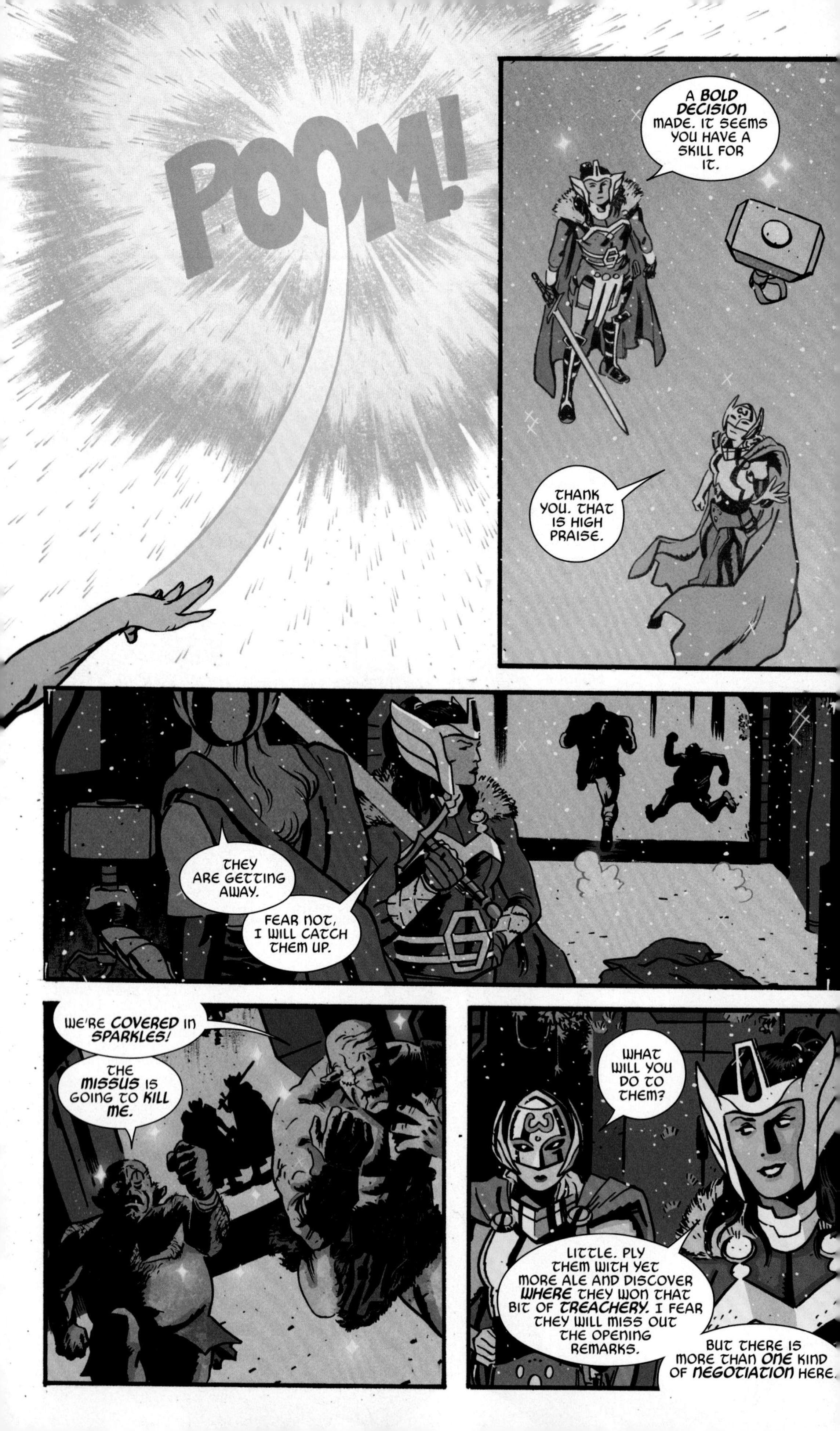
POOM!
A BOLD DECISION MADE. IT SEEMS YOU HAVE A SKILL FOR IT.
THANK YOU. THAT IS HIGH PRAISE.
THEY ARE GETTING AWAY.
FEAR NOT, I WILL CATCH THEM UP.
WE'RE COVERED IN SPARKLES!
THE MISSUS IS GOING TO KILL ME.
WHAT WILL YOU DO TO THEM?
LITTLE. PLY THEM WITH YET MORE ALE AND DISCOVER WHERE THEY WON THAT BIT OF TREACHERY. I FEAR THEY WILL MISS OUT THE OPENING REMARKS.
BUT THERE IS MORE THAN ONE KIND OF NEGOTIATION HERE.

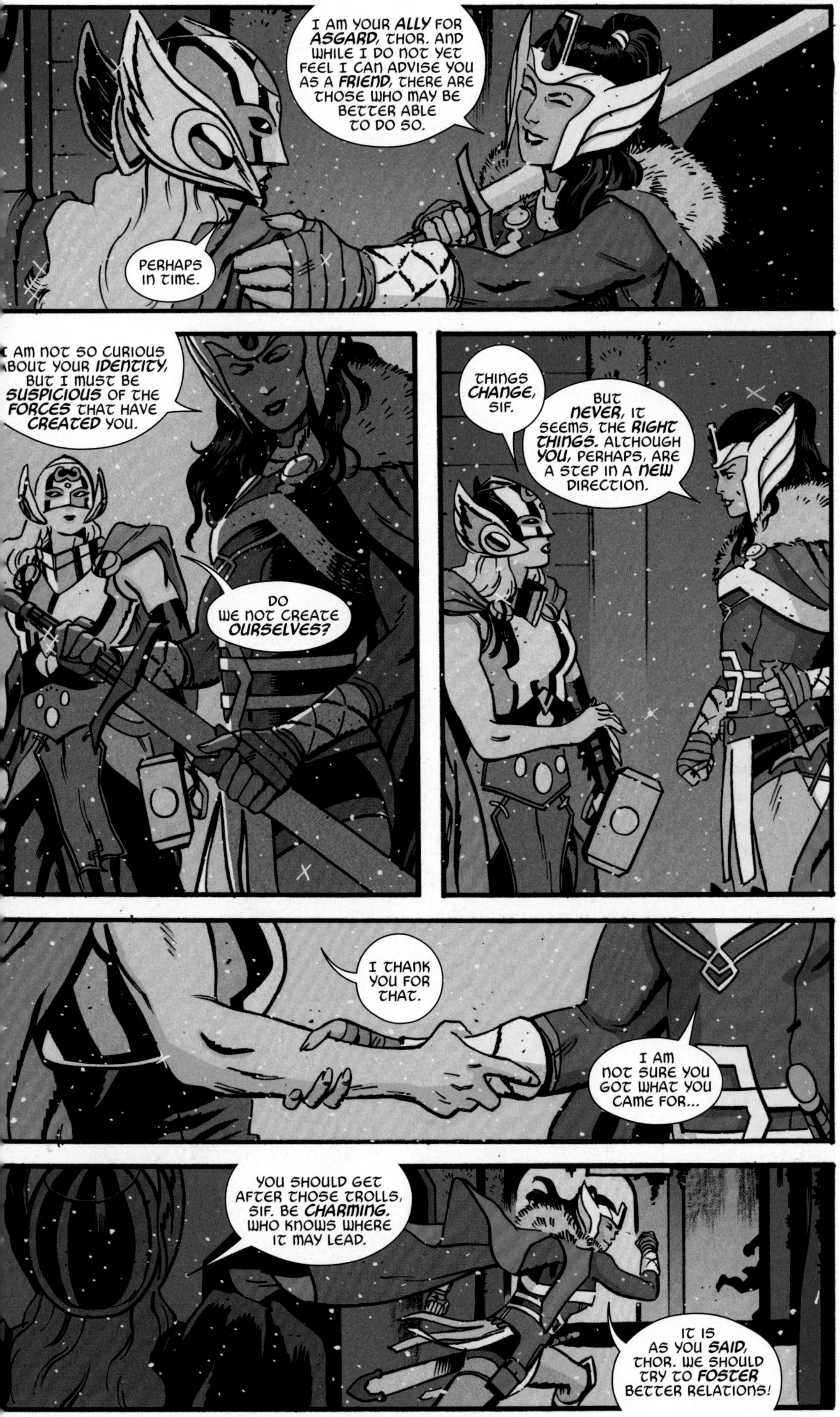
I AM YOUR ALLY FOR ASGARD, THOR. AND WHILE I DO NOT YET FEEL I CAN ADVISE YOU AS A FRIEND, THERE ARE THOSE WHO MAY BE BETTER ABLE TO DO SO.
PERHAPS IN TIME.
I AM NOT SO CURIOUS ABOUT YOUR IDENTITY, BUT I MUST BE SUSPICIOUS OF THE FORCES THAT HAVE CREATED YOU.
DO WE NOT CREATE OURSELVES?
THINGS CHANGE, SIF.
BUT NEVER, IT SEEMS, THE RIGHT THINGS. ALTHOUGH YOU, PERHAPS, ARE A STEP IN A NEW DIRECTION.
I THANK YOU FOR THAT.
I AM NOT SURE YOU GOT WHAT YOU CAME FOR...
YOU SHOULD GET AFTER THOSE TROLLS, SIF. BE CHARMING. WHO KNOWS WHERE IT MAY LEAD.
IT IS AS YOU SAID, THOR. WE SHOULD TRY TO FOSTER BETTER RELATIONS!

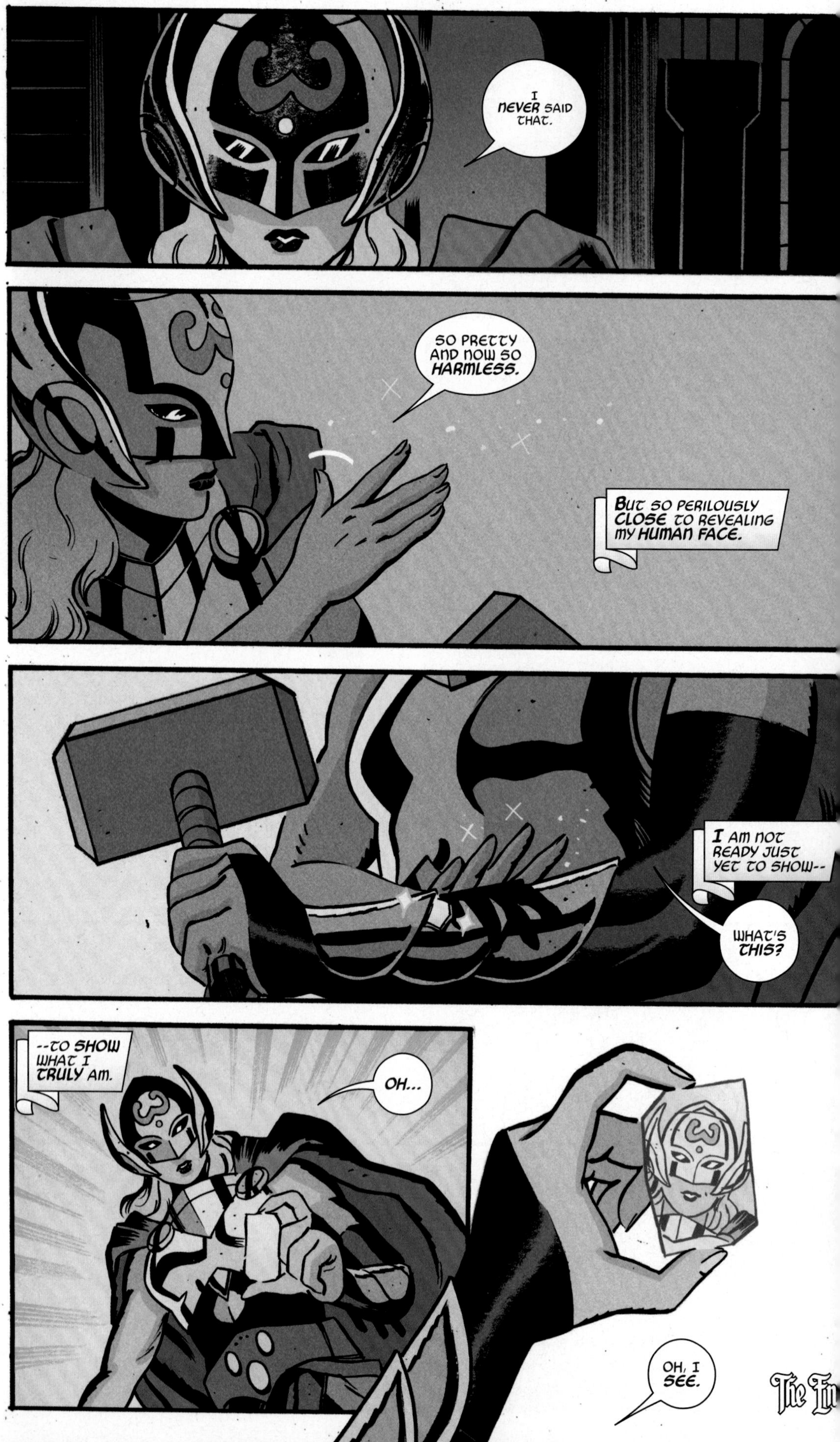

I NEVER SAID THAT.
SO PRETTY AND NOW SO HARMLESS.
BUT SO PERILOUSLY CLOSE TO REVEALING MY HUMAN FACE.
I AM NOT READY JUST YET TO SHOW--
WHAT'S THIS?
--TO SHOW WHAT I TRULY AM.
OH...
OH, I SEE.

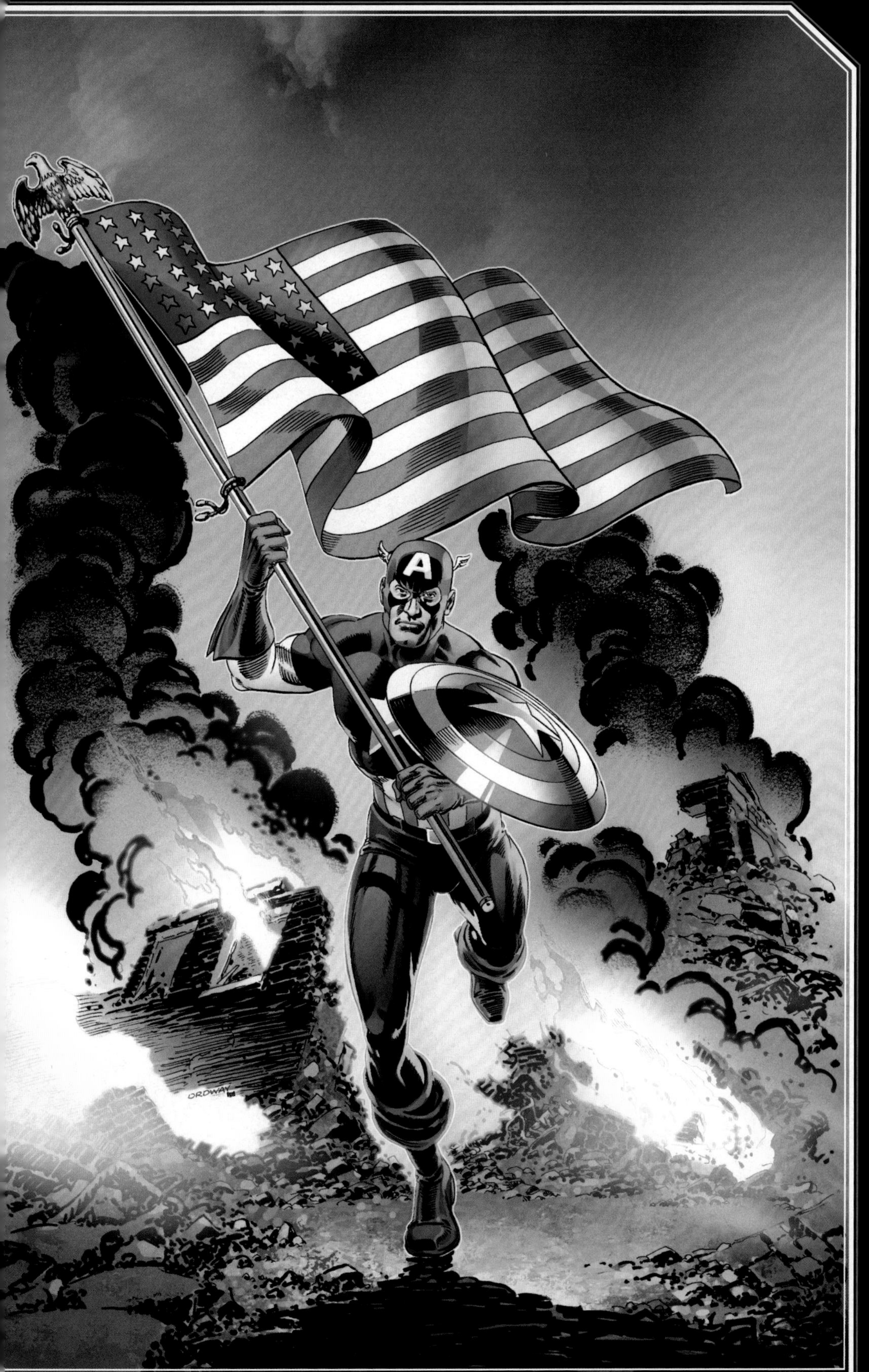
A
ORDWAY

CAPTAIN AMERICA & THE INVADERS: BAHAMAS TRIANGLE

AFTER UNDERGOING A SECRET MILITARY EXPERIMENT, STEVE ROGERS RE-EMERGED A SUPER-SOLIDER — THE EVER-FEARLESS CAPTAIN AMERICA! IT'S 1941, AND THE THREAT OF WORLD WAR II LINGERS OVER THE UNITED STATES OF AMERICA. AND WHEN IT COMES TO SERVING HIS COUNTRY, THERE'S NO MISSION STEVE WILL TURN DOWN...

Roy Thomas
WRITER

Jerry Ordway
ARTIST

Jay David Ramos
COLOR ARTIST

VC's Joe Caramagna
LETTERER

Jerry Ordway & Frank D'Arm
COVER ART

Shannon Andrews Ballesteros
ASSISTANT EDITOR

Alanna Smith
ASSOCIATE EDITOR

Tom Brevoort
EDITOR

AVENGERS CREATD BY Stan Lee & Jack Kirby   SPECIAL THANKS TO Roger Stern & John Byrne

**CAPTAIN AMERICA & THE INVADERS:
BAHAMAS TRIANGLE**
variant by Patch Zircher & Frank D'Armata

**CAPTAIN AMERICA & THE INVADERS:
BAHAMAS TRIANGLE**
variant by Ron Lim & Israel Silva

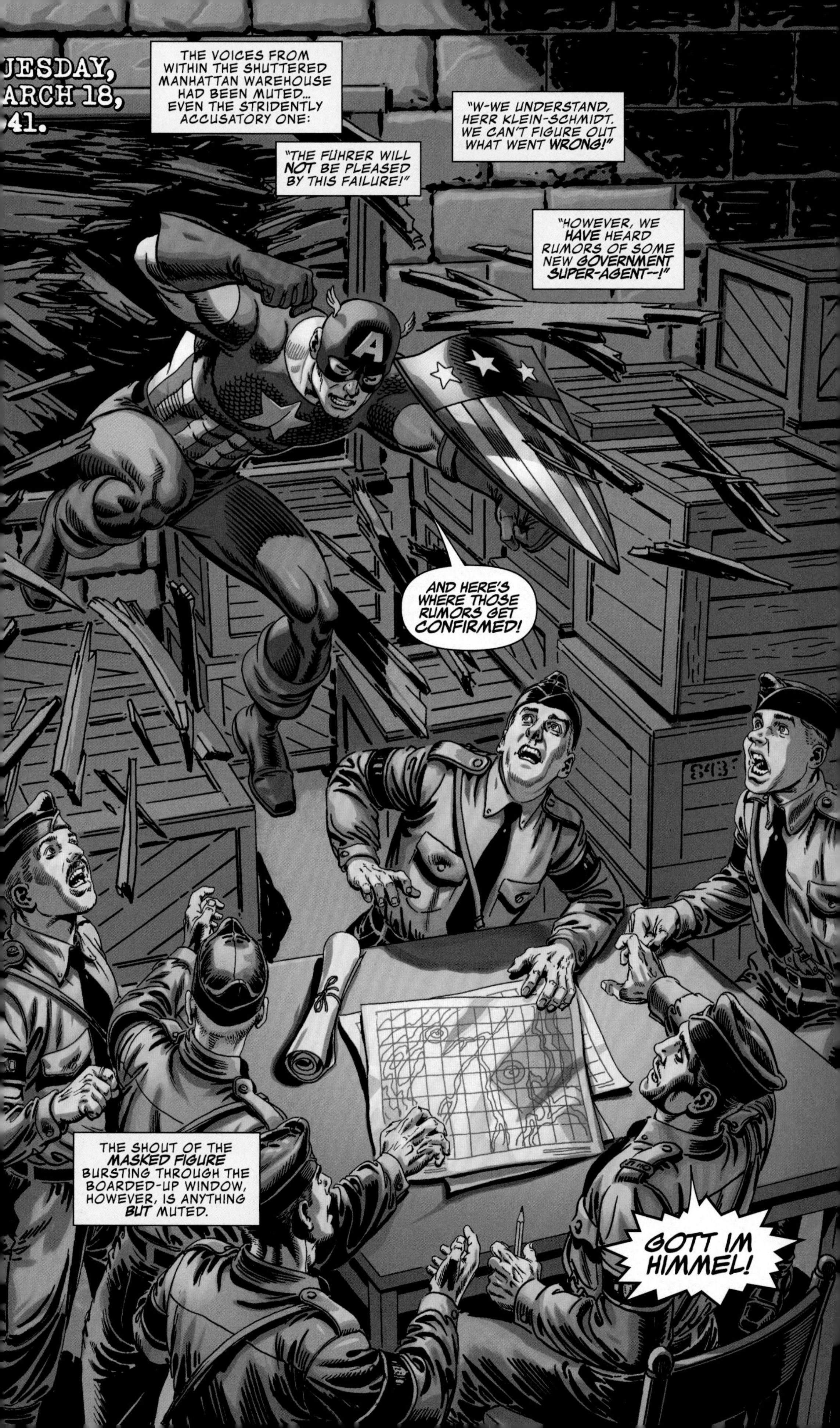
JESDAY, ARCH 18, 41.
THE VOICES FROM WITHIN THE SHUTTERED MANHATTAN WAREHOUSE HAD BEEN MUTED... EVEN THE STRIDENTLY ACCUSATORY ONE:
"THE FÜHRER WILL NOT BE PLEASED BY THIS FAILURE!"
"W-WE UNDERSTAND, HERR KLEIN-SCHMIDT. WE CAN'T FIGURE OUT WHAT WENT WRONG!"
"HOWEVER, WE HAVE HEARD RUMORS OF SOME NEW GOVERNMENT SUPER-AGENT--!"
AND HERE'S WHERE THOSE RUMORS GET CONFIRMED!
THE SHOUT OF THE MASKED FIGURE BURSTING THROUGH THE BOARDED-UP WINDOW, HOWEVER, IS ANYTHING BUT MUTED.
GOTT IM HIMMEL!

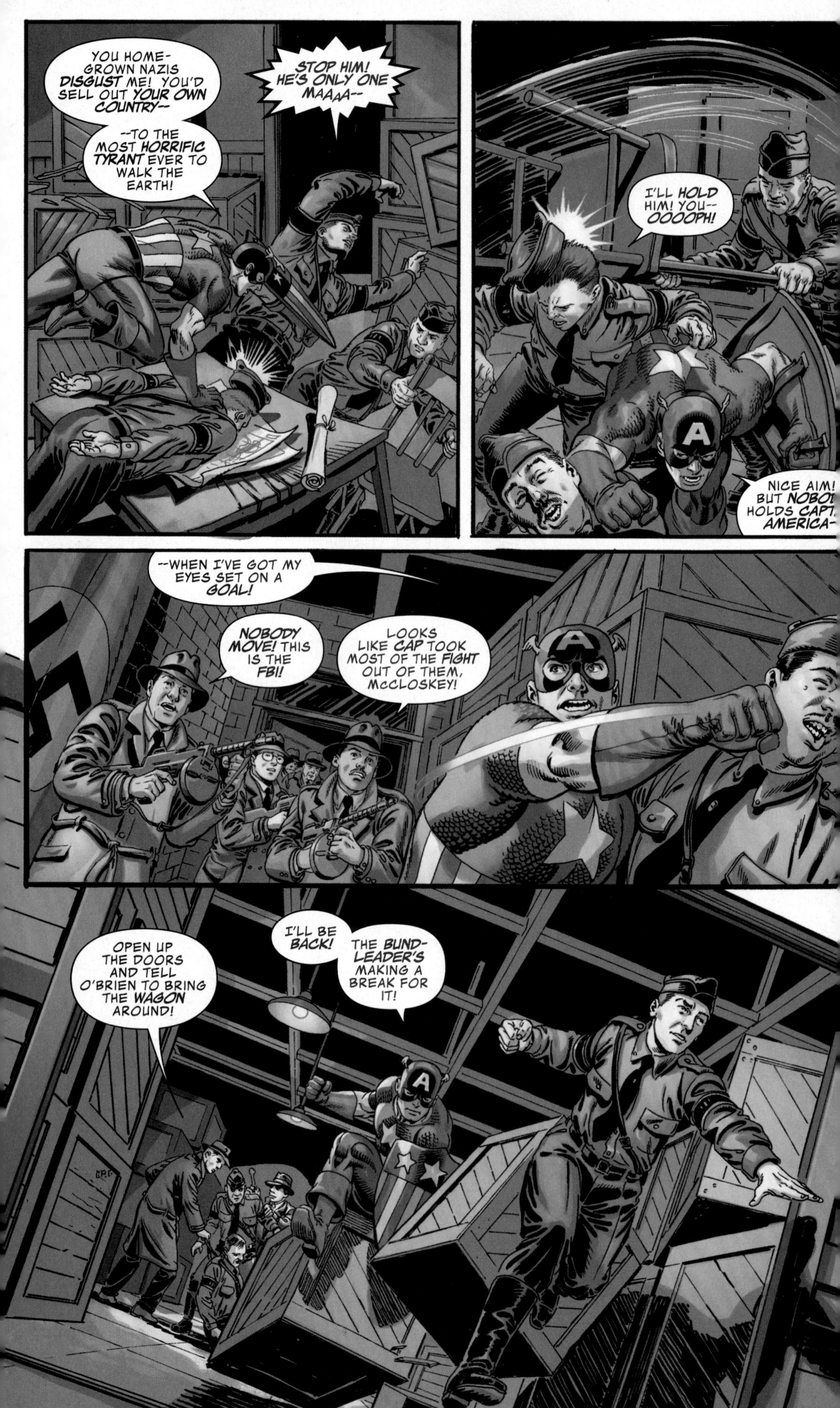
YOU HOME-GROWN NAZIS DISGUST ME! YOU'D SELL OUT YOUR OWN COUNTRY--
STOP HIM! HE'S ONLY ONE MAAAA--
--TO THE MOST HORRIFIC TYRANT EVER TO WALK THE EARTH!
I'LL HOLD HIM! YOU-- OOOOPH!
NICE AIM! BUT NOBOD HOLDS CAPT AMERICA-
--WHEN I'VE GOT MY EYES SET ON A GOAL!
NOBODY MOVE! THIS IS THE FBI!
LOOKS LIKE CAP TOOK MOST OF THE FIGHT OUT OF THEM, McCLOSKEY!
OPEN UP THE DOORS AND TELL O'BRIEN TO BRING THE WAGON AROUND!
I'LL BE BACK!
THE BUND-LEADER'S MAKING A BREAK FOR IT!

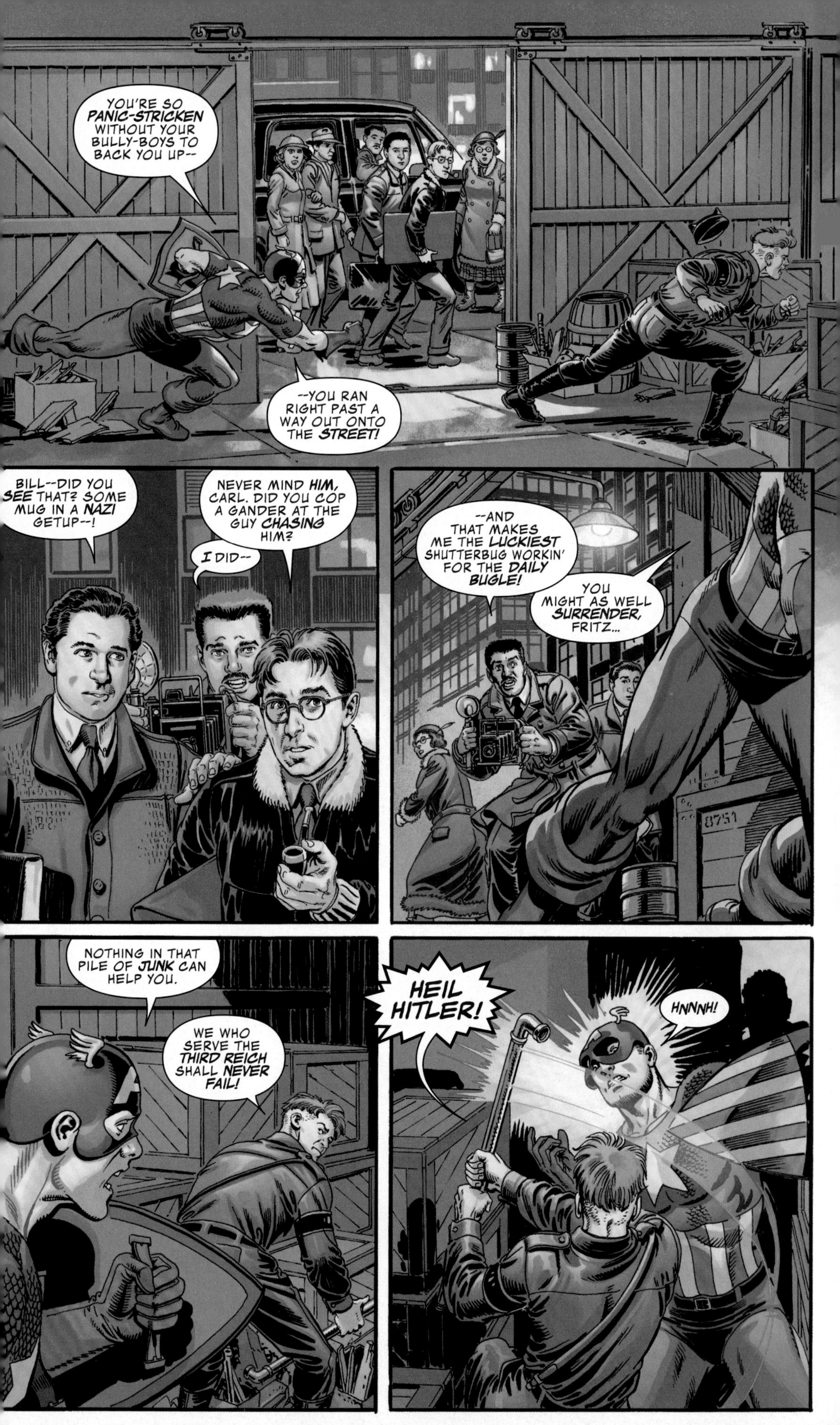

YOU'RE SO PANIC-STRICKEN WITHOUT YOUR BULLY-BOYS TO BACK YOU UP--
--YOU RAN RIGHT PAST A WAY OUT ONTO THE STREET!
BILL--DID YOU SEE THAT? SOME MUG IN A NAZI GETUP--!
NEVER MIND HIM, CARL. DID YOU COP A GANDER AT THE GUY CHASING HIM?
I DID--
--AND THAT MAKES ME THE LUCKIEST SHUTTERBUG WORKIN' FOR THE DAILY BUGLE!
YOU MIGHT AS WELL SURRENDER, FRITZ...
8751
NOTHING IN THAT PILE OF JUNK CAN HELP YOU.
WE WHO SERVE THE THIRD REICH SHALL NEVER FAIL!
HEIL HITLER!
HNNNH!

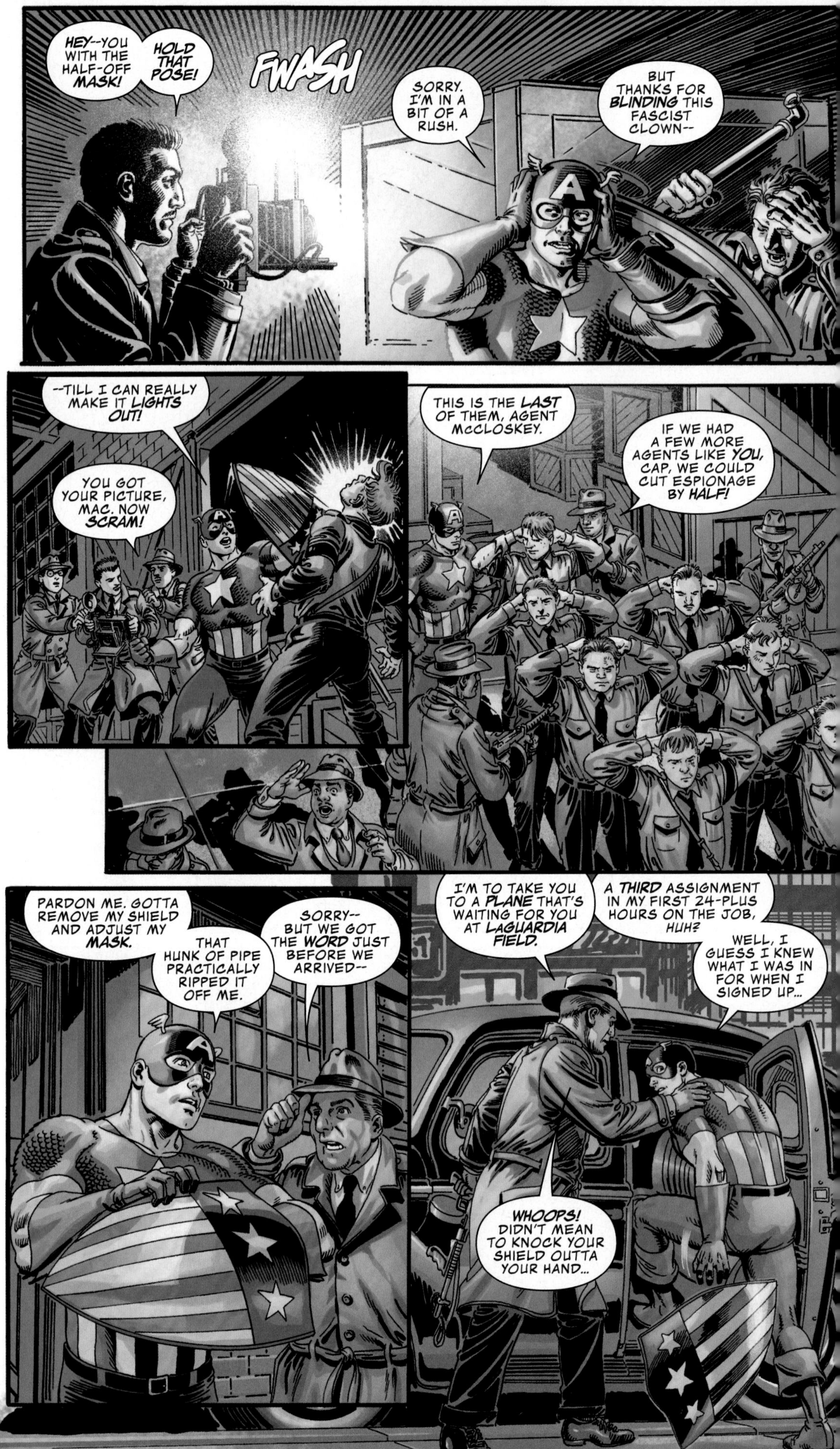
HEY--YOU WITH THE HALF-OFF MASK!
HOLD THAT POSE!
FWASH
SORRY. I'M IN A BIT OF A RUSH.
BUT THANKS FOR BLINDING THIS FASCIST CLOWN--
--TILL I CAN REALLY MAKE IT LIGHTS OUT!
YOU GOT YOUR PICTURE, MAC. NOW SCRAM!
THIS IS THE LAST OF THEM, AGENT McCLOSKEY.
IF WE HAD A FEW MORE AGENTS LIKE YOU, CAP, WE COULD CUT ESPIONAGE BY HALF!
PARDON ME. GOTTA REMOVE MY SHIELD AND ADJUST MY MASK.
THAT HUNK OF PIPE PRACTICALLY RIPPED IT OFF ME.
SORRY-- BUT WE GOT THE WORD JUST BEFORE WE ARRIVED--
I'M TO TAKE YOU TO A PLANE THAT'S WAITING FOR YOU AT LAGUARDIA FIELD.
A THIRD ASSIGNMENT IN MY FIRST 24-PLUS HOURS ON THE JOB, HUH?
WELL, I GUESS I KNEW WHAT I WAS IN FOR WHEN I SIGNED UP...
WHOOPS! DIDN'T MEAN TO KNOCK YOUR SHIELD OUTTA YOUR HAND...

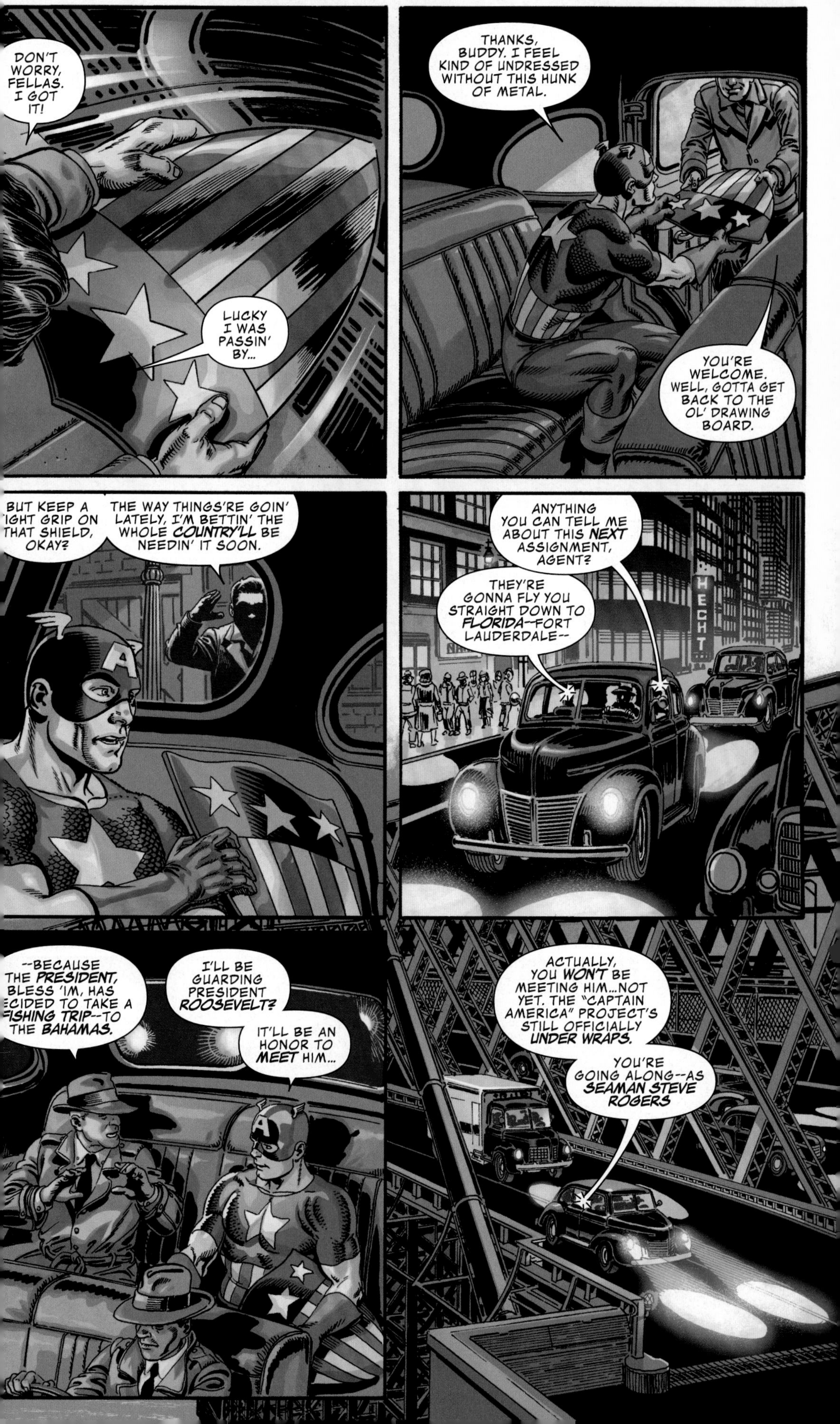

DON'T WORRY, FELLAS. I GOT IT!
LUCKY I WAS PASSIN' BY...
THANKS, BUDDY. I FEEL KIND OF UNDRESSED WITHOUT THIS HUNK OF METAL.
YOU'RE WELCOME. WELL, GOTTA GET BACK TO THE OL' DRAWING BOARD.
BUT KEEP A TIGHT GRIP ON THAT SHIELD, OKAY?
THE WAY THINGS'RE GOIN' LATELY, I'M BETTIN' THE WHOLE COUNTRY'LL BE NEEDIN' IT SOON.
ANYTHING YOU CAN TELL ME ABOUT THIS NEXT ASSIGNMENT, AGENT?
THEY'RE GONNA FLY YOU STRAIGHT DOWN TO FLORIDA--FORT LAUDERDALE--
HECHT
--BECAUSE THE PRESIDENT, BLESS 'IM, HAS DECIDED TO TAKE A FISHING TRIP--TO THE BAHAMAS.
I'LL BE GUARDING PRESIDENT ROOSEVELT?
IT'LL BE AN HONOR TO MEET HIM...
ACTUALLY, YOU WON'T BE MEETING HIM...NOT YET. THE "CAPTAIN AMERICA" PROJECT'S STILL OFFICIALLY UNDER WRAPS.
YOU'RE GOING ALONG--AS SEAMAN STEVE ROGERS

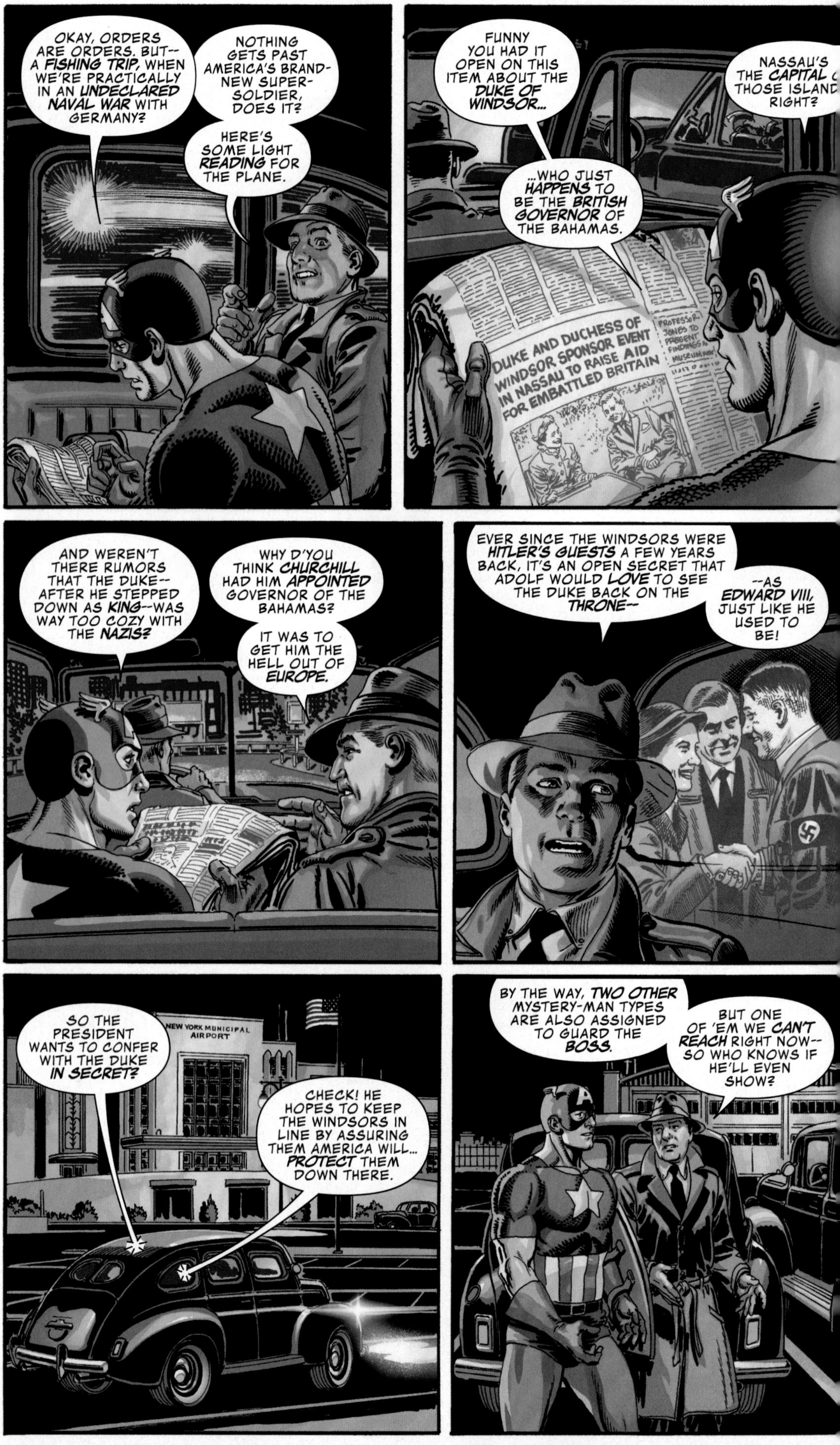
OKAY, ORDERS ARE ORDERS. BUT-- A FISHING TRIP, WHEN WE'RE PRACTICALLY IN AN UNDECLARED NAVAL WAR WITH GERMANY?
NOTHING GETS PAST AMERICA'S BRAND-NEW SUPER-SOLDIER, DOES IT?
HERE'S SOME LIGHT READING FOR THE PLANE.
FUNNY YOU HAD IT OPEN ON THIS ITEM ABOUT THE DUKE OF WINDSOR...
...WHO JUST HAPPENS TO BE THE BRITISH GOVERNOR OF THE BAHAMAS.
DUKE AND DUCHESS OF WINDSOR SPONSOR EVENT IN NASSAU TO RAISE AID FOR EMBATTLED BRITAIN
PROFESSOR JONES TO PRESENT FINDINGS AT MUSEUM
NASSAU'S THE CAPITAL OF THOSE ISLANDS, RIGHT?
AND WEREN'T THERE RUMORS THAT THE DUKE-- AFTER HE STEPPED DOWN AS KING--WAS WAY TOO COZY WITH THE NAZIS?
WHY D'YOU THINK CHURCHILL HAD HIM APPOINTED GOVERNOR OF THE BAHAMAS?
IT WAS TO GET HIM THE HELL OUT OF EUROPE.
EVER SINCE THE WINDSORS WERE HITLER'S GUESTS A FEW YEARS BACK, IT'S AN OPEN SECRET THAT ADOLF WOULD LOVE TO SEE THE DUKE BACK ON THE THRONE--
--AS EDWARD VIII, JUST LIKE HE USED TO BE!
NEW YORK MUNICIPAL AIRPORT
SO THE PRESIDENT WANTS TO CONFER WITH THE DUKE IN SECRET?
CHECK! HE HOPES TO KEEP THE WINDSORS IN LINE BY ASSURING THEM AMERICA WILL... PROTECT THEM DOWN THERE.
BY THE WAY, TWO OTHER MYSTERY-MAN TYPES ARE ALSO ASSIGNED TO GUARD THE BOSS.
BUT ONE OF 'EM WE CAN'T REACH RIGHT NOW-- SO WHO KNOWS IF HE'LL EVEN SHOW?

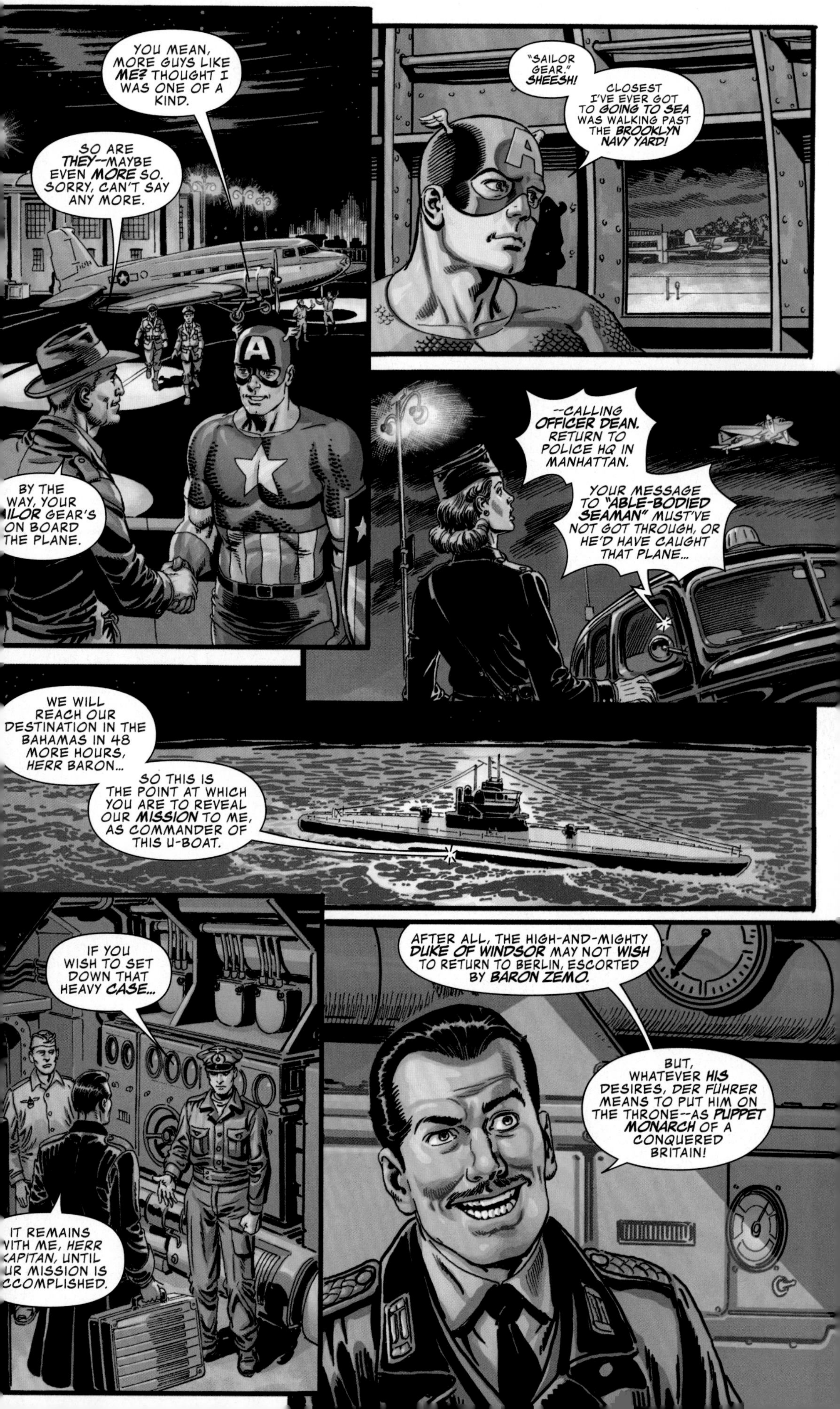
YOU MEAN, MORE GUYS LIKE ME? THOUGHT I WAS ONE OF A KIND.
SO ARE THEY--MAYBE EVEN MORE SO. SORRY, CAN'T SAY ANY MORE.
BY THE WAY, YOUR ILOR GEAR'S ON BOARD THE PLANE.
"SAILOR GEAR." SHEESH!
CLOSEST I'VE EVER GOT TO GOING TO SEA WAS WALKING PAST THE BROOKLYN NAVY YARD!
--CALLING OFFICER DEAN. RETURN TO POLICE HQ IN MANHATTAN.
YOUR MESSAGE TO "ABLE-BODIED SEAMAN" MUST'VE NOT GOT THROUGH, OR HE'D HAVE CAUGHT THAT PLANE...
WE WILL REACH OUR DESTINATION IN THE BAHAMAS IN 48 MORE HOURS, HERR BARON...
SO THIS IS THE POINT AT WHICH YOU ARE TO REVEAL OUR MISSION TO ME, AS COMMANDER OF THIS U-BOAT.
IF YOU WISH TO SET DOWN THAT HEAVY CASE...
IT REMAINS VITH ME, HERR KAPITAN, UNTIL UR MISSION IS CCOMPLISHED.
AFTER ALL, THE HIGH-AND-MIGHTY DUKE OF WINDSOR MAY NOT WISH TO RETURN TO BERLIN, ESCORTED BY BARON ZEMO.
BUT, WHATEVER HIS DESIRES, DER FÜHRER MEANS TO PUT HIM ON THE THRONE--AS PUPPET MONARCH OF A CONQUERED BRITAIN!

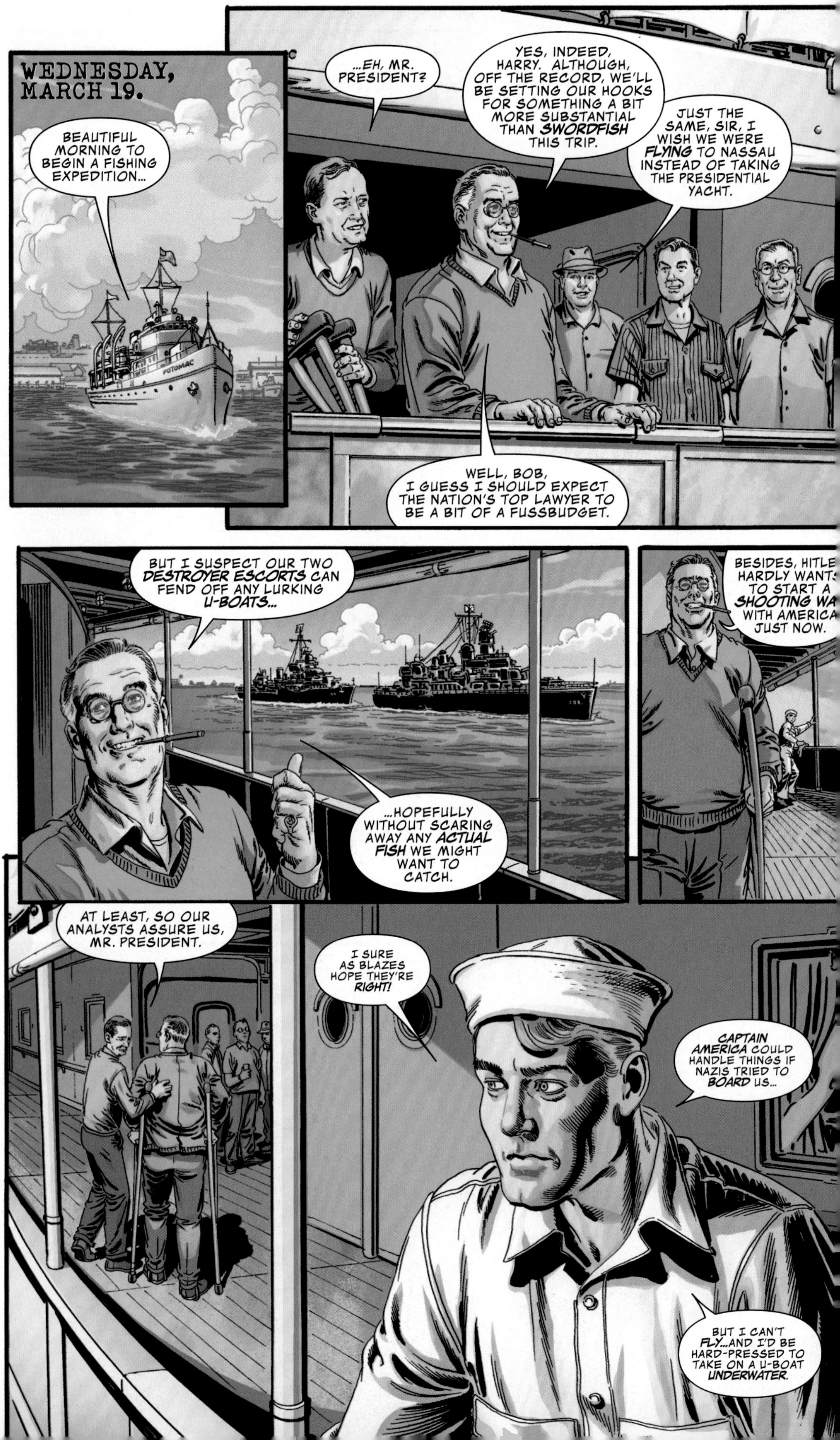
WEDNESDAY, MARCH 19.
BEAUTIFUL MORNING TO BEGIN A FISHING EXPEDITION...
POTOMAC
...EH, MR. PRESIDENT?
YES, INDEED, HARRY. ALTHOUGH, OFF THE RECORD, WE'LL BE SETTING OUR HOOKS FOR SOMETHING A BIT MORE SUBSTANTIAL THAN SWORDFISH THIS TRIP.
JUST THE SAME, SIR, I WISH WE WERE FLYING TO NASSAU INSTEAD OF TAKING THE PRESIDENTIAL YACHT.
WELL, BOB, I GUESS I SHOULD EXPECT THE NATION'S TOP LAWYER TO BE A BIT OF A FUSSBUDGET.
BUT I SUSPECT OUR TWO DESTROYER ESCORTS CAN FEND OFF ANY LURKING U-BOATS...
...HOPEFULLY WITHOUT SCARING AWAY ANY ACTUAL FISH WE MIGHT WANT TO CATCH.
BESIDES, HITLE HARDLY WANTS TO START A SHOOTING WA WITH AMERICA JUST NOW.
AT LEAST, SO OUR ANALYSTS ASSURE US, MR. PRESIDENT.
I SURE AS BLAZES HOPE THEY'RE RIGHT!
CAPTAIN AMERICA COULD HANDLE THINGS IF NAZIS TRIED TO BOARD US...
BUT I CAN'T FLY...AND I'D BE HARD-PRESSED TO TAKE ON A U-BOAT UNDERWATER.

STILL, WHATEVER IT TA—

SORRY, FELLA. DIDN'T SEE YOU. JUST FEELING A BIT... QUEASY.

AS IN "SEASICK"?

THAT'S NOT SUPPOSED TO *HAPPEN* IN OUR LINE OF WORK, IS IT, SAILOR?

DON'T WORRY ABOUT IT. I'LL BE ALL RIGHT.

BY THE WAY, MY NAME'S STEVE ROGERS.

MINE'S HAMMOND...JIM HAMMOND.

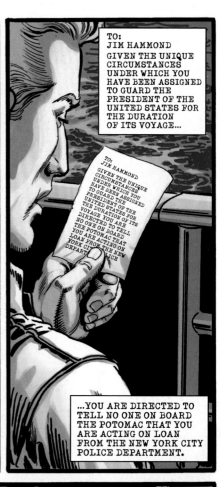

TO: JIM HAMMOND

GIVEN THE UNIQUE CIRCUMSTANCES UNDER WHICH YOU HAVE BEEN ASSIGNED TO GUARD THE PRESIDENT OF THE UNITED STATES FOR THE DURATION OF ITS VOYAGE...

...YOU ARE DIRECTED TO TELL NO ONE ON BOARD THE POTOMAC THAT YOU ARE ACTING ON LOAN FROM THE NEW YORK CITY POLICE DEPARTMENT.

WHAT DO THEY THINK—I'M SOME KIND OF IDIOT?

UH-OH! THERE GO MY SECRET ORDERS!

OH, WELL... I WAS PROBABLY *SUPPOSED* TO BURN THEM AFTER READING, ANYWAY.

I'VE EVEN GOT A MOP TO SWEEP UP THE ASHES!

NIGHT IN THE ATLANTIC.

THIS DAMN *STORM'S* TOSSIN' US LIKE A CORK IN A WATERFALL.

TELL EVERYONE ABOARD WE'RE MAKING FOR LANDFALL AT *NASSAU*-- IMMEDIATELY!

BUT WE AREN'T EXPECTED THERE TILL *DAWN,* CAP'N.

RA-KOOOOOM

IF WE TRY TO RIDE OUT THIS TEMPEST, SAILOR, ALL THAT'S LIABLE TO MAKE IT TO SHORE IS *FLOTSAM* AND *JETSAM!*

RADIO NASSAU THAT, GOD WILLING, WE'LL BE THERE BY 0200 HOURS!

YESSIR!

REALLY SEASICK THIS TIME, *HUH,* ROGERS?

H-HOW LONG DID IT TAKE *YOU* TO GET YOUR--YOU KNOW--*SEA LEGS?*

ACTUALLY, I DOUBT I'VE BEEN A SWABBIE ANY LONGER THAN *YOU* HAVE.

JUST NOT *BUILT* TO GET MOTION SICKNESS, I GUESS.

YOU'RE LUCKY. BUT... I'M OKAY NOW.

I'LL... GET OVER IT...

WE DON'T KN WHAT MIG WAITING F IN NASS

NOW WHAT DO WE DO?

I SAID--

I HEARD YOU, DEAR EDWARD.

WE'LL DO WHAT WE ALWAYS DO WHEN DIGNITARIES VISIT US HERE IN EXILE ON OUR PERSONAL ST. HELENA.

WE'LL PLAY THE GRACIOUS HOSTS...AS IF THIS WERE BUCKINGHAM PALACE, AND NOT SOME DESOLATE ISLAND IN THE MIDST OF NOWHERE.

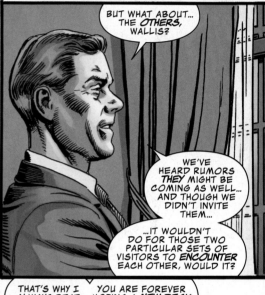

BUT WHAT ABOUT... THE OTHERS, WALLIS?

WE'VE HEARD RUMORS THEY MIGHT BE COMING AS WELL... AND THOUGH WE DIDN'T INVITE THEM...

...IT WOULDN'T DO FOR THOSE TWO PARTICULAR SETS OF VISITORS TO ENCOUNTER EACH OTHER, WOULD IT?

THAT'S WHY I ALWAYS BEAT YOU AT CARDS, EDWARD.

YOU ARE FOREVER HOPING A NEW DECK WILL PROVE THE ANSWER TO YOUR PROBLEMS...

...WHILE I PLAY THE CARDS THAT ARE DEALT ME...

...AS BEST I CAN.

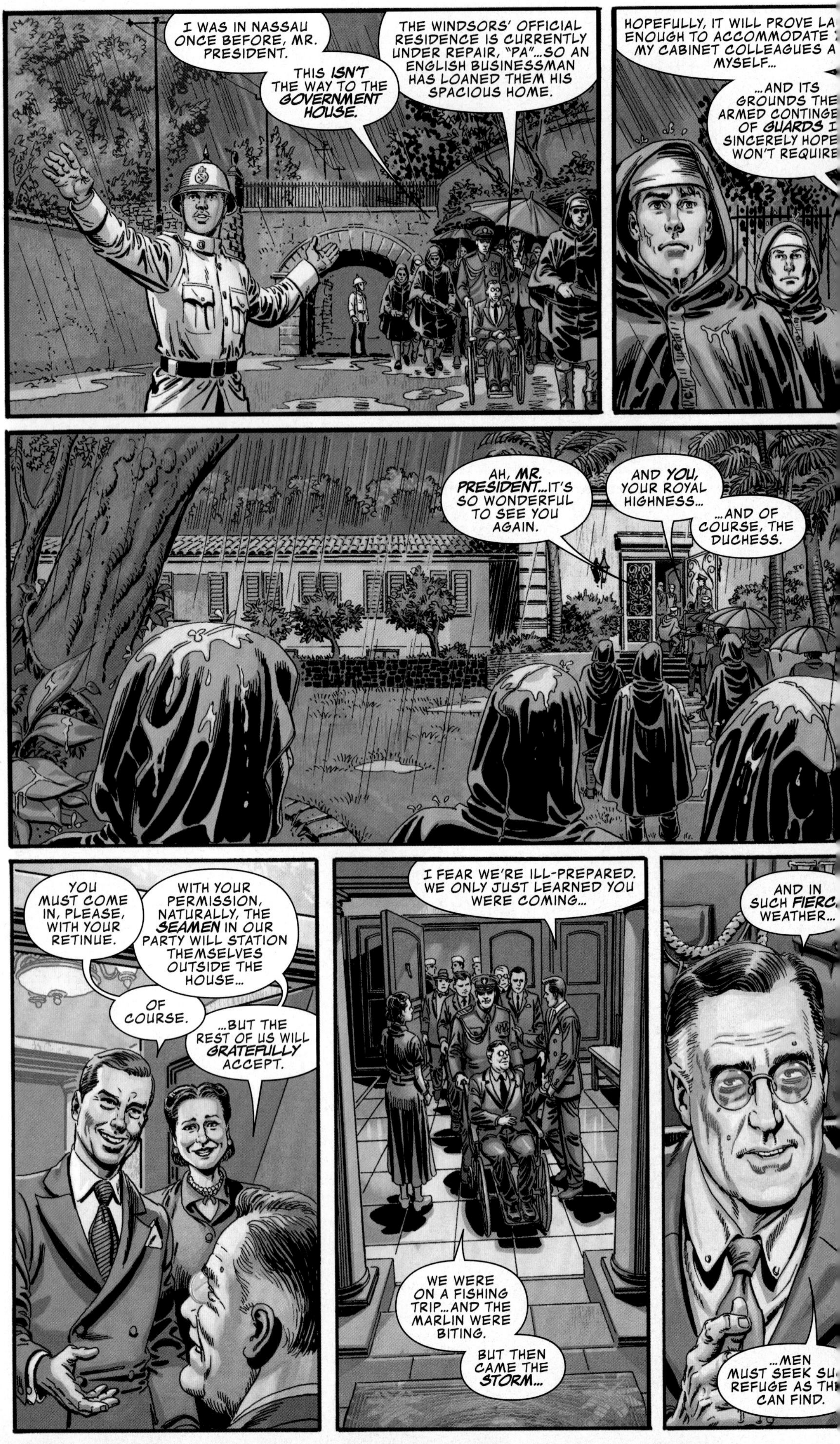
I WAS IN NASSAU ONCE BEFORE, MR. PRESIDENT.
THIS ISN'T THE WAY TO THE GOVERNMENT HOUSE.
THE WINDSORS' OFFICIAL RESIDENCE IS CURRENTLY UNDER REPAIR, "PA"...SO AN ENGLISH BUSINESSMAN HAS LOANED THEM HIS SPACIOUS HOME.
HOPEFULLY, IT WILL PROVE LA ENOUGH TO ACCOMMODATE MY CABINET COLLEAGUES A MYSELF...
...AND ITS GROUNDS THE ARMED CONTINGE OF GUARDS I SINCERELY HOPE WON'T REQUIRE
AH, MR. PRESIDENT...IT'S SO WONDERFUL TO SEE YOU AGAIN.
AND YOU, YOUR ROYAL HIGHNESS...
...AND OF COURSE, THE DUCHESS.
YOU MUST COME IN, PLEASE, WITH YOUR RETINUE.
WITH YOUR PERMISSION, NATURALLY, THE SEAMEN IN OUR PARTY WILL STATION THEMSELVES OUTSIDE THE HOUSE...
OF COURSE.
...BUT THE REST OF US WILL GRATEFULLY ACCEPT.
I FEAR WE'RE ILL-PREPARED. WE ONLY JUST LEARNED YOU WERE COMING...
WE WERE ON A FISHING TRIP...AND THE MARLIN WERE BITING.
BUT THEN CAME THE STORM...
AND IN SUCH FIERC WEATHER...
...MEN MUST SEEK SU REFUGE AS TH CAN FIND.

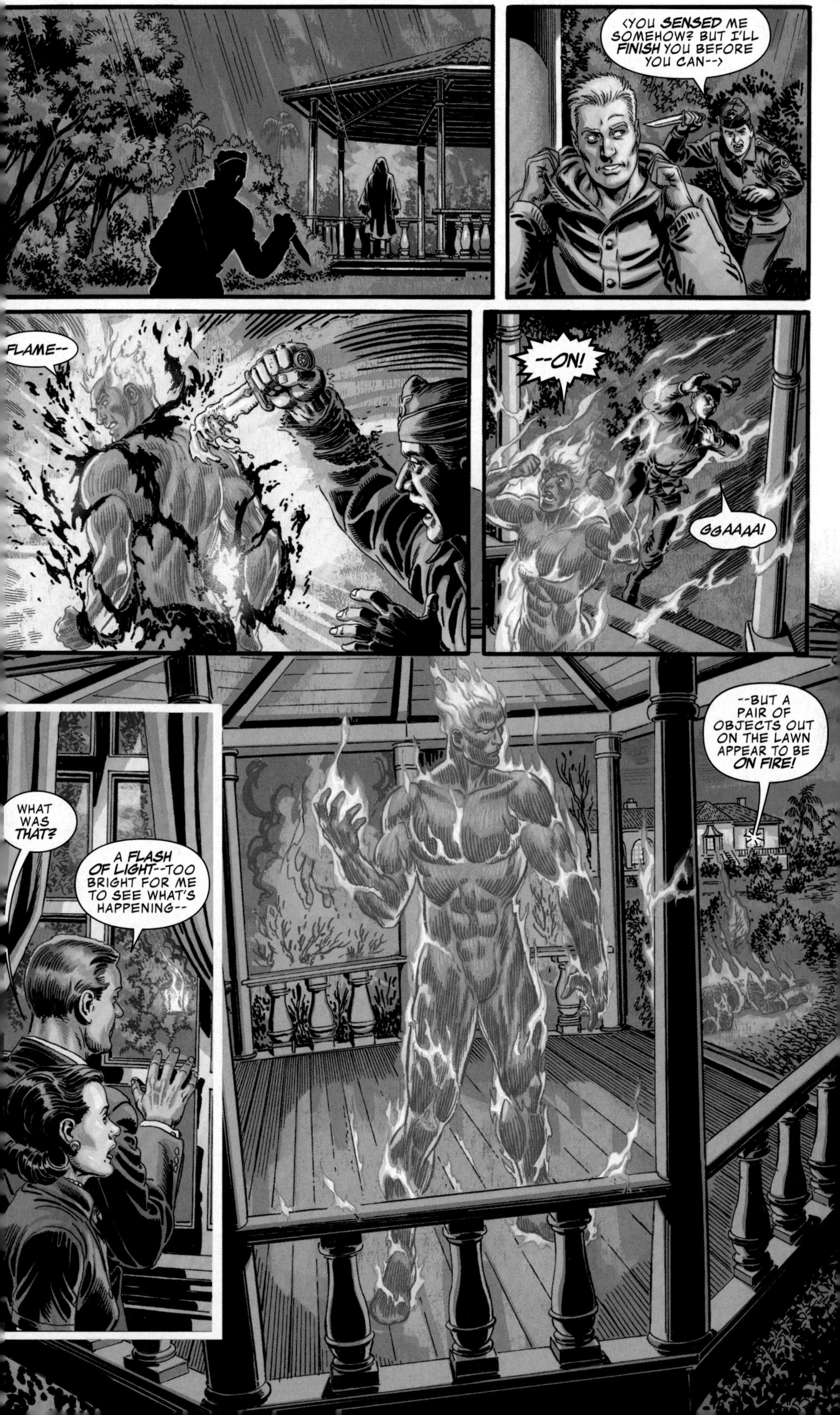

‹YOU SENSED ME SOMEHOW? BUT I'LL FINISH YOU BEFORE YOU CAN--›
FLAME--
--ON!
GGAAAA!
WHAT WAS THAT?
A FLASH OF LIGHT--TOO BRIGHT FOR ME TO SEE WHAT'S HAPPENING--
--BUT A PAIR OF OBJECTS OUT ON THE LAWN APPEAR TO BE ON FIRE!

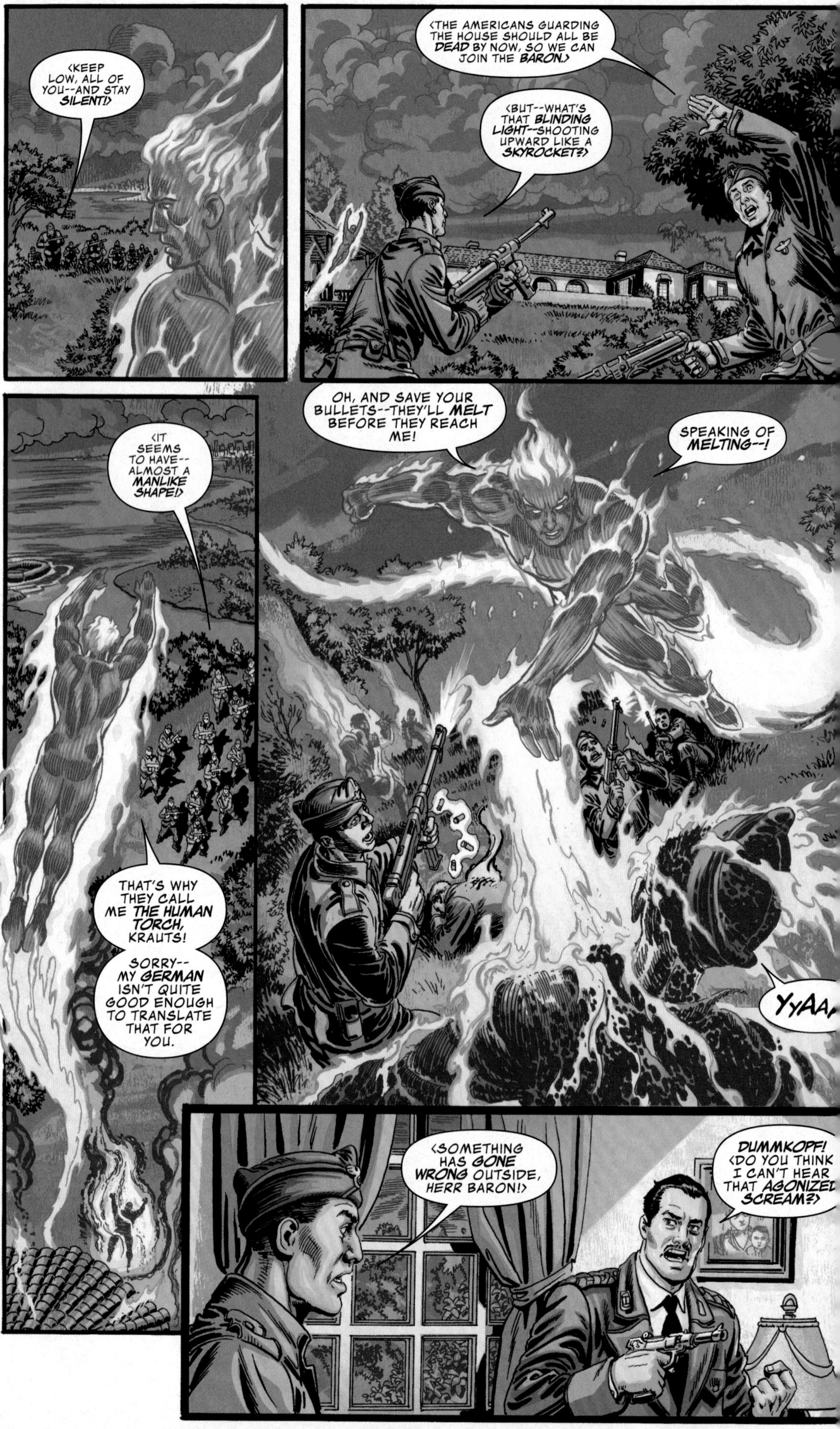

<KEEP LOW, ALL OF YOU--AND STAY SILENT!>
<THE AMERICANS GUARDING THE HOUSE SHOULD ALL BE DEAD BY NOW, SO WE CAN JOIN THE BARON.>
<BUT--WHAT'S THAT BLINDING LIGHT--SHOOTING UPWARD LIKE A SKYROCKET?>
<IT SEEMS TO HAVE--ALMOST A MANLIKE SHAPE!>
THAT'S WHY THEY CALL ME THE HUMAN TORCH, KRAUTS!
SORRY--MY GERMAN ISN'T QUITE GOOD ENOUGH TO TRANSLATE THAT FOR YOU.
OH, AND SAVE YOUR BULLETS--THEY'LL MELT BEFORE THEY REACH ME!
SPEAKING OF MELTING--!
YYAA
<SOMETHING HAS GONE WRONG OUTSIDE, HERR BARON!>
DUMMKOPF! <DO YOU THINK I CAN'T HEAR THAT AGONIZED SCREAM?>

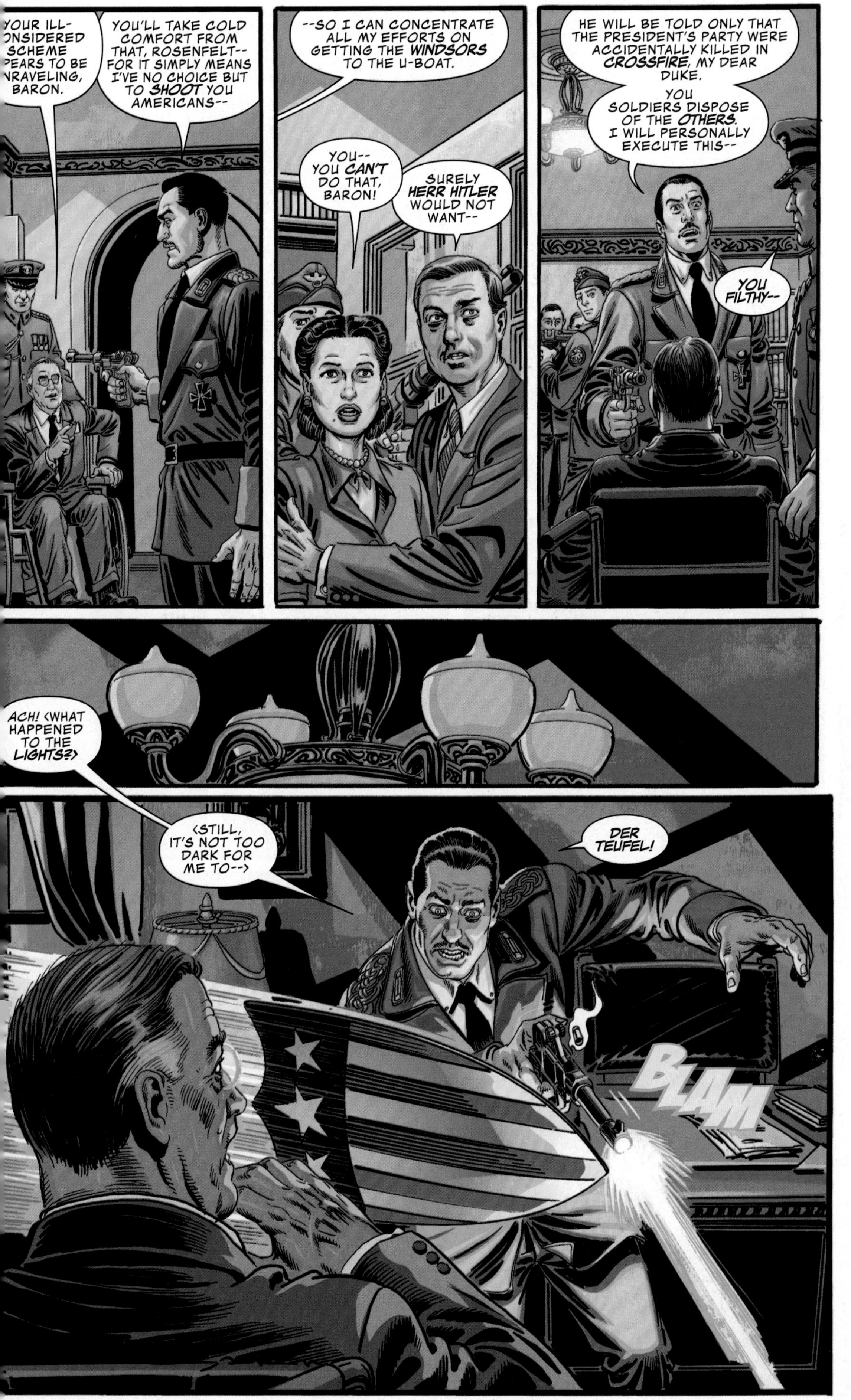
YOUR ILL-
ONSIDERED SCHEME PEARS TO BE NRAVELING, BARON.
YOU'LL TAKE COLD COMFORT FROM THAT, ROSENFELT-- FOR IT SIMPLY MEANS I'VE NO CHOICE BUT TO SHOOT YOU AMERICANS--
--SO I CAN CONCENTRATE ALL MY EFFORTS ON GETTING THE WINDSORS TO THE U-BOAT.
YOU-- YOU CAN'T DO THAT, BARON!
SURELY HERR HITLER WOULD NOT WANT--
HE WILL BE TOLD ONLY THAT THE PRESIDENT'S PARTY WERE ACCIDENTALLY KILLED IN CROSSFIRE, MY DEAR DUKE.
YOU SOLDIERS DISPOSE OF THE OTHERS. I WILL PERSONALLY EXECUTE THIS--
YOU FILTHY--
ACH! <WHAT HAPPENED TO THE LIGHTS?>
<STILL, IT'S NOT TOO DARK FOR ME TO-->
DER TEUFEL!
BLAM

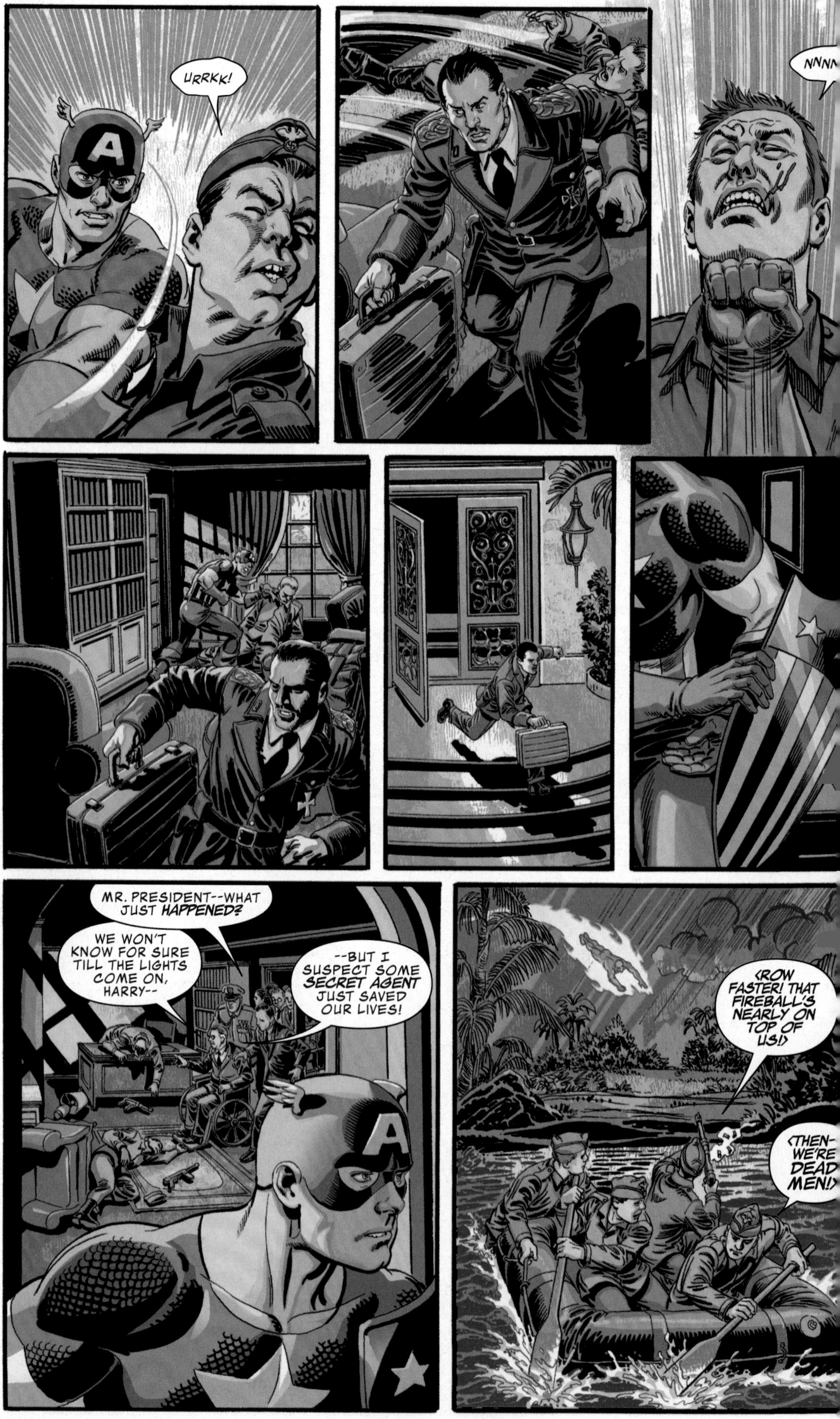

URRKK!
NNNN
MR. PRESIDENT--WHAT JUST HAPPENED?
WE WON'T KNOW FOR SURE TILL THE LIGHTS COME ON, HARRY--
--BUT I SUSPECT SOME SECRET AGENT JUST SAVED OUR LIVES!
‹ROW FASTER! THAT FIREBALL'S NEARLY ON TOP OF US!›
‹THEN-WE'RE DEAD MEN!›

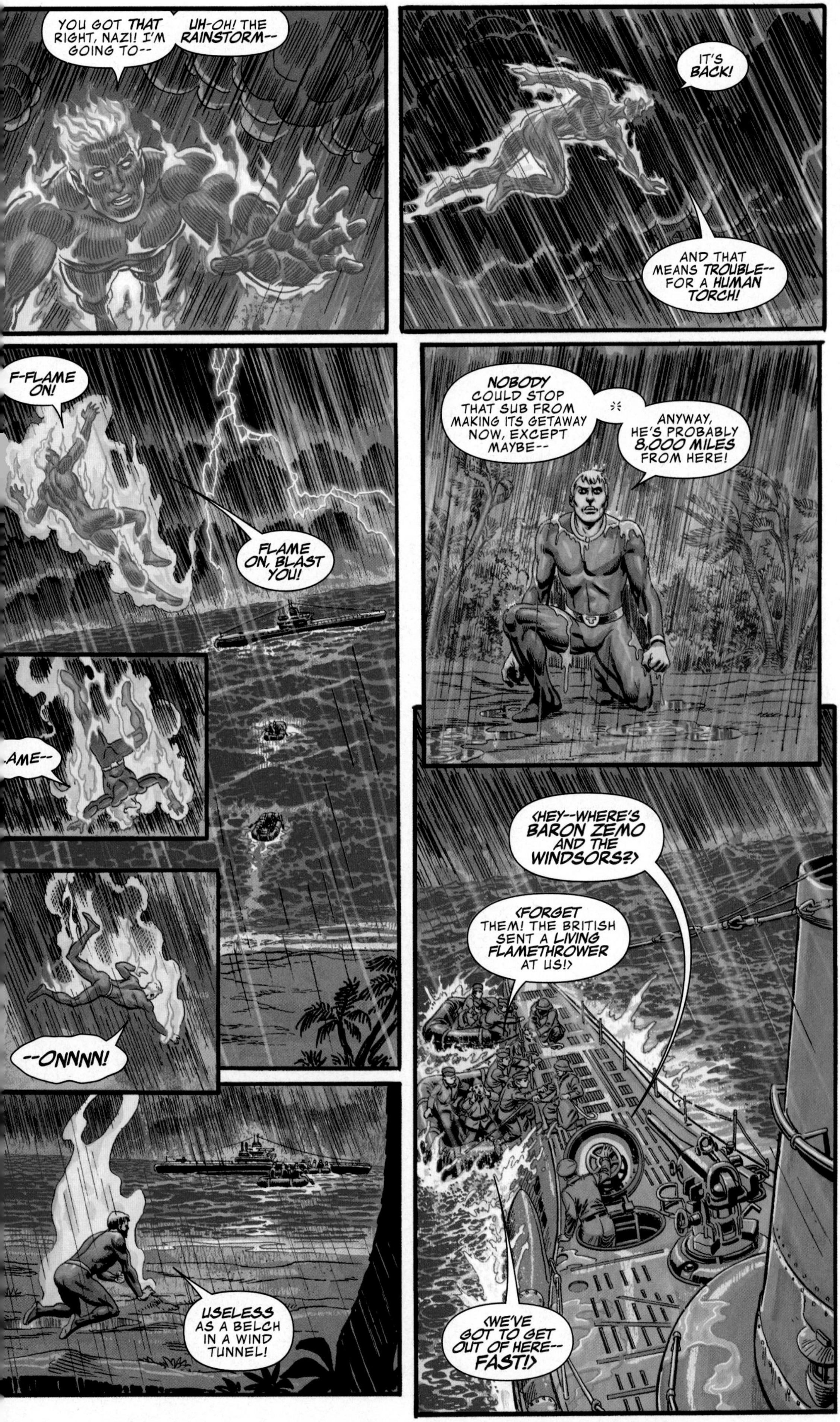
YOU GOT THAT RIGHT, NAZI! I'M GOING TO--
UH-OH! THE RAINSTORM--
IT'S BACK!
AND THAT MEANS TROUBLE-- FOR A HUMAN TORCH!
F-FLAME ON!
FLAME ON, BLAST YOU!
-AME--
--ONNNN!
USELESS AS A BELCH IN A WIND TUNNEL!
NOBODY COULD STOP THAT SUB FROM MAKING ITS GETAWAY NOW, EXCEPT MAYBE--
ANYWAY, HE'S PROBABLY 8,000 MILES FROM HERE!
<HEY--WHERE'S BARON ZEMO AND THE WINDSORS?>
<FORGET THEM! THE BRITISH SENT A LIVING FLAMETHROWER AT US!>
<WE'VE GOT TO GET OUT OF HERE-- FAST!>

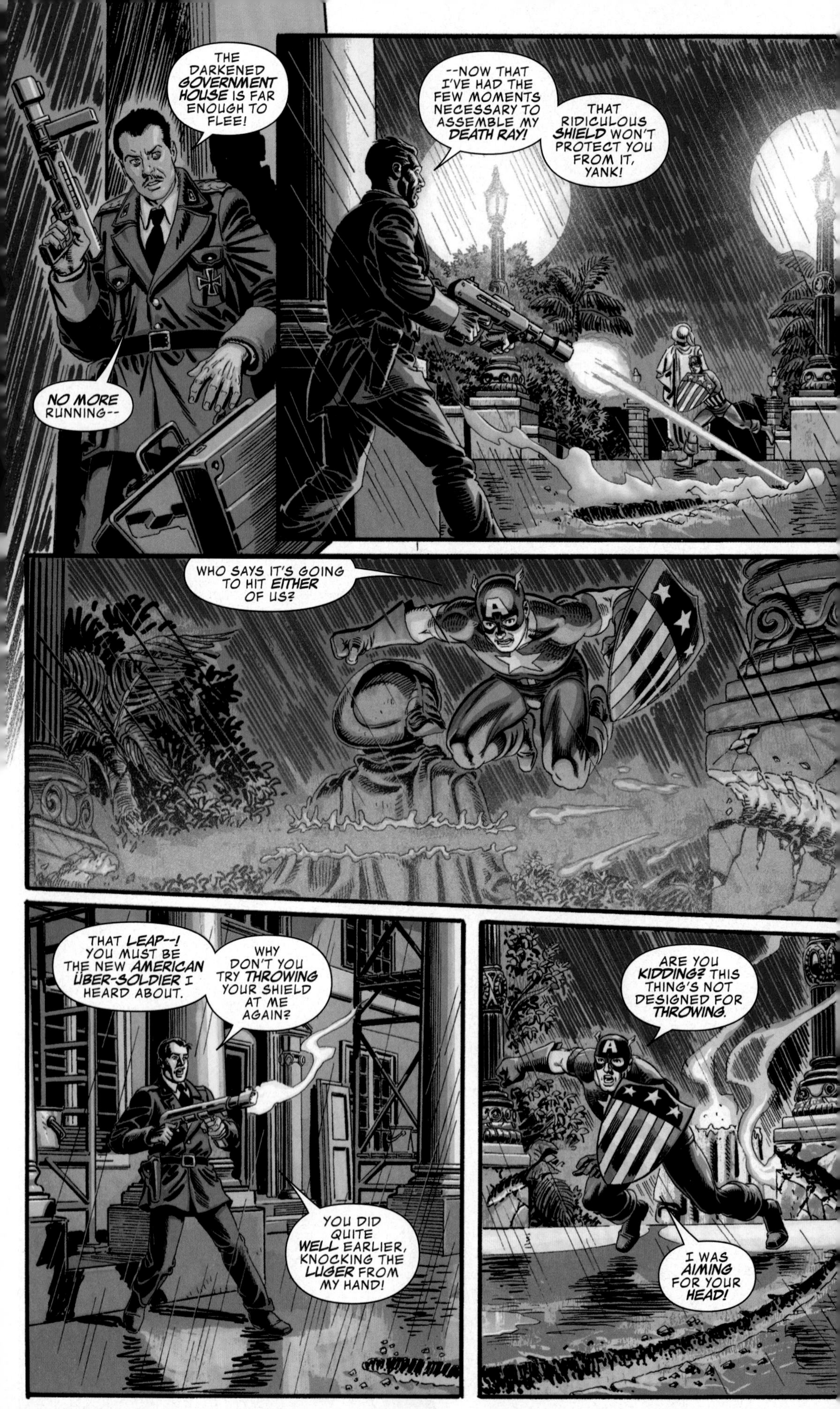
THE DARKENED GOVERNMENT HOUSE IS FAR ENOUGH TO FLEE!
NO MORE RUNNING--
--NOW THAT I'VE HAD THE FEW MOMENTS NECESSARY TO ASSEMBLE MY DEATH RAY!
THAT RIDICULOUS SHIELD WON'T PROTECT YOU FROM IT, YANK!
WHO SAYS IT'S GOING TO HIT EITHER OF US?
THAT LEAP--! YOU MUST BE THE NEW AMERICAN ÜBER-SOLDIER I HEARD ABOUT.
WHY DON'T YOU TRY THROWING YOUR SHIELD AT ME AGAIN?
YOU DID QUITE WELL EARLIER, KNOCKING THE LUGER FROM MY HAND!
ARE YOU KIDDING? THIS THING'S NOT DESIGNED FOR THROWING.
I WAS AIMING FOR YOUR HEAD!

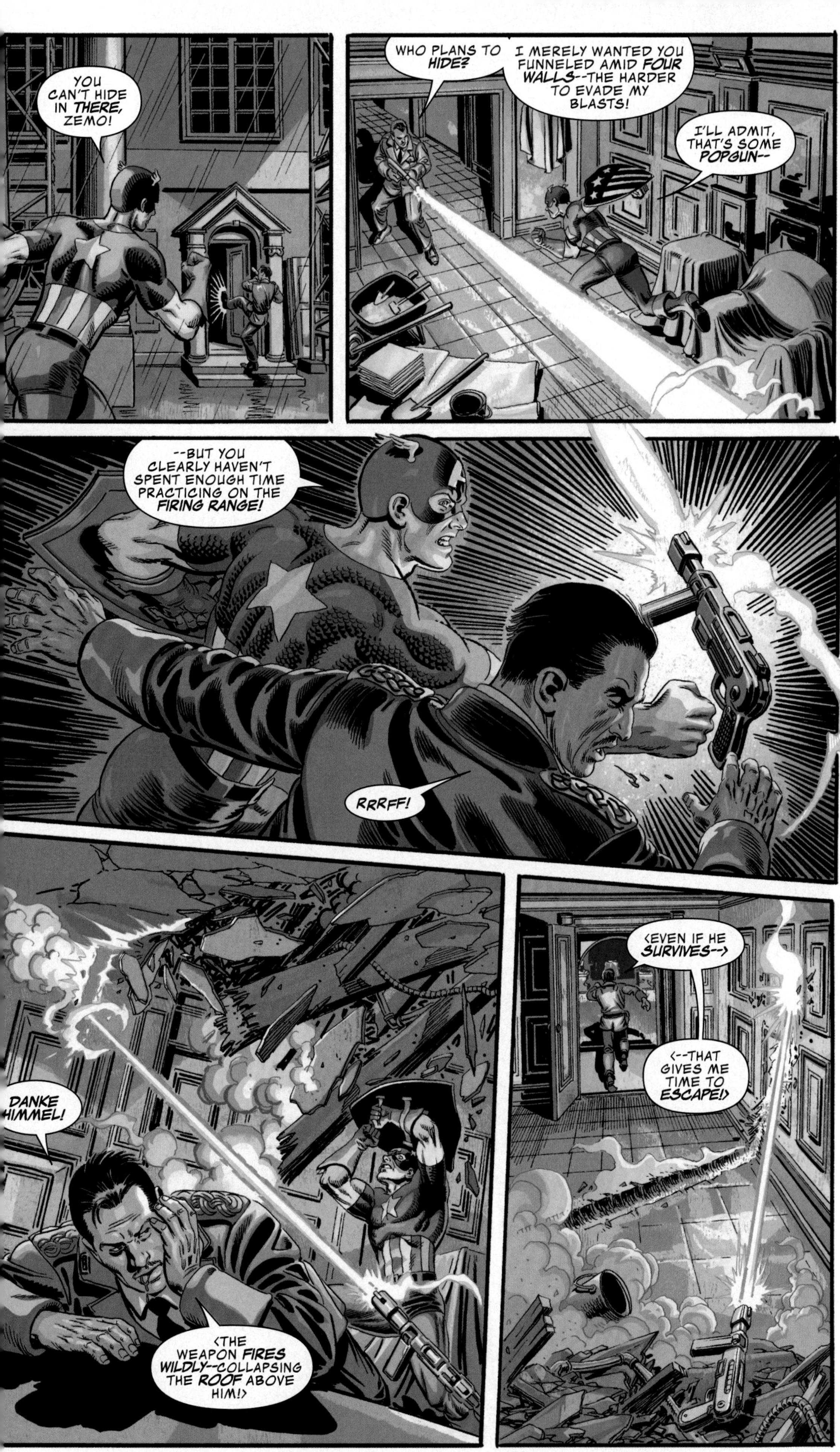

YOU CAN'T HIDE IN THERE, ZEMO!
WHO PLANS TO HIDE?
I MERELY WANTED YOU FUNNELED AMID FOUR WALLS--THE HARDER TO EVADE MY BLASTS!
I'LL ADMIT, THAT'S SOME POPGUN--
--BUT YOU CLEARLY HAVEN'T SPENT ENOUGH TIME PRACTICING ON THE FIRING RANGE!
RRRFF!
DANKE HIMMEL!
<THE WEAPON FIRES WILDLY--COLLAPSING THE ROOF ABOVE HIM!>
<EVEN IF HE SURVIVES-->
<--THAT GIVES ME TIME TO ESCAPE!>

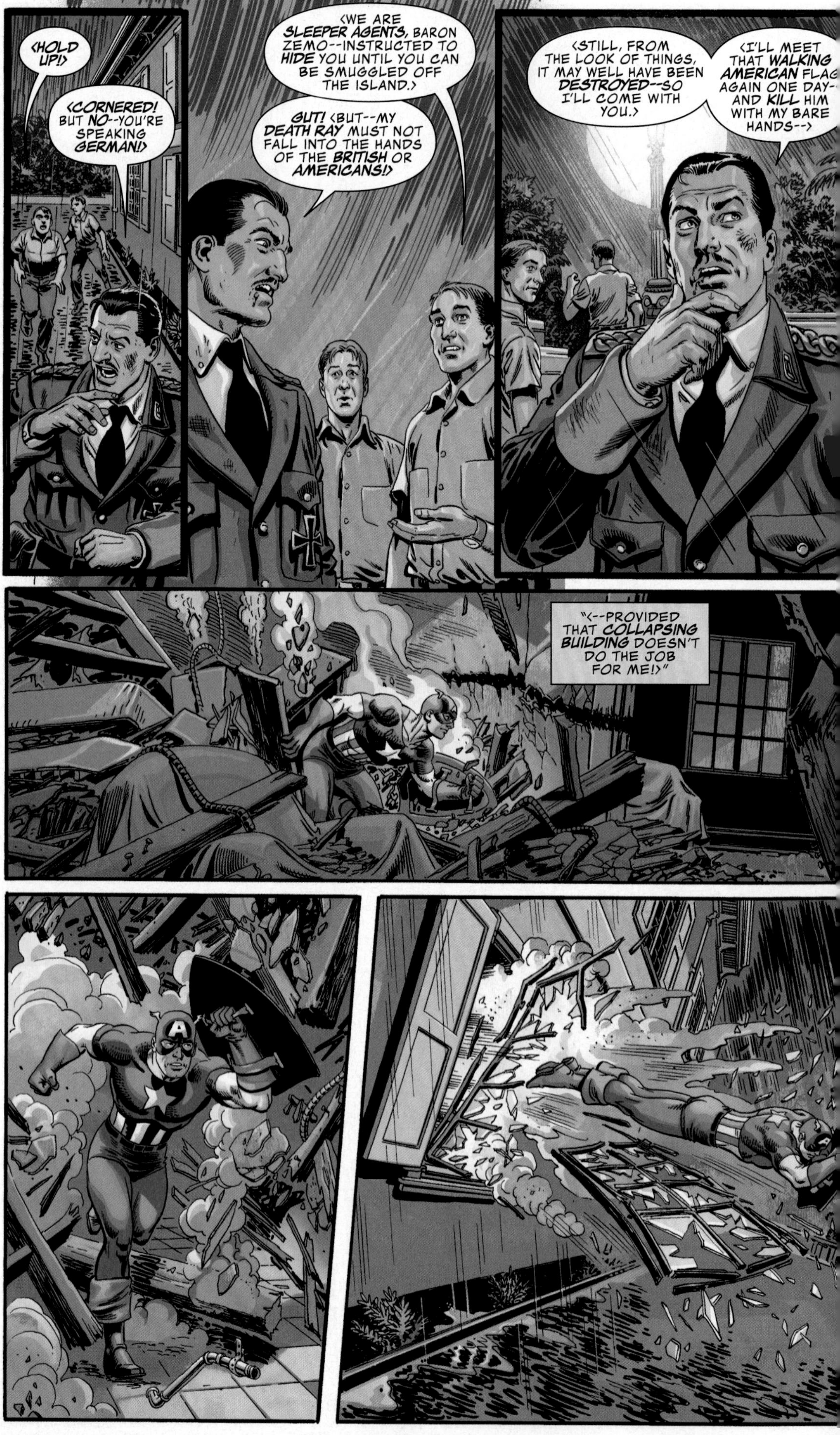

<HOLD UP!>
<CORNERED! BUT NO--YOU'RE SPEAKING GERMAN!>
<WE ARE SLEEPER AGENTS, BARON ZEMO--INSTRUCTED TO HIDE YOU UNTIL YOU CAN BE SMUGGLED OFF THE ISLAND.>
GUT! <BUT--MY DEATH RAY MUST NOT FALL INTO THE HANDS OF THE BRITISH OR AMERICANS!>
<STILL, FROM THE LOOK OF THINGS, IT MAY WELL HAVE BEEN DESTROYED--SO I'LL COME WITH YOU.>
<I'LL MEET THAT WALKING AMERICAN FLAG AGAIN ONE DAY--AND KILL HIM WITH MY BARE HANDS-->
"<--PROVIDED THAT COLLAPSING BUILDING DOESN'T DO THE JOB FOR ME!>"

DONE A *RUNNER*, EH, ZEMO? WELL, NOT MUCH CHANCE THAT *DEATH RAY GADGET'S* STILL INTACT IN THERE.

BUT WHILE *YOU'RE* FREE, YOU CAN ALWAYS BUILD *ANOTHER* ONE--

--SO I'M GOING TO MAKE IT MY BUSINESS TO *STOP* YOU!

NO... NOT MY BUSINESS.

MY *DESTINY*.

FIRST, THOUGH--GOT TO MAKE SURE FDR AND THE OTHERS ARE ALL RIGHT!

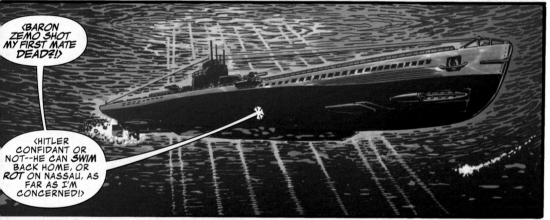

<BARON ZEMO SHOT MY FIRST MATE *DEAD?!*>

<HITLER CONFIDANT OR NOT--HE CAN *SWIM* BACK HOME, OR *ROT* ON NASSAU, AS FAR AS I'M CONCERNED!>

<SET THE COORDINATES FOR THE U-BOAT PENS AT *SAINT-NAZAIRE!*>

<EVEN WITH A PAIR OF *U.S.* DESTROYERS IN THE AREA--

<--OR ANYTHING *ELSE* THE AMERICANS CAN THROW AT US--

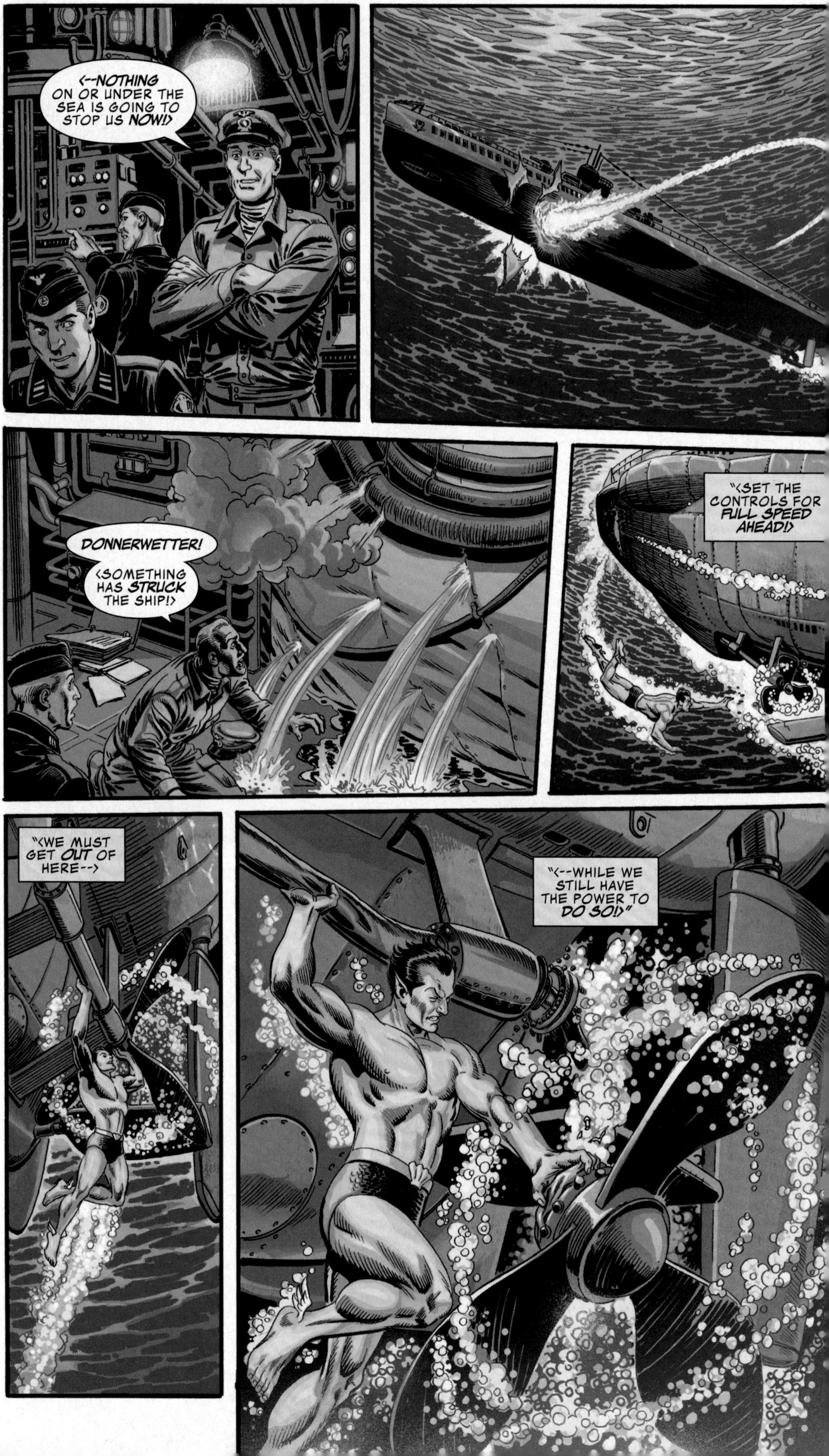

<--NOTHING ON OR UNDER THE SEA IS GOING TO STOP US NOW!>
DONNERWETTER!
<SOMETHING HAS STRUCK THE SHIP!>
"<SET THE CONTROLS FOR FULL SPEED AHEAD!>
"<WE MUST GET OUT OF HERE-->
"<--WHILE WE STILL HAVE THE POWER TO DO SO!>"

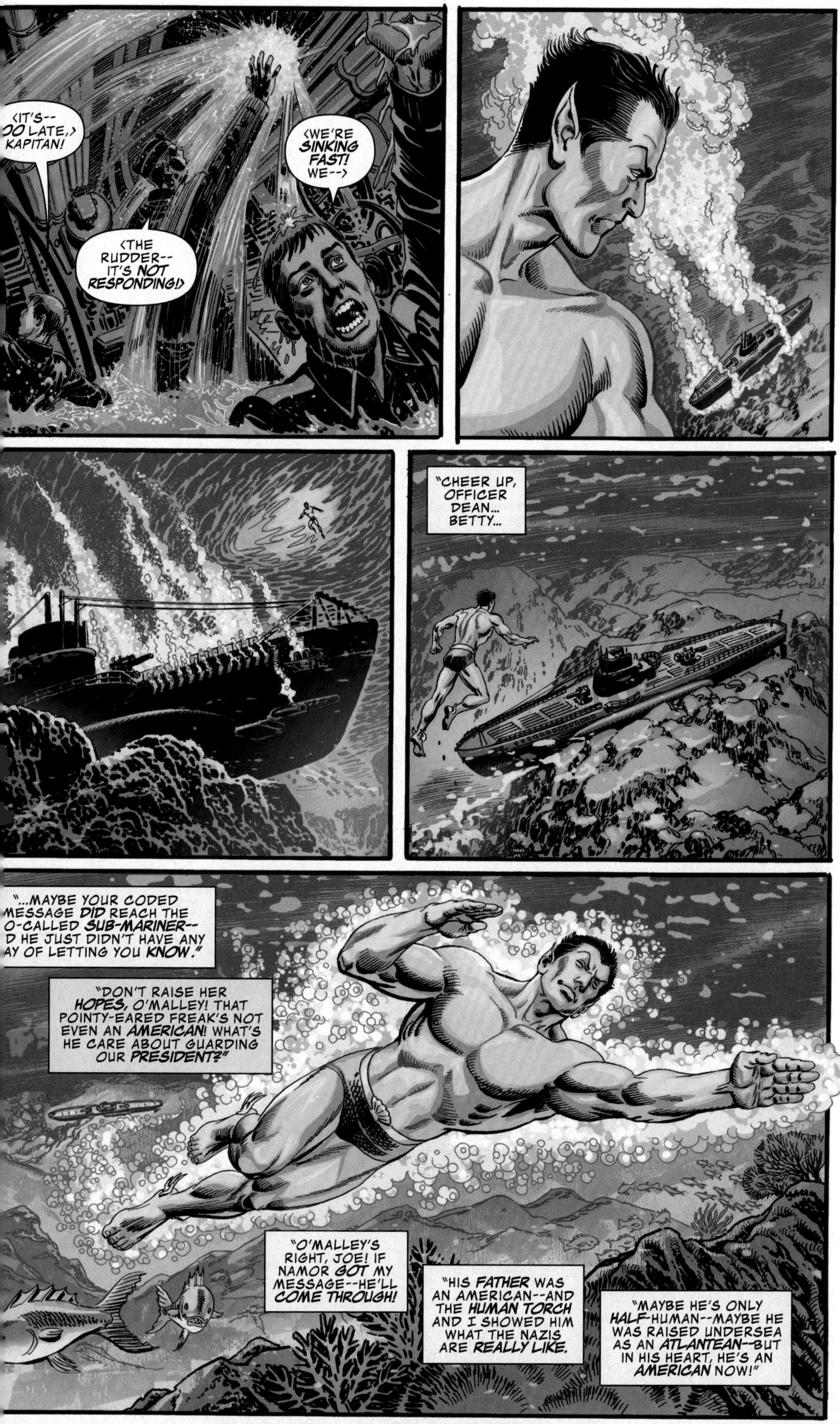

<IT'S-- OO LATE,> KAPITAN!
<WE'RE SINKING FAST! WE-->
<THE RUDDER-- IT'S NOT RESPONDING!>
"CHEER UP, OFFICER DEAN... BETTY...
"...MAYBE YOUR CODED MESSAGE DID REACH THE O-CALLED SUB-MARINER-- D HE JUST DIDN'T HAVE ANY AY OF LETTING YOU KNOW."
"DON'T RAISE HER HOPES, O'MALLEY! THAT POINTY-EARED FREAK'S NOT EVEN AN AMERICAN! WHAT'S HE CARE ABOUT GUARDING OUR PRESIDENT?"
"O'MALLEY'S RIGHT, JOE! IF NAMOR GOT MY MESSAGE--HE'LL COME THROUGH!
"HIS FATHER WAS AN AMERICAN--AND THE HUMAN TORCH AND I SHOWED HIM WHAT THE NAZIS ARE REALLY LIKE.
"MAYBE HE'S ONLY HALF-HUMAN--MAYBE HE WAS RAISED UNDERSEA AS AN ATLANTEAN--BUT IN HIS HEART, HE'S AN AMERICAN NOW!"

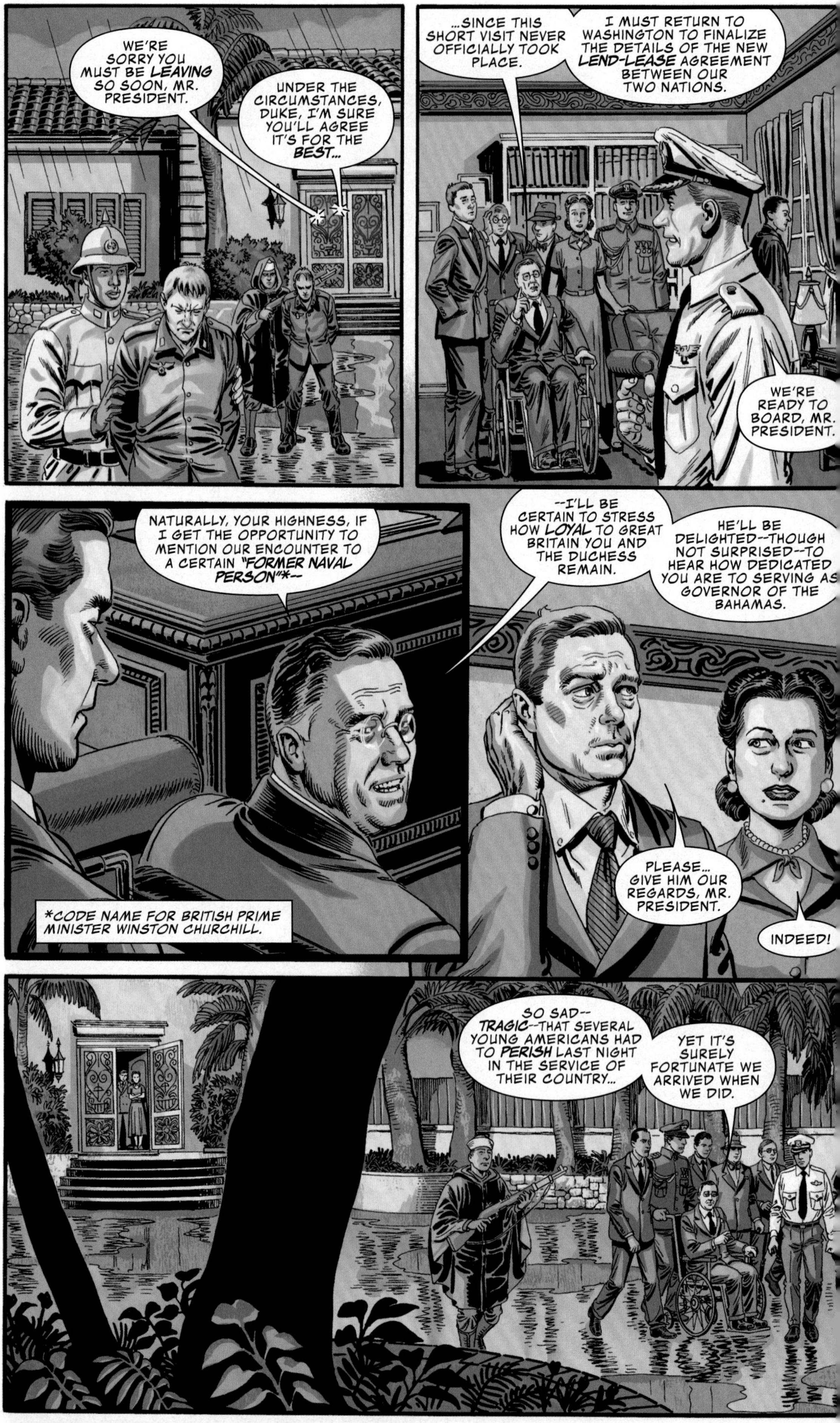
WE'RE SORRY YOU MUST BE LEAVING SO SOON, MR. PRESIDENT.
UNDER THE CIRCUMSTANCES, DUKE, I'M SURE YOU'LL AGREE IT'S FOR THE BEST...
...SINCE THIS SHORT VISIT NEVER OFFICIALLY TOOK PLACE.
I MUST RETURN TO WASHINGTON TO FINALIZE THE DETAILS OF THE NEW LEND-LEASE AGREEMENT BETWEEN OUR TWO NATIONS.
WE'RE READY TO BOARD, MR. PRESIDENT.
NATURALLY, YOUR HIGHNESS, IF I GET THE OPPORTUNITY TO MENTION OUR ENCOUNTER TO A CERTAIN "FORMER NAVAL PERSON"*--
--I'LL BE CERTAIN TO STRESS HOW LOYAL TO GREAT BRITAIN YOU AND THE DUCHESS REMAIN.
HE'LL BE DELIGHTED--THOUGH NOT SURPRISED--TO HEAR HOW DEDICATED YOU ARE TO SERVING AS GOVERNOR OF THE BAHAMAS.
*CODE NAME FOR BRITISH PRIME MINISTER WINSTON CHURCHILL.
PLEASE... GIVE HIM OUR REGARDS, MR. PRESIDENT.
INDEED!
SO SAD--TRAGIC--THAT SEVERAL YOUNG AMERICANS HAD TO PERISH LAST NIGHT IN THE SERVICE OF THEIR COUNTRY...
YET IT'S SURELY FORTUNATE WE ARRIVED WHEN WE DID.

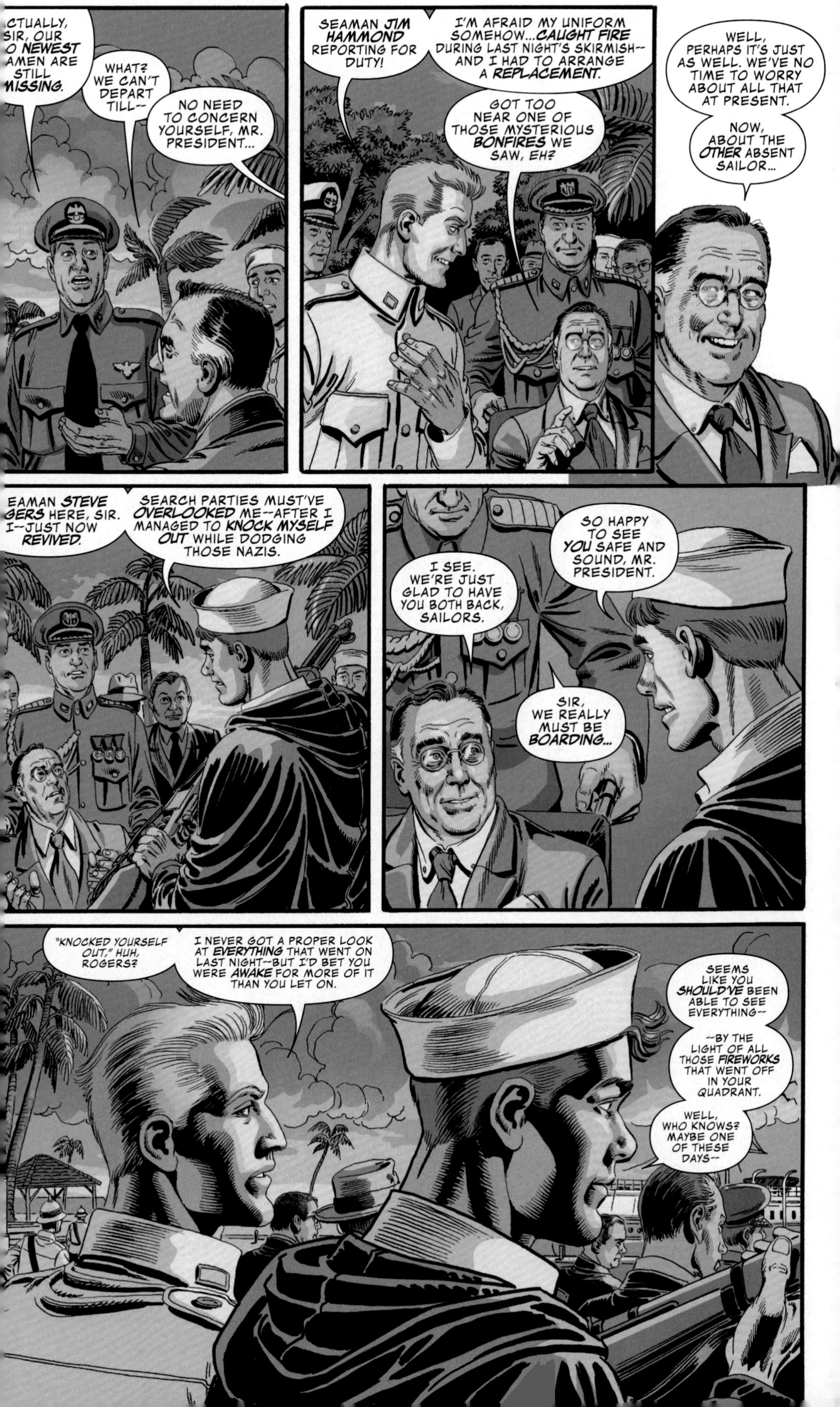

CTUALLY, SIR, OUR O NEWEST AMEN ARE STILL MISSING.
WHAT? WE CAN'T DEPART TILL--
NO NEED TO CONCERN YOURSELF, MR. PRESIDENT...
SEAMAN JIM HAMMOND REPORTING FOR DUTY!
I'M AFRAID MY UNIFORM SOMEHOW...CAUGHT FIRE DURING LAST NIGHT'S SKIRMISH--AND I HAD TO ARRANGE A REPLACEMENT.
GOT TOO NEAR ONE OF THOSE MYSTERIOUS BONFIRES WE SAW, EH?
WELL, PERHAPS IT'S JUST AS WELL. WE'VE NO TIME TO WORRY ABOUT ALL THAT AT PRESENT.
NOW, ABOUT THE OTHER ABSENT SAILOR...
EAMAN STEVE GERS HERE, SIR. I--JUST NOW REVIVED.
SEARCH PARTIES MUST'VE OVERLOOKED ME--AFTER I MANAGED TO KNOCK MYSELF OUT WHILE DODGING THOSE NAZIS.
SO HAPPY TO SEE YOU SAFE AND SOUND, MR. PRESIDENT.
I SEE. WE'RE JUST GLAD TO HAVE YOU BOTH BACK, SAILORS.
SIR, WE REALLY MUST BE BOARDING...
"KNOCKED YOURSELF OUT," HUH, ROGERS?
I NEVER GOT A PROPER LOOK AT EVERYTHING THAT WENT ON LAST NIGHT--BUT I'D BET YOU WERE AWAKE FOR MORE OF IT THAN YOU LET ON.
SEEMS LIKE YOU SHOULD'VE BEEN ABLE TO SEE EVERYTHING--
--BY THE LIGHT OF ALL THOSE FIREWORKS THAT WENT OFF IN YOUR QUADRANT.
WELL, WHO KNOWS? MAYBE ONE OF THESE DAYS--

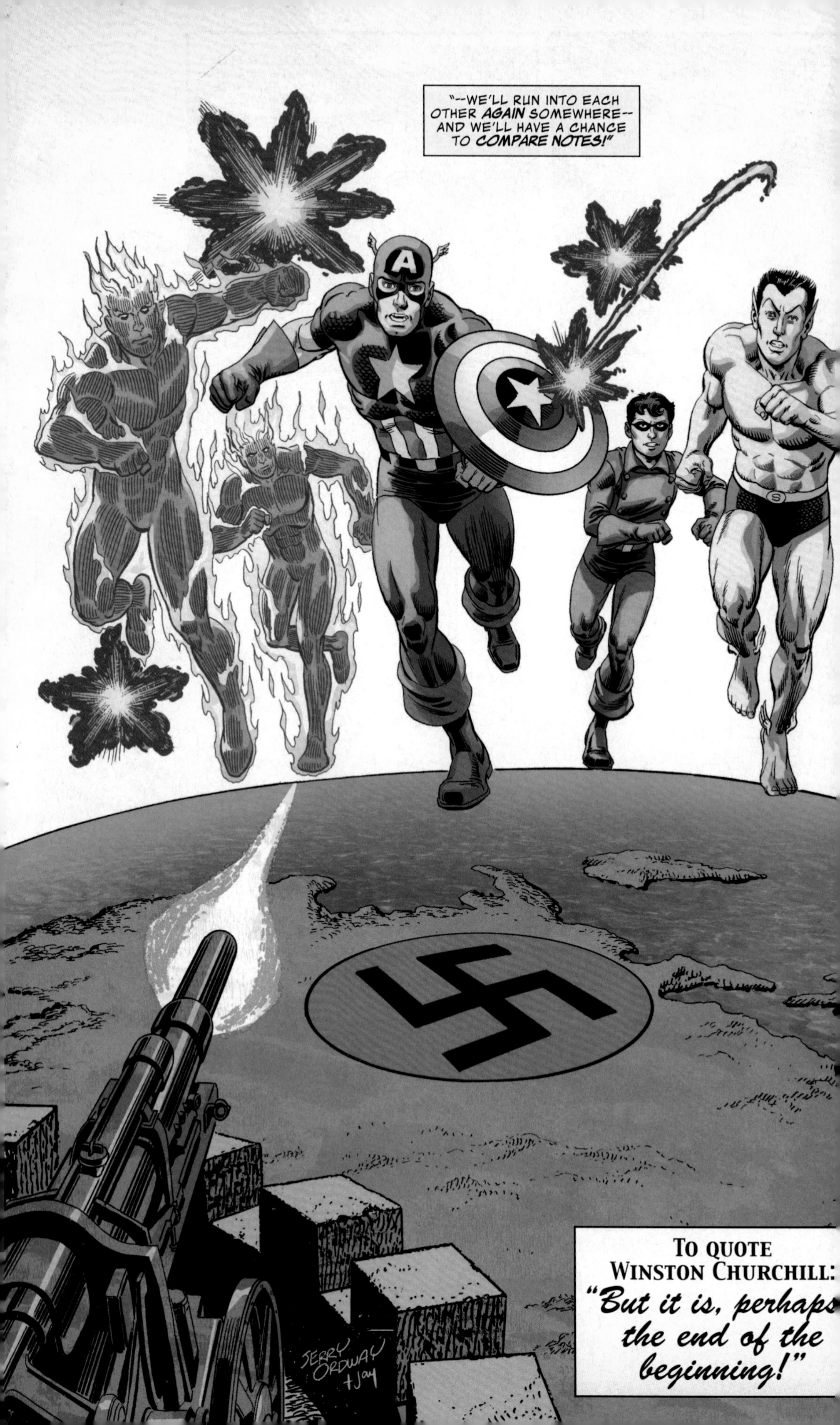
"--WE'LL RUN INTO EACH OTHER AGAIN SOMEWHERE-- AND WE'LL HAVE A CHANCE TO COMPARE NOTES!"
TO QUOTE WINSTON CHURCHILL: "But it is, perhaps the end of the beginning!"
JERRY ORDWAY +Jay